Peter Fjellstedt

Picture of landscape from Sillerud

STUDIA MISSIONALIA UPSALIENSIA   XXXVI

PETER FJELLSTEDT
Missionary Mentor to Three Continents

by

Emmet E. Eklund

Augustana Historical Society
Rock Island, Illinois
1983

**Augustana Historical Society
Publication No. 30
Ross Paulson, General Editor**

ISBN: 0-910184-30-5
Library of Congress Card Number: 83-71472

Printed in the United States of America
by
Graphic Publishing Co., Inc.
Lake Mills, Iowa 50450

*To My Marion
Companion on the way*

Contents

List of Illustrations

Acknowledgements

To conduct research and to write on the subject of Peter Fjellstedt's life and contributions have made me aware of the many persons to whom I am indebted. Without the work they have done, this study would have been impossible.

Important work has been done in Sweden on Fjellstedt. Carl Anshelm has done the most extensive work in his three volumes entitled: *Peter Fjellstedt, hans barndoms och ungdomstid samt utländska missionsverksamhet* [*His Childhood, Youth and Foreign Missionary Activity*] *Peter Fjellstedt, hans verksamhet i hemlandet för den yttre missionen* [*His Activity in the Homeland for Foreign Missions*]; and *Peter Fjellstedt, hans verksamhet för kyrklig väckelse och inre mission 1850-1881* [*His Work in Behalf of Churchly Revival and Inner Missions 1850-1881*].

A much shorter work but also of considerable value is Emilia Ahnfelt-Laurin's *Peter Fjellstedt, hans verksamhet i fosterlandet mellan åren 1843-1881* [*Peter Fjellstedt and His Work in His Homeland between the Years 1843-1881*]. This book is basically a compilation of letters from Fjellstedt's correspondence and, although somewhat sketchy, it is deserving of the scholar's attention.

Other reputable scholars have written about various aspects of Fjellstedt's work. His contribution to the formation of the missionary movement in Sweden was ably assessed by Bengt Sundkler in his study of the Swedish Missionary Society. His relationship to the Lund Missionary Society was explored by Gustaf W. Lindeberg. In his pioneering studies of Swedish emigration to America, Gunnar Westin gave an important place to Fjellstedt. Ruben Josefson, former Director of the Fjellstedt School and later Archbishop of Sweden, made a specific study of Fjellstedt's missionary theology and of the latter's belief in the possibility of the salvation of heathen outside of the Church.

Resources are also present in America among which is Eric Norelius' highly valuable work, *De Svenska Luterska församlingarnas och Svenskarnes historia i Amerika* [*The History of the Swedish Lutheran Congregations and the Swedes in America*]. These two volumes are indispensable. They cover roughly the first seven and one-half decades of Swedish emigration to America which began about 1840. Norelius' primary objective was to relate that movement to the origin and development of the Augustana Lutheran Church.

Others whose research and writing have furnished fine resources include: O. Fritiof Ander, G. Everett Arden, Conrad Bergendoff, Emeroy Johnson, Emory K. Lindquist, Ernst W. Olson, Oscar N. Olson, Sam Rönnegård and George M. Stephenson.

This is the first attempt to make a full assessment of Fjellstedt's relation to the Augustana Lutheran Church. In addition, I have sought to give a full presentation of his theology in its relationship to the *Augustana (Augsburg) Confession.*

Certain persons must be identified for special thanks. The kindness and cooperation I received from the staff in the library of Augustana College, Rock Island, Illinois and at the Carolina Redivivi, Uppsala, Sweden were greatly appreciated.

Two of my former teachers, Conrad Bergendoff and Emory Lindquist, contributed so much to this project and in so many ways. Inspiration from their classrooms now more than three decades ago continues to be of great value to me. Dr. Bergendoff's initial counsel and help in the beginning of this project saved me many hours of search for relevant material. Dr. Lindquist's careful examination of the manuscript with many fine comments saved me from many serious errors.

Three persons in Sweden also deserve special thanks. Professor Carl Hallencreutz, Professor of Missiology at Uppsala University, was a great source of encouragement to me and gave me much guidance. The opportunity he gave me to present a portion of this work in one of his seminars did much to clarify the direction of the manuscript. Furthermore, his fine knowledge of the Swedish Church and mission history as well as his remarkably thorough reading of the manuscript with many helpful comments have been invaluable.

Rector Allen Parkman of the Fjellstedt School was most gracious to my requests. Generous with his time, he helped me with material including pictures as well as information about the School and the man for whom it was named. He, too, gave useful suggestions after reading the work.

To Bishop Bengt Sundkler I am grateful both for his encouragement and the help which his writings, so well researched and written, gave to me.

I am also thankful to Pacific Lutheran University, its president, William O. Rieke, and its Board of Regents. President Rieke has been unfailing in his words of encouragement during the course of the enterprise. In 1978-79, I was granted by the Board of Regents the Regency Professorship. The generous stipend and leave of absence associated with that award gave me the opportunity to launch this research. In addition, President Rieke generously provided a substantial subsidy from the University for publication costs of this manuscript.

Finally, I am most grateful to my wife Marion to whom I dedicate this book. She has been at my side constantly, finding material, and typing the manuscript. Without her companionship and encouragement, it is doubtful if this work could have been completed.

July 17, 1981

Introduction

Peter Fjellstedt (1802-1881), churchman, educator, linguist, missionary, preacher, writer, was a leading figure in the nineteenth century evangelicial revival in Sweden. Some scholarly work has been done on him in that country, the most extensive of which was by Carl Anshelm. Those who make subsequent studies of Fjellstedt are obligated to make frequent references to the results of his research. These volumes are a basic resource. A work of considerably shorter length but also of value has been produced by Emilia Ahnfelt-Laurin.

By contrast, no significant study has been made of Fjellstedt in the English language. In view of his great contribution to, and interest in, the Swedish Lutheran immigrants and the church they formed, the Augustana Lutheran Church, and absence of such a work represents a serious void.

The Augustana Lutheran Church became the largest immigrant community among all Swedish people in America whether church or secular. To the character and development of that body, Fjellstedt made great contributions. He inspired financial support, helped secure leadership, and contributed to the theological development of this Church as it simultaneously made terms with the frontier environment and retained its Lutheran identity. In this second instance, Fjellstedt played an important role through his loyalty to the Bible and the Lutheran confessions. His counsel to the early leaders of Augustana on the basis of these resources was valuable.

It is largely because there is no work on Fjellstedt in the English language that this study has been made. It is directed particularly to the heirs of the Augustana Lutheran Church which in 1962 was incorporated into the larger Lutheran Church in America. This new body is of heterogeneous ethnic background consisting of Lutherans from Danish, Finnish, German and Swedish traditions.

Each of these four groups is to be valued for its uniqueness. Although each arose in relation to the common Lutheran faith, different nuances emerged. Consequently, the Lutheran Church in America can know its history only as it searches for its roots in the Danish, Finnish, German and Swedish bodies from which it grew. Hence, to state that a study of Peter Fjellstedt in the English language "is directed particularly to the heirs of the Augustana Lutheran Church" includes not only the descendants of the Swedish immigrants who organized Augustana. This work is also related to the some 3,000,000 members of the Lutheran Church in America. The awareness of its identity will be all the clearer as each of these roots is explored. It should be of value also to the people of Sweden who desire to know more clearly their own history.

As always, the ones who are expected to read a book guide in some degree the plan of the book. I have written on the assumption that the prospective readers know very little about Peter Fjellstedt. The first chapter is therefore biographical. To readers in Sweden, this portion of the book may seem repetitious. In view of English readers in America, however, it is necessary. For this first chapter I have depended heavily upon Anshelm's research and, to a lesser degree, upon that of Ahnfelt-Laurin. This chapter concludes with a description of his work as a pioneer in several areas.

The main thrust of the book is not biographical, important and necessary as that is. The central concern is to set forth the unique contributions which Peter Fjellstedt gave to the character and life of the Augustana Church and, indirectly, to the Lutheran Church in America. To assess these contributions, one must know what shaped the contributor and what the formulation of those shaping factors were. Chapter two deals with the first of these and chapter three with the latter where the theology of Fjellstedt is described.

In terms of the central intention, chapter four is the heart of the book. Here, the specific contributions of Fjellstedt to Augustana are articulated. The attempt has been made to show what was significant in Fjellstedt's influence in Augustana's formulation of its theology. Especially does this uniqueness appear in its understanding of the ministry and the Church, a view which Fjellstedt transmitted to the Swedish Lutheran immigrants.

The appendix is most closely related to chapter four. All of the men whose brief biographies are presented came to America to serve Augustana. They came from the Fjellstedt School or its predecessor, the Mission Institute. Almost without exception, they served the Augustana Lutheran Church faithfully, some with distinction.

I have followed the plan of using the Swedish words as they have appeared in the original source even when the same word appears differently from one document to another: for example, in the May-July (1847) issue of *Lunds Missions-Tidning*, Fjellstedt wrote an article against slave-trading. The term he used for that practice was "slafhandeln." Nine years later, in the same paper for July 1856, he spelled the word "slavehandeln." In the development of the Swedish language during the last half of the nineteenth century and into this century, "f" when not the first letter in the alphabet often came to be displaced by the letter "v." A similar change occurred in the displacement of the letter "w" by "v," and the letter "e" by "a." For example, Växjö today was formerly Wexjö." Words, especially in titles, where it was deemed necessary have been translated.

It is my hope that this book may be a salute to Peter Fjellstedt. It is likely there would have been an Augustana apart from Fjellstedt. That belongs to the realm of speculation. Historians are not speculators; they try rather to show what happened. The Augustana Lutheran Church was an historical fact. It has influenced the lives of thousands including the author of this book. What it was was in no small measure due to Peter Fjellstedt. For Augustana, he was among those persons who labored and into whose labors we have been called upon to enter.

Chapter I
An Overview of Peter Fjellstedt's Life

To Sweden as to the United States and much of Europe came the great nineteenth century religious revival. Swedish immigrants in America who had been greatly influenced by this movement established the largest organization in North America among Swedish-American citizens, the Augustana Lutheran Church.[1] In general, the person in Sweden who has been regarded as the spiritual father to this American church was Carl Olof Rosenius. But there were others who in their way were equally important to Augustana's origin and development. They were mentors without whose aid this immigrant group may not have survived and formed a history of its own which covered 102 years. One of these persons was Peter Larsson who became known as Peter Fjellstedt.

1. Fjellstedt's Childhood and Early Youth (1802-1818)

Peter Larsson was born September 17, 1802 in Värmland, in the parish of Sillerud which lay west of the northernmost shores of Lake Vänern, about thirty-five miles east of the Norwegian border. His father was Lars Larsson and his mother, before her marriage, was Catherina Petersson.[2]

The family's limited income was from farming which, however, had to be supplemented by the father's work as a carpenter. The poverty of the Larssons was severely deepened when one dark night in 1806, their home was completely destroyed by fire. The mother was home alone. Through tremendous effort, Catherina saved Marta, Peter's older sister by a year, Peter and her father-in-law but the exertion permanently affected her health. Few of their meager possessions were saved.

[1]For most of its history, the Augustana Church was officially called the "Augustana Synod." At its organizational convention at Jefferson Prairie, Wisconsin (June 5-11, 1860), its constitution was entitled: "Constitution of the Scandinavian Ev. Lutheran Augustana Synod in North America" (G. Everett Arden, *Augustana Heritage: A History of the Augustana Lutheran Church* [Rock Island, Ill.: Augustana Press, 1963], p. 84, fn. 23). Even as late as 1935, "Synod" and "Church" were made synonomous. When Dr. P. O. Bersell was installed as president on October 2, 1935, he said: "There is something distinctive about the Augustana Synod, even in the family of Lutheran Churches in America" (*Ibid.*, P. 330). In 1948, the distinction was correctly made that "Church" refers to the community of believers who identify themselves according to the scriptures and the beliefs which flow from that source whereas "Synod" is a reference to the Church in meeting to determine policy by and for a particular church body. The name was changed officially to "Augustana Lutheran Church." I shall use this designation unless a specific quotation includes the term "Synod."

[2]Carl Anshelm, *Peter Fjellstedt*, Vol. 1: *hans barndoms-och ungdomstid samt utländska missionsverksamhet* [*Peter Fjellstedt: His Childhood, Youth and Foreign Missions Work*] (Stockholm: Svenska Kyrkans Diakonistyrelses Bokförlag, 1930), pp. 13, 16, 42.

From Fjällane
Ruins of house where Fjellstedt was born

Fjellstedt's first pulpit

Economic hardships forced the family to move often within the Sillerud parish (e. g., Solberga, Sandtegen, Tranhem, Fjällane, Takena, Byn). Not only individual conditions contributed to their poverty. National disaster worked its hardship. In 1812, all of Sweden suffered from a severe famine. Many persons starved to death. The Larssons along with many others were forced to eat bread made from the bark of trees.

Under such circumstances, Peter was forced to leave home at the age of nine to support himself. He hired out to herd cattle and sheep. Even at so early a stage, he showed inclinations toward becoming a preacher. In later years, he remembered: "Once in awhile, I would step up on a large stone and try to preach to cows, sheep and lambs but I did not find them very remarkable listeners. Quickly I would have to finish my preaching and again assemble my scattered herd."[3]

With the end of summer came also the end of Peter's job. With many other Swedes, including children, he was reduced to beggary, a most offensive ordeal for a boy who was basically very bashful, a trait which characterized him through all his student days. Fortunately, Peter was rescued from this unwelcome form of livelihood by his engagement by a neighboring farmer for his services as a tutor for the farmer's children. This was evidence of a precocious boy who at the age of ten was able to teach other children. Since the age of six, "a burning desire to read was . . . in him" and he read everything he could lay his hands upon. Within a year he was able to read without stumbling.[4]

For the next five years, Peter alternated between the work of a tutor during the winter months and a herdsman in the summer. He also developed skills as a carpenter, woodsman, tailor and farmer.

At the age of fourteen, he prepared himself for confirmation and his first communion, an experience which he later said had not been entirely satisfying as a religious experience. At the age of sixteen, the death of his mother at the early age of forty-four hastened his departure from home. Through the help of his pastor, Nils Sillén, Peter went to Karlstad where he began his formal education. When he matriculated there, he signed his name "Peter Fjellstedt." Thereafter he was thus known.

2. Education at Karlstad (1819-1823)

Peter's early years as a student were marked by great proverty. A teacher, a friend of the Larsson family, arranged with the owner of a foundry to contribute toward Peter's education. The donor agreed to give ten *riksdalar* if he completed the first term.[5] It is not clear whether that promise was fulfilled. Fortunately, he obtained from other sources twenty *riksdalar* for his needs.

At the beginning, because of limited means, he was forced to engage a corner room in a public house. Quietness was at a premium if not nonexistent. His bed was the top of a chest; the only cover was his coat. His

---

[3]"Sjelfbiografi af P. Fjellstedt," *Dr. P. Fjellstedt's samlade skrifter*, Vol. 3: *i ordnadt: Predikninar. Föredrag om yttre och inre missionen. Profetiorna. Enskilda bibliska ämmen. Bibliska personligheter* ["The Autobiography of P. Fjellstedt," *Dr. Fjellstedt's Collected Writings According to a Selected Order. Sermons. Discourses on Outer and Inner Missions, the Prophets. Personal Biblical Subjects. Biblical Personalities*] (Stockholm: Nya Tryckeri-Aktiebolaget, 1884). Anshelm employed an interesting photograph of the stone (opposite page 16, Vol. 1) from which the boy Peter preached. He called it: "Fjellstedt's first pulpit." P. 582.

[4]"Kort teckning af d:r Fjellstedt's lif och verksamhet," ["A Short Sketch of Dr. Fjellstedt's Life and Work"], *Biblia det är all den Heliga Skrift, med förklaringar,* Vol. I: *Gamla Testamentet* [*The Bible: the Complete Holy Scriptures with Commentary: The Old Testament*] (Stockholm: F. and G. Reijers förlag, 1890), p. 1.

[5]The *riksdalar* was minted in Sweden beginning in the seventeenth century. The last of this coin was produced in 1871. Its value was about one-fourth of an American dollar. See Svensk Upplagsbok (Malmö: Förslagshuset Norden AB, 1952), 24:143.

diet consisted of bread, butter and water. Hence, it was a great event when his father visited and brought him cheese to add to his fare.

Conditions improved as his instructors came to recognize his diligence and his promise as a student. Arrangements were made for him to be a guest periodically in the homes of various families. He received clothes which with his tailor's skill he altered to fit properly. Eventually, through the efforts of faculty members, he received a position as a tutor to two boys. He was given board, room and fifty crowns.[6] The length of time he was so occupied is not specified. He used the money to buy books. In spite of his poverty, the opportunity to study was so meaningful to him that any hardship from economic privation was almost overlooked. He wrote: "I never lost courage. Hunger and cold were my old companions so I was not frightened. I kept my health and rejoiced each day that I could remain in the town and attend school."[7]

It is not quite true that he kept his health. At the end of the first semester, he contracted measles. He left his bed prematurely to go home to his father's house. He suffered a severe reaction: his face swelled so that his eyes were swollen shut. Refused acceptance at places where he asked, he found shelter in a barn. After two days of refuge there, a woman found him. She too had no sympathy for him and drove him from the building with the comfortless words: "Get out of here immediately, boy. You cannot stay here. If you should die here, it would be terribly difficult to get rid of you."[8] Surprisingly, after he received the command to leave the barn, his condition soon became much better. "Amazingly, I was helped. An hour after I was commanded to leave, I actually became so well that I could go. The fever left me, the swelling went down and my eyes opened. I could not thank the Lord enough."[9]

Fjellstedt related that his beginnings at Karlstad were scarcely auspicious. His education to that point had been confined to the Bible and the Psalmbook which scarcely prepared him for the question at matriculation as to who Gustavus Vasa was. "Had I been asked when Nebuchadnezzar was born, I could have given a better answer."[10] Before the end of his days at Karlstad, however, he had proved himself to be a fine student. He stood at the head of his class in both his second and third years. His ability as a linguist was demonstrated in that by the end of his Karlstad years, he had mastered five languages: German, French, Latin, Hebrew and Greek.

Peter had a personal difficulty in his shyness—a trait which he certainly overcame in his later life. "It was my fortune to be so shy and sensitive, yes, so awkward in fellowship with others that I did not come into close relationship with any of my schoolmates."[11] This negative relation with his peers

---

[6]During the last century the Swedish crown ranged in relation to the American dollar from three to four crowns to one dollar.

[7]Anshelm, 1:42.

[8]*Ibid.*, p. 23-24.

[9]"Autobiography," p. 586.

[10]*Ibid.*, p. 587.

[11]*Ibid.*, p. 591.

led him to believe his fellow students were jealous of him because of his academic accomplishments. So uncomfortable did he feel that he asked and received faculty permission to complete his studies in private away from Karlstad (winter term and part of the summer of 1822). He moved out into the country with a companion.

3. The Years From Lund to Basel (1823-1828)

Because of financial needs, Fjellstedt's studies at Lund were divided into three periods. After a short initial residence at Lund, through the influence of his adviser, the brilliant Lund professor, Esaias Tegnér (1782-1846), Fjellstedt received a position as tutor to the sons of two prominent citizens, Lieutenant-Colonel C. Kuylenstierna and Major C. J. von Mentzer. Since these persons lived in another area, Fjellstedt had to move to Lilla Segerstad in the adjoining province of Småland. His intention was to study theology in private toward the achievement of the coveted profession of the ministry.

Economically, his new position was delightful. "Such a position was for me completely new. Neither hunger nor any other destitute condition plagued me and I lived among men who treated me with goodness and respect."[12] His reference to the behavior toward him no doubt reflects on his bad experiences with fellow students at Karlstad.

In another respect, however, his residence at Lilla Segerstad was less than satisfactory. Academically, he suffered. Tegnér, authority in Greek literature, had been close enough to awaken in Fjellstedt a taste for poetry. Later he felt that he had wasted his time in reading only that type of literature. "My former zeal for serious study was crippled so that I instead turned my ardent imagination in my free time to such activities as reading poetry which had no worth and was an occasion for a waste of time."[13]

The idyllic life in Småland did not, however, extinguish his desire to be a minister. In fact, because of the impact of the religious revival, opportunities for laymen to preach gave him a chance to proclaim the Gospel in the Långaryds parish. His ability as a preacher drew members from as many as a dozen parishes and filled the church to overflowing. "Although only twenty-two years old, Fjellstedt was well along the way to becoming a folk-and-revival preacher."[14]

After sixteen months away from Lund, his determination to become a minister drew him back to the University. By that time, he had developed a strong desire to become a missionary. This was an unusual desire for a person in the Sweden of that day since there was a disturbingly cool attitude toward missions. Only two Swedes in 1825 were missionaries neither of whom was able to receive support from the Church in Sweden. Hans Peter Hallbeck went to South Africa in 1817 under the auspices of the Herrnhuters (the Moravians). Cornelius Rahm was in Siberia from 1817 until 1825. He worked under the Church of England through its London

---

[12]*Ibid.*, p. 591.

[13]*Ibid.*, p. 594.

[14]Anshelm, 1:44.

The old Junior College in Karlstad

Missionary Society, the same organization which later gave support to Fjellstedt who also could not depend upon his own Church in Sweden.

Fjellstedt began his second stint at Lund in the autumn of 1825. He studied church history, Hebrew, Greek, dogmatics and other theological subjects. In early 1826, economic limitations again forced him to seek employment and leave Lund. He moved to Göteborg where he taught English, French, German and Latin at the Herrnhuter school there. The school was under the leadership of the Moravian, Efraim Stare.[15] The influence of this man and the Herrnhuters left a life along impression upon Fjellstedt. Their spiritual warmth, intense interest in missions and sympathy for the Augsburg Confession all appealed to him. He actually for awhile became a member of the Society of the Moravian Brethren. Because of the Society's friendliness to the Augsburg Confession, this action of Fjellstedt did not necessitate a break with his own church.

Not only his spiritual life but his academic commitment was stimulated in Göteborg. He read through the Old Testament in Hebrew. He also studied Icelandic, Italian, Spanish and Portuguese and thus added to his skills four more languages (beside the five he already knew).

He returned to Lund University as a student for the last time in September 1827 after an absence of more than a year and a half. By the end of the year, he had completed his studies. He was examined by the faculty and received the highest academic award, two *riksdalar*.

In early 1828, he returned to Karlstad to be ordained there. Ordination was delayed because he had not fulfilled the requirement of parish service under the supervision of a pastor. This demand was met by a ministry of two months under pastoral supervision from the minister in Millesvik,

---

[15]"Moravian" and "Herrnhut" refer to the same religious group.

Värmland. Finally, on May 1, 1828, he was ordained at Karlstad. As at Lund, Fjellstedt did very well. Bishop Bjurbäck said: "Fjellstedt will be ordained for he knows more theology than the masters."[16]

Although offered an assistantship at Millesvik, he was determined to go out as a missionary. Through the help of Johan Christian Moritz who had been converted from his native Judaism and whom he had met in the summer of 1827, Fjellstedt was accepted by the Mission Institute at Basel, Switzerland. Money from unexpected sources enabled him to travel there. "Once again," he confessed, "the concern of God our Father has been shown for his child."[17] The Institute was still under the leadership of its founder, Christian G. Blumhardt, a warm-hearted and zealously mission oriented man. Fjellstedt was deeply moved by the lively religious spirit of the northern Swiss and southern German piety. He always regarded Basel as his spiritual home, "the home of his heart."[18]

Academically, however, Basel could offer Fjellstedt little. At the end of five months, he left Basel and came under the supervision and support of the Anglican Church Missionary Society for which the Basel Institute educated missionaries. His intention was to go to Abyssinia. With that purpose, he left Basel for London via Sweden in December 1828.

4. From Basel to South India (1828-1835)

The Basel Society followed the practice of sending its prospective missionaries back to their homeland before they left for their first assignment. This arrangement was not only out of the humane consideration that the servants of the Church would be away from their native land for a long time; the Society also felt their visits would be a means of fostering missionary interest in the home countries.

Fjellstedt arrived in Malmö on (the day of) Christmas Eve, 1828. He concentrated on three centers: Lund, Göteborg and Stockholm. Only in Göteborg did he feel the message for missions received an encouraging hearing. This may have been because of the influence in that area of both Henric Schartau (1757-1825) and the Moravians. He succeeded in organizing the first missionary society in Sweden, *Svenska Missions Sällskapet* of Göteborg. Six years later, in 1835, a society of the same name but national in scope was brought into being. Fjellstedt also participated in the celebration of the 1,000th anniversary of the arrival of Ansgar, the young Benedictine monk, as missionary to Sweden. His arrival is generally regarded as the beginning of the Christianization of this northern country. In a tone of discouragement, he reported to the Basel Society: "I have tried through God's grace in accordance with my instruction to light a fire. That is all I could do. Whether it goes out or through the Saviour's breath of grace flames up, He

---

[16]Anshelm *Peter Fjellstedt*, Vol. II: *hans verksamhet i hemlandet för den yttre missioner* [*His work in the Homeland for Outer Missions*] (Stockholm: Svenska Kyrkans Diakonistyrelses Bokförlag, 1935), p. 85.

[17]"Autobiography," p. 598.

[18]Anshelm, I, 145.

alone knows. I pray that it will blow upon these small sparks."[19] Subsequent developments showed Fjellstedt's work had been blessed far more than he thought.

Slightly more than two months after his arrival in Sweden, he left for London on February 28, 1829. The size and culture of the large city impressed him. Even more, he was moved by the great missionary interest he found there. There were three missionary societies, one of which was to support him for several years, the Church Missionary Society.

He stayed in London from the spring of 1829 to early autumn of 1830 in order to study languages. To the nine with which he was equipped, he added five more: Arabic, Ethiopian, Amharic (the official language of Ethiopia), Coptic and Persian. He also studied medicine, botany, chemistry, astronomy, mineralogy and zoology. Samuel Lee, professor of Arabic and later of Hebrew at Cambridge, said of Fjellstedt: "It seems that he has such good ability in all kinds of disciplines because he makes such rapid progress in all of them."[20]

War in Abyssinia prevented Fjellstedt from going there. Just at that time, the Institute at Basel needed a teacher. He was called there and from the autumn of 1830 to the end of that year, he taught Hebrew, Greek and exegesis in the Old and New Testament. He found his work very unsatisfactory. "I was seldom really composed or happy."[21]

He was, therefore, very happy when the Church Missionary Society called him to become director of the Protestant seminary for the education of native teachers in Pallamcottah, South India. He returned to London to make final arrangements for his leave-taking. Although the Church Society was Anglican, Fjellstedt's ordination in the Lutheran Church of Sweden, was acceptable. Had the orders been of the Lutheran Church in Germany, he would have had to be ordained in the Anglican Church.

In March 1831, Fjellstedt was married to Christiana Schweizerbart, the daughter of a professor at the Karlsinstitut in Stuttgart, Germany. The marriage service was celebrated by an Anglican priest in London.

Peter and Christiana left for South India shortly after their marriage. A sea voyage of five months around the South African Cape of Good Hope brought them to Madras on the east coast of India in September 1831. For the next four months, Peter studied two new languages: Sanskrit and Tamil, the latter of which he found difficult to read.

In January 1832, they left for their new home about 380 miles south of Madras, Pallamcottah. They stayed there for a little more than three years. Peter found satisfaction in his work. In spite of opposition from Hindu Brahmans, the number of converts grew. Revolutionary for that time and in that place, girls as well as boys were educated. He taught the Bible, the Christian faith, Greek, English, Sanskrit, natural science and also made tours to congregations where he preached in the native language, Tamil.

Both the Fjellstedts suffered ill health from the extremely hot climate they

[19]*Ibid.*, p. 118.

[20]*Ibid.*, p. 131.

[21]*Ibid.*, p. 142.

encountered there. Almost from the beginning, Christiana was sick and had to move to a cooler climate on the southeast coast of India. Before long, Peter suffered from boils which had the frightening effect of causing lapses of memory. Warned by doctors that the boils could go inward and cause death, the Fjellstedts left Pallamcottah on February 20, 1835.

In India, two daughters, Theodora Eugenia and Selma Natalie, had been born. On the return sea voyage, ten month old Selma died. With no other pastor on board, Fjellstedt had to conduct the funeral for his little daughter. "The thoughts which filled my fatherly heart as the little casket sank into the deep, I will not try to write. But one day, when the deep shall give up its dead, all who are asleep in the Lord shall be reunited and be with him forever, never again to be separated."[22]

5. From South India to Asia Minor (1836-1840)

After their arrival in London May 19, 1835, the Fjellstedts remained there until the autumn of that year. October 1 their first son, Victor Nathaniel, was born. Shortly thereafter, Fjellstedt took his family to Christiana's home at Kornthal in Stuttgart. The family remained there until Christiana and the children rejoined the husband and father in the second field where the London Missionary Society sent him.

On April 11, 1836, he arrived in Smyrna (Izmir) Turkey. He worked among the Islamic as well as Eastern Orthodox people. He found the enterprise difficult. "Missionary work among the Mohammedans is different but no more so than the task to carry the Gospel to the members of the benighted Greek Church."[23] (From twentieth century perspective, it is difficult to justify the missionary efforts among fellow Christians of the Eastern Orthodox communion).

On August 10, 1837, Fjellstedt was joined by his family. They made their home in the village of Bouja, a few miles away from Smyrna. In August 1838, their fourth child, Richard, was born.

One of Fjellstedt's great joys was the opportunity to visit the seven cities mentioned in the second and third chapters of Revelation: Smyrna, Laodicea, Sardis, Philadelphia, Pergamum, Thyatira and Ephesus. At the same time, the experience was painful for him because all he found was "representative of a weak remnant of Christianity as it is still found in the Greek Church."[24]

Together with a fellow missionary, Mr. Jetter, Fjellstedt labored to communicate the Gospel. Opportunities to preach were minimal. Conversation in such places as coffee houses was more satisfactory. Followers of Islam enjoyed such dialogue. The written word was another avenue. Fjellstedt basically used portions of scripture. A-B-C books, and geography and science books were distributed among children who seemed to enjoy the materials thoroughly.

Hostility to their work was active. The Archbishop of Ephesus was representative of the opposition to Fjellstedt and Jetter: "I have burned your false

[22]"Autobiography," p. 606.

[23]*Ibid.*, p. 607.

[24]*Ibid.*, p. 610.

gospel and shall burn it wherever I come across it."[25] By mid 1840, Fjellstedt was persuaded missionary work in Turkey was futile. On July 20, 1840, the Fjellstedts left. Peter was deeply despondent. How could both attempts to serve in the mission field have ended so badly? Had he misinterpreted the divine calling? He asked such questions in relation to his service in both South India and Turkey. On the occasion of his departure from South India, a fellow missionary from America, Levi Spaulding, wrote a letter of encouragement which turned out to be prophetic: "Although it is now hidden to you at this moment, perhaps you are to do greater work in Europe and in America than in your present work in India."[26] So it was to be.

6. From London to Basel and Back to Sweden (1840-1845)

In Turkey, Fjellstedt had completed a translation into the Turkish language of the Anglican Book of Common Prayer. Upon their arrival in London, this work was accepted by the Society for the Propagation of Christian Knowledge. It was decided, however, that the book should be printed in Leipzig. So, following the birth of their fifth child, Carlotta, the family moved there in order for Fjellstedt to make arrangements for its printing.

In the autumn of 1841, while the Fjellstedts were still in London, Peter was approached by the Basel Mission Society to become one of its travelling preachers to heighten interest in missions. In March, 1842, he was assigned the vast territory of Switzerland, southern Germany, the Baltic States, Sweden, Denmark, Norway, Scotland and England. He still hoped he might be able to return to the mission field and kept his association with the Church Missionary Society. To the credit of this organization, it continued for several years after Fjellstedt's return from Turkey to pay him a stipend. As long as he was with the Basel Mission Society, the Church Society paid him 1800 crowns a year on the grounds he had lost his health while in its service. This was of great help to Fjellstedt since now the family had grown to six living children with the birth of Marie in Leipzig.

He moved his family from Leipzig to Basel in November of 1842. In his deputation work, he held meetings and services not only in churches but in homes and schools also. Weekdays as well as Sundays were employed as he worked for the cause of missions. On a typical Sunday he would preach in the morning. In the afternoon, he gave missionary presentations. He also gave Bible studies and counseled troubled people. Although he met some opposition, the cause of missions prospered under his ministry.

As time went on, he longed to go back to Sweden. Since this was one of the countries which had been assigned to him, the opportunity was open to him. Hence, on July 22, 1843, he landed in Malmö. Visits with his aged father and his old acquaintances in Karlstad were heartwarming. During the next nine months, he preached in approximately one hundred congregations in the provinces of Värmland, Dalarna, Småland, Blekinge and Skåne as well as in such important centers as Linköping, Uppsala, Stockholm and Gävle.

[25]Anshelm, 1:261.

[26]*Ibid.*, pp. 179-80.

Wherever he went, the response was enthusiastic. In one instance, he preached to 3000 people for three hours. It was estimated that during his stay in Sweden, he preached to at least 100,000 people. About 5000 Swedish crowns were collected for the Basel Mission Society and at least eleven persons registered their desire to enter into missionary service. To his good friend, Peter Wieselgren, Fjellstedt wrote: "I am in the inner depths of my soul a Swede. On the basis of my travels through Sweden, I have seen that much good can be done through and for the cause of missions by continuing, or, after a time, taking up this work again."[27] Clearly, this second visit in Sweden gave Fjellstedt the feeling of elation in contrast to the despair he had felt during his earlier effort to arouse missionary interest in his homeland.

Fjellstedt left Sweden. By September 1844, he was back in Basel with his family but the urge to live in Sweden deepened. Since his work was in northern Europe and since he wanted his children to be educated in Sweden, he decided to move there with his family. Unable to find suitable living quarters in Lund, they were invited to live with Mrs. Emilie Petersen who, like Mrs. Fjellstedt, was a German by birth. Mrs. Petersen and her late husband had opened at Herrestad near Jönköping a school for poor children. Fjellstedt had become friends with Mrs. Petersen on his recent visit to Sweden. He continued his work for the Basel Mission Society until early 1846. He travelled extensively on the continent and succeeded well to promote missions although he felt that interest was more difficult to arouse than when he had begun his work in 1842. During this period, a seventh child, Joel Elisama, was born in August 1845.

Sufficient missionary interest had grown in Sweden so that a group of people including Peter Wieselgren conceived of the idea of forming a missionary society which would have three features: it would be self-supporting; it would be national in scope; and it would sponsor an institute where persons could be educated for missionary service. Fjellstedt was called to the position of director of the institute which was to be located in Lund. After some hesitation, he accepted the call in February 1846.

7. His Work in Sweden (1846-1872)

Upon his return to Sweden in early 1846, Fjellstedt, with the exception of four years when he lived in Kornthal, Würtemberg, Germany, was to spend the rest of his life ministering in his native land. He did much travelling for the cause of missions. Though his travels were concentrated in the provinces of Blekinge, Skåne and Småland, he also travelled into Dalarna, Gastrikland, Öland and as far north as Gävel and Härnösand. This work was very successful both spiritually and financially for the cause of missions.

i. Fjellstedt—Author, Editor, Educator and "Travelling Preacher"

Fjellstedt, as director of the Institute, believed the students educated for missionary service should receive as rigorous a discipline as pastors. He also

---

[27]Anshelm, II, 170.

favored a close relationship between the Institute and the University at Lund. Missionaries, as pastors, should be firmly grounded in biblical and theological studies.

Beside directing the Institute, Fjellstedt taught courses in Old and New Testament, in biblical analysis and English. He engaged in journalism. In 1846, he launched *Lunds Mission-Tidning* (*Lunds Mission Newspaper*) for the purpose of informing people about the newly formed Lund Missionary Society and to stimulate interest in the cause of missions. A second paper, *Bibelvännen* (*The Bible's Friend*), was begun in 1848 as a companion to *Missions-Tidning* for the purpose of enlightening the laity in "the world of the Bible."[28] For more than twenty years until 1868, he was the sole editor of these papers. In 1848, he began a third paper, *Folkskolan* (*The Folk School*), to be used by parents in teaching their children as a supplementary resource to the public schools which had been established by the government in 1842. He continued the publication of this paper for four years. Finally, for a short time, he edited *Samaritan* (*The Samaritan*) which was sent to prisons, work-houses, factories and the poor. Since his salary from the Institute was not guaranteed, he depended on the income from his papers. The response to these publications was extraordinary. The combined subscription to *Lunds Missions-Tidning and Bibelvännen* reached a total of from 14,000 to 20,000 and they were second in popularity only to the national paper, *Aftonbladet* (*The Evening Paper*).

The Mission Institute at Lund, though financially solvent, never attracted many students. Various reasons were given. Some critics, including Lars Paul Esbjörn, then pastor at Hille who would later be the first ordained pastor from Sweden to come to America as one of the founders of the Augustana Lutheran Church, felt the standards of the school were too high. Others felt the high church orientation of the Lund Missionary Society was an obstacle.

In October 1855, it was decided to move the Institute to the larger city of Stockholm. The Lund Society would become an associate society with the older Swedish Missionary Society located there. From the Lund Society, one half of its resources of 40,000 *riksdalar* was to be held in trust by the older Society from which only the interest could be used. Should the Lund Society at any time again become an independent unit, it could take back the 20,000 *riksdalar*. The other half was given without condition to the Swedish Missionary Society.

The Institute had a promising first year in Stockholm (1856). Forty-nine students—far more than Lund had ever had—were enrolled, thirty in P. A. Ahlberg's catechetical class and nineteen in the preparatory school for ministers and missionaries. After one year, for health reasons, Ahlberg moved and established his own school at Ahlsborg. From his school many later enrolled in the Augustana Seminary and eventually became pastors in the Augustana Lutheran Church in America. At the end of the second year, only twelve students remained. The educational climate for the Institute was not as favorable as Fjellstedt had hoped. The standards may have been too high as some felt they had been in Lund. Education for laity with less rigorous

---

[28]*Ibid.*, p. 266.

Peter Fjellstedt
The original youth portrait in Basels mission institute

theological standards seems to have been more popular. So the experience of P. A. Ahlberg as well as others who stressed this approach suggested.[29]

At the close of the term in 1859, the Institute was moved to Uppsala. Then Fjellstedt, tired and perhaps discouraged, asked to be relieved of his duties. He wanted to become a parish priest. His health was not robust. Beside the deteriorating efffects of his health from the years in South India, a seven week tour of the schools of the Swedish Missionary Society in Lapland for which the Society commissioned Fjellstedt had had negative effects. He contracted an illness which affected his feet. From this malady he never fully recovered.

In 1861, Fjellstedt left Uppsala and thus closed an era in his life. His critical view of the Church had mellowed. In 1855, he had expressed the view that the Church in Sweden ought to adopt the model of the Scotland Free Church. He was close to being a separatist. Even his friend, C. O. Rosenius, considered him too revolutionary. Just four years later, June 1859, Fjellstedt addressed a group of pastors in Uppsala. Although still critical, he was also encouraged "because it is the nature of the Church to outgrow those faults so that it can become what it ought to be."[30] In the previous year, the hated Conventicle Decree of 1726 which had severely restricted religious meetings apart from Church authority had been repealed. Though some of its tenets were adhered to for awhile, the ecclesiastical climate toward freedom was greatly improved.

Beside his work as editor, Fjellstedt distinguished himself as an author. By 1855, he had produced his three volume work, *Biblia det är all den Heliga Skrift, med förkläring* (*The Bible: The Complete Holy Scriptures With Commentary*) and a translation of Luther's *Small Catechism*. The first of these works in its first printing of 4000 copies sold out immediately. It has gone through twelve editions, the last in 1919, thirty-eight years after the author's death. Both of these works were used widely by pastors in the Augustana Lutheran Church. The *Catechism* was one of the first books T. N. Hasselquist, president of Augustana College and Theological Seminary from 1863 to 1889, printed on his press in Galesburg. In 1854, Fjellstedt translated the *Book of Concord* (*Evangelisk lutherska kyrkans symboliska böcker*) which for several decades was the standard work in Sweden. His doctoral dissertation, *Några grunddrag of Nya Testamentets lära om det andelig presterskapet och församlingens embeten* (*Some Essential Features of the New Testament Teaching Regarding the Spiritual Priesthood and the Office of the Congregation*), was published in 1857.

In 1853, Halle University conferred on Peter Fjellstedt a doctor's degree. His reputation as a preacher and teacher was great and was established nationwide. Peter Wieselgren, spoke of his preaching as if it were "the purest of water, that which kings ask for their table, that which shepherds

---

[29]For example, two years after the departure of the Institute from Stockholm to Uppsala, Pastor H. J. Lundborg founded a school a hundred miles north and a little east of Stockholm at Grythyttan. It was a school for colporteurs and it was well received.

[30]Anshelm, *Peter Fjellstedt*, Vol. 3: *hans verksamhet för kyrklig väckelse och inre mission 1850-1881* [*His Work for Church Revival and Inner Missions*] (Stockholm: Svenska Krykans Diakonistyrelses Bokförlag, 1957), p. 219.

seek at the foot of the mountain."[31] And Archbishop Wingård referred to him as "a respected voice in the Church."[32]

During this period also, Fjellstedt began to make contacts and to lend his valuable support to the leaders of the young Augustana Lutheran Church in America. To this body he would become a great theological mentor, defender, supporter—in a word, a wonderful friend.

These years were not without sorrow. In January 1854, their youngest child, Joel, died at the age of nine of scarlet fever. Fjellstedt was away on a preaching mission which made the bereavement more intense. Joel seems to have been a favorite of his father. Already the little boy had expressed his intention to become a minister. Just six years later, in January 1860, the oldest son, Victor, died probably of tuberculosis.

ii. Fjellstedt, Parish Priest

His desire to be a parish priest was met in two places. First, in 1861, he became pastor in Överum, Småland. His tenure there was short. Apparently, Fjellstedt was not as prepared to settle down as he had imagined. In 1866, he left Överum. One observer noted that as a parish pastor, it was "impossible for him to make preaching tours for missions which he continually saw his duty to do."[33]

His second parish ministry was more favorable. From 1866 to 1872, he served as associate with Peter Wieselgren who recognized the need for his friend to make preaching tours. As fellow-worker with Wieselgren at Göteborg, Fjellstedt became the pastor of a new church, Johanneskyrkan. He was also free to travel. For example in 1867, he made an extended tour into Germany and Switzerland to the churches he had visited more than twenty years earlier.

His reputation had spread internationally. His ecumenical spirit attracted the noted church historian of America, Philip Schaff, to invite Fjellstedt to attend the Evangelical Alliance meeting at New York in 1870. Likely because of his age (he was then seventy), Fjellstedt declined. The School at Uppsala was named for him. All his life the Fjellstedt School continued as a chief concern and constantly he spoke in favor of its support.

Emigrants leaving for America from Göteborg, an important place of embarkation, were ministered to by Fjellstedt as well as Wieselgren. Both felt a commitment to the Augustana Lutheran Church. In a letter to T. N. Hasselquist in the spring of 1870, Wieselgren wrote:

> Now your old friend lies panting on the sofa since he has given two
> farewell talks to a thousand or eleven hundred who sailed at eleven
> o'clock this morning and this evening at seven o'clock . . . Such talks I

[31]Emilia Ahnfelt-Laurin, *Peter Fjellstedt: hans verksamhet i fosterlandet mellan åren 1843-1881* [*His Work in the Fatherland Between the Years 1843-1881*] (Stockholm: A. V. Carlsons Förlag, 1881), p. 179.

[32]Anshelm, 3:52.

[33]Ahnfelt-Laurin, p. 196.

have also given when I am able but Fjellstedt gives them every sailing day no matter how weak he is.[34]

That same year, Hasselquist made a visit to Sweden. In Fjellstedt, he found a capable supporter in Augustana's need for funds as well as in its struggle against the attempted inroads into Augustana's work by the American Episcopalian Church, an effort, unfortunately, which seemed to have had some support from officials of the Lutheran Church in Sweden.

These were enjoyable years in Göteborg, but he was also reminded of the reality of mortality. He invited his friend, C. O. Rosenius, to preach for him on May 9, 1867. Rosenius collapsed in the pulpit; his left side remained paralyzed. He lingered for nine months and died the following February. Of him Fjellstedt wrote:

> The beloved and intimately missed and now departed brother was especially dear to my heart . . . . His memory is blessed among us and yet he speaks with power for many thousands though he is dead. No, not dead! I Thess. 4:14: Blessed are those who dwell in the courts of the Lord; they are not dead. They sleep.[35]

Too, his own strength was failing. He surrendered the editorship of *Lunds Missions-Tidning* and *Bibelvännen* though both continued under new direction. In March 1869, he wrote to his son-in-law, Axel Hermelin: "Here in Göteborg there is too much unrest and almost more work than I can endure."[36] Three more years were spent in that city. Finally in September 1872, he left the last parish he was ever to serve and moved to Kornthal, a suburb of Stuttgart.

8. Life in Kornthall, Würtemberg (1872-1876)

The Fjellstedts had hoped to spend their declining years in Mrs. Fjellstedt's home city. She had never felt at home in Sweden. During several and sometimes long periods of time while Fjellstedt was associated with the Institute, she had lived in Kornthal. To retire there seemed advisable.

They were destined to be disappointed. A number of conditions contributed to that situation. The remaining Fjellstedt son, Richard, caused anxiety on two grounds. First, there was concern for his spiritual life. On one occasion, Fjellstedt wrote: "The most important of all, my dear beloved Richard, is the concern for your immortal soul . . . . I entreat you, my dear son, turn to the Lord! . . . Think of the old word: 'Abandon bad company! Flee from evil' "[37]

The other cause for worry was Richard's apparent inability to care for his

---

[34]Peter Wieselgren to T. N. Hasselquist, autumn 1870, in Gunnar Westin, *Emigranterna och kyrkan: brev från och till Svenskar i Amerika 1849-1892* [*The Emigrants and the Church: Letters from and to Swedes in America*] (Stockholm: Svenska Kyrkans Diakonistyrelses Bokförlag, 1932), p. 266.

[35]Anshelm, 3:327.

[36]*Ibid.*, p. 338.

[37]*Ibid.*, p. 335.

finances. He had a yen for beautiful horses. In 1867, even before the Fjellstedt's moved to Kornthal, it had been necessary for Fjellstedt's son-in-law, Axel Hermelin, to act as guardian over the financial affairs of Richard and his wife.

Secondly, during this period several of his dear friends passed away. In 1875, Baron Axel Rappe died. He had generously supported Fjellstedt's work for missions. That same year, Rappe's sister, Elise, who had done so much in the publication of Fjellstedt's *Lunds Missions-Tidning* and *Bibelvännen*, also died.

Thirdly, the hope that Christiana's health would be improved in Kornthal was not fulfilled. And fourthly, economic conditions were more severe than the Fjellstedts had anticipated. The inflationary effects of the Franco-Prussian War had made residence in Germany very expensive. "Rent and other prices for those things needed for life have nearly doubled in amount since the last war."[38]

Not all was unpleasant in Kornthal. He rejoiced when he heard of the good progress of the Fjellstedt School in Uppsala. Through the generous contributions of Baron Adolf Rappe of Strömserum, the institution could build better facilities and enjoyed improved solvency. He had the joy of geographical nearness to some of his grandchildren. Little Gertrud, child of his youngest daughter, Marie, and her husband, Captain Philip Klett, lived nearby. In 1874, their nine-year-old grandson, child of Eugenia and Axel Hermelin who lived in Bo, Sweden, came to live with his grandparents in order to attend a noted institute in Kornthal. Also, Fjellstedt could indulge in his fond desire to travel. On four separate occasions (1873, 1874, 1875, 1876) he visited Sweden. Did he perhaps miss his native land more than he had assumed would be the case?

By 1876, the Fjellstedt's decided to return to Sweden. Even Christiana who had so long expressed nostalgia for Kornthal when living away from there now seemed to have a similar feeling toward the native land of her husband. He wrote: "My wife, especially, but also I, both wish to return and set up our home in Hälsingborg, for nowhere has she felt such well-being as there."[39]

Their plans were not to be fulfilled. Before they could leave for Sweden, Christiana died on July 11, 1876. Of her death, Fjellstedt wrote: "The sorrow is deep and difficult. But God is love. Though he takes, yet he also gives. He has shown his grace and mercy in mamma's journey home. It was a quiet, blessed death."[40]

9. His Final Residence in Uppsala (1877-1881)

All the more, following his wife's death, Fjellstedt was drawn to Sweden. He was invited to make his home in a variety of places including the home of his daughter Eugenia. It was, however, the school at Uppsala that drew

[38]*Ibid.*, p. 379.

[39]*Ibid.*

[40]*Ibid.*, p. 383.

Christiana (Nanny) Fjellstedt born, Schweizerbart,
from portrait of year 1841, in Baron J. Hermelins
collection, Gripenberg.

him. There he spent his last years in fruitful activity, quiet and happiness. It must have been with a depth of feeling he received the invitation from seven students there: "With the heartiest plea, we urge Dr. Fjellstedt to take up his dwelling with us here at the School. How ardently we would thank God if such great grace should attend us. He knows that we need such support. May his holy will be done."[41]

In January 1877, he took up residence at the School and during the last full year of his life, 1880, he was provided with more commodious quarters in the newly completed building. He worked for eleemosynary projects such as children's homes. He conducted Bible studies: among those who attended was Princess Eugenia. He helped gather funds for the School, taught some courses in biblical interpretation and assisted in the conduct of morning devotions. He continued to write. He became involved in the Waldenströmian controversy and took a position against Waldenström in his *Hvad lärer Bibeln om försoningen?* [*What Does the Bible Teach About the Atonement?*]. His last published work was entitled: *Bibliska framtids-vinkar* [*The Biblical Signs of the Future*].

Fjellstedt continued to preach. During these last years, he carried out at

41*Ibid.*, p. 385.

least six itineraries. The last official act he did was to preach. On December 12, 1880, he conducted worship in a church outside of Uppsala. The unheated building contributed to the cold he caught. He became very ill and on the early morning of January 4, 1881, surrounded by his children, he died at the age of seventy-eight years, three months and fifteen days.

On January 10, his funeral service was held at the Uppsala cathedral. Many leaders from Church, university and government were in attendance. He was buried near his beloved Fjellstedt School. Tributes came from many places within his homeland and abroad. Of special interest toward the purpose of this book, Fjellstedt's contribution to the Augustana Lutheran Church was the message from T. N. Hasselquist, Olof Olsson and A. R. Cervin, all pioneer pastors of Augustana to whom Fjellstedt had meant so much:

> He more than any living Swede was permitted to be chosen as an instrument in the Lord's hand to awaken a true Christian life. At the same time, he has also been a means to make the holy cause of missions known and loved. He himself for a long time gave his personal power and gifts.[42]

Thus ended the life of one deeply dedicated to the ministry of the Church both in Sweden and beyond its borders. Rich were the effects of his life. His contribution was clearly shown in the Augustana Lutheran Church by its very character and existence.

10. Peter Fjellstedt: The Pioneer

Peter Fjellstedt was a man of many gifts. Vocationally, he was committed to the cause of the Christian Church. He expressed that vocation as preacher, tutor, educator, teacher, missionary, scholar and pastor. But he was something more. He was also a pioneer and this dimension of his career enhanced his vocation.

Who is a pioneer? Webster's Third International Dictionary gives a twofold definition of the noun form: one that "originates or helps open up a new line of thought or activity" and "one of the first to settle in a primitive territory." As a verb, pioneer means: "to act as a pioneer" and "to open or prepare for others to follow."[43]

Fjellstedt fulfilled these traits. In his criticism of the Lutheran Church in Sweden and his sympathy for a free church on the pattern of the Free Church of Scotland, he was opening up "a new line of thought or activity" which was foreign to Swedish history.

He did not literally become "an early settler in a primitive territory"—unless one counts his years in South India and Asia Minor. That could scarcely be a justifiable application of the term "pioneer." Metaphorically, however, he was an "early settler in a primitive territory" in his determination that missions, heretofore of scant concern to the

---

[42]*Augustana och missionären: veckotidning för kyrka och mission* [*Augustana and the Missionary: Weekly Paper for Church and Mission*], 26 (February 23, 1881), 114.

[43]*Webster's Third International Dictionary of the English Language*, 1961, p. 1721.

Lutheran Church in Sweden, must become an important imperative in the life of that Church.

Certainly also he was one "to open or prepare for others to follow." By the combination of his many gifts, his charisma, and his commitment, he not only prepared the way where others might follow but was sufficiently persuasive to motivate them to do so. In the light of these qualities, Fjellstedt did indeed "act as a pioneer."

To these traits must be added one more characteristic, the willingness to leave the security of an established order and risk the dangers of a new and often unfriendly environment. This, too, marked much of his ministry. One need only recall the dangers he experienced during the missionary phase of his career especially in Asia Minor. Likewise, it would have been easier to have kept silent about the faults of his Church. That he refused to do. Though he was a loving critic of Swedish Lutheranism, his was one of the few voices raised in protest against its weaknesses.

The quality of his vocation as a pioneer runs like a thread throughout his career. Had it not been for this trait, it is scarcely likely that Peter Fjellstedt would have emerged into the prominence he did. His courage as a pioneer was demonstrated in a number of significant ways.

i. Inspired the First Missionary Society in Sweden

Following the practice of the Basel Mission Society, Fjellstedt, as one of its missionaries, was allowed to return to his homeland before he departed for his assignment in South India. While in Sweden, he held several meetings to promote the cause of missions. He inspired the formation of the Swedish Missionary Society in Göteborg. A later Swedish churchman, Bengt Sundkler, saw that as a significant pioneering venture.

> After Fjellstedt had visited Sweden in 1829, he had doubts as to whether he had been effective. Yet he had been instrumental in organizing one society, *Svenska Missions-Sällskapet* in Göteborg and this *was the first such society ever to have been organized there* [in Sweden]. Six years later, the Swedish Missionary Society in Stockholm was organized from which flowed significant consequences.

The "consequences" of which Sundkler wrote included the important work done by the Society in Lapland and in many parts of the globe. Sundkler concluded: "It is entirely necessary to take account . . . of the preparation for this work which began with Fjellstedt's visit which resulted in the SMS."[44]

ii. Organized the First Mission Institute in Sweden

Fjellstedt was a pioneer in the organization of the first mission institute in Sweden. This occurred in 1846 and was important for Fjellstedt's ability to continue his work for the cause of missions when, because of ill health, he

---

[44]Bengt Sundkler, *Svenska missionssällskapet: 1835-1876: missionstankens genombrott och tidigare historia i Sverige* [*The Swedish Mission Society: 1835-1876: Thoughts on the Breakthrough of Missions and the Earlier History in Sweden*] (Stockholm: Svenska Kyrkans Diakonistyrelses Bokförlag, 1937), p. 35.

Peter Fjellstedt
From portrait, painted in Stuttgart 1835 by
Holder. In Baron J. Hermelin's collection,
Gripenberg.

could no longer be a missionary in a foreign land. He was not a pioneer in the sense that the concept of a mission institute originated with him. He obtained the idea from Basel. Nevertheless, not only the notion itself but also the high academic standards and expectations which he saw in Basel were transferred to the Institute at Lund.

The character of the Institute as Fjellstedt conceived it also had a pioneer element about it. There were those who thought all that was needed was a radical religious experience. In the power and strength of that, one could go immediately as a missionary to a foreign people. In opposition to those who desired lower academic standards at Lund, Fjellstedt argued cogently that the educational requirements for missionaries were great and that the academic discipline of the school must be rigorous. The need to live in a strange country, to learn a new language and to be able to translate required thorough preparation. Furthermore, the need for a solid foundation in biblical, historical and theological studies placed upon sending agencies the grave responsibility to educate their missionaries well. Fjellstedt never surrendered that position.

Because of Fjellstedt's pioneering work and the good foundations he established, the Lund Institute eventually became the Fjellstedt School. That Institution served the Augustana Lutheran Church well.

iii. The Establishment of St. Johannes Church

A third pioneering venture was the erection of St. Johannes Church in the
Göteborg area. This was in no small measure the work of the Dean of
Göteborg, Peter Wieselgren, who wanted to assure the continuing ministry
of Fjellstedt in that vicinity. But Fjellstedt was by no means opposed to the
idea.

St. Johannes Church was of an independent character, the first of that
type to be built in Sweden.[45] One of the constituencies of that particular
church was seamen to whom it ministered. The free-standing church was
non-territorial in that it was not restricted to territorial (parochial) lines. St.
Johannes came out of the revival and was built not from state funds but
from monies raised from among congregations.

Carl Anshelm pointed out further that St. Johannes stood under the
authority of the Dean—in this case, Wieselgren—instead of the Bishop of
the diocese. This arrangement was not altogether pleasing to Bishop Björk.
He raised the question as to the danger of allowing colporteurs to come into
St. Johannes and exercise their ministry. Since he, the Bishop, had no
authority to close the doors to those workers and since he recognized both
Fjellstedt and Wieselgren were sympathetic to that kind of lay activity,
Bishop Björk expressed concern over the ministry at St. Johannes. He
thought its ministry might "glide out into crude ways of error."[46]

Another issue caused Björk even greater anxiety. He knew large crowds
of people would be attracted to St. Johannes with its free access to a wider
variety of spokesmen for the Gospel. The Bishop expressed his confidence
in both Wieselgren and Fjellstedt to supervise adequately this freer ministry.
"But," he wrote, "how shall it go when Brother [Wieselgren] and Fjellstedt
are no longer around to exercise supervision over this?" Wieselgren assured
the Bishop that if he were to go first, then Fjellstedt would still be around to
exert his influence to procure a dean adequate to the task. And, if both
should be gone, Wieselgren expressed confidence in the changed spirit of the
Church as had been demonstrated in the general Church meeting of 1868.[47]

iv. Women Teachers in School in South India

A fourth area of pioneering activity was Fjellstedt's engagement of
women as teachers in the Protestant Seminary at Pallamcottah, South
India, where he was the director from 1831 to 1835. It is true that the
practice did not begin there with Fjellstedt. It was not altogether a new

[45]I am indebted to Dr. Carl Hallencreutz who shared this information with me on
November 12, 1979.

[46]Anshelm, 3:339.

[47]*Ibid.* This followed by two years the important decision of 1866 when the Church in
Sweden was given greater right to direct its affairs through General Assemblies.

initiative.[48] Still, Fjellstedt's support of the policy reflected his sympathy with the advanced views in contemporary India missions. This was a reflection of Fjellstedt's pioneering spirit.

v. The Missionary Movement in Sweden

There were two phases of Fjellstedt's missionary activity: the decade when he served in South India and Asia Minor and his work in Sweden to stimulate the Church's interest in missions. The Church in Sweden had been notably late in sending out missionaries. Its excuse for that neglect included the shortage of pastors in its own land. That its concern for missions had been all but lacking was shown in the need for Fjellstedt to go to other countries (Basel Mission Society and the English Church Missionary Society) for his support when he went out as a missionary.

Fjellstedt was a pioneer in the stimulation of missionary interest in Sweden. Among the papers he edited, one was dedicated especially to that cause—the *Lunds Missions-Tidning*. Through that medium, Fjellstedt informed his readers of a wide range of missionary activities and concerns. Some articles were devoted to non-Christian religions, some, to the character of the land and the people where missionary activity was carried on, and some dealt with missionaries. Letters from those working in foreign countries were reprinted. Appeals for funds and financial reports of monetary gifts received were included. All these features served to arouse and nurture missionary interest.

Not only the journalistic aspect of his vocation but also other expressions of his life work were devoted to the end that Sweden's interest in missions might be heightened. Much of his preaching was dedicated to that end. As a travelling representative of the Basel Mission Society and later in his many preaching tours in Sweden, he emphasized the importance of missions. The people heard and responded with generosity.

It is undeniably true that as a pioneer, it was Fjellstedt who first aroused the national interest in missions in nineteenth century Sweden. He widened the vision of the Church in Sweden so that even before his death in 1881 that Church was gaining a place of prominence among the Western Churches in the missionary enterprise. The Church in Sweden still occupies such a position.[49]

[48]Again, it is to Professor Hallencreutz that I am indebted for this information. The existence of a school for girls at that time over against the prevailing custom in India of educating only boys was heartily supported by Fjellstedt. His attitude belonged to a pioneering spirit. Such a school was a part of the educational institution over which Fjellstedt presided. See above, beginning on page 22.

[49]In late 1971, I had the opportunity in Geneva, Switzerland to converse with Dr. Herbert Schaffer, the head of education for the Lutheran World Federation. He informed me that the Church in Sweden is one of the most generous contributors to missions. Fjellstedt himself lived to see this occur. Toward the end of his life, he wrote: "The Swedish Church has recognized the authority and necessity of the work of missions and has taken a big step forward in that important area of the Christian work of love such as no other state church with the exception of a couple has dared to take. May the Lord in rich measure bless this work!" *Augustana och missionären*, 26 (May 18, 1881), 309.

vi. A Pioneer Among Pioneers

Finally, in his relation to the Augustana Lutheran Church, Fjellstedt was a pioneer—in fact, a pioneer among pioneers. Although he never went to America, the aid, sympathy and support he gave to Augustana fulfilled every trait of a pioneer. Certainly he acted as one. Even with his doubts about the advisability of emigrating to America, he was in spirit "an early settler in a primitive territory" and in his significant support of the work among Swedish Lutheran immigrants, beginning a decade before the organization of the Augustana Lutheran Church, he thus worked "to open or prepare for others to follow." This was accomplished through the several men he persuaded to go to America and serve as pastors.

Other expressions of his role as pioneer in relation to Augustana were as originator or helper to "open up a new line of thought or activity" and "the willingness to leave the security of an established order and to risk the dangers of a new and often unfriendly environment." He took the risk of supporting a people and a form of church polity which Swedish authorities held in high suspicion. Many had little confidence in the survival of the Augustana Lutheran Church.[50] In spite of this, Fjellstedt took a position beside the Swedish Lutheran pioneers in America. He procured for them both money and men for the ministry. He raised their vision beyond themselves from the earliest days of their history as a Church to become aware of the Great Commission to support missionary work. He influenced significantly their view of themselves by doing much to shape their doctrine of the Church.

Peter Fjellstedt above all was a man committed to Christ and his kingdom. For a small group of pioneers in mid-America from which would come an important American Christian community, the Augustana Lutheran Church, he was a pioneer among pioneers.

[50]George Stephenson, *The Religious Aspects of Swedish Immigration* (Minneapolis: University of Minnesota Press, 1932). Stephenson wrote: ". . . Archbishop Wingård, Reuterdahl and Sundberg had strong leanings toward the Anglican Church and looked with no little distrust on the Augustana Synod" (p. 221). He also wrote: "He [Reuterdahl] believed that the Augustana Synod would disintegrate and that the Swedes would be swallowed up by the sects, there being no episcopate to stabilize it" (p. 224).

Old quarter with Spalenthor in Basel, where Fjellstedt lived around 1840.

Chapter II
The Shaping of Fjellstedt's Religious Commitment

As one looks at the accomplishments, commitment and integrity of Peter Fjellstedt, important and intriguing questions arise: "How did he become the person he was?" What were the influences that shaped his commitment?" Or, to put it otherwise, "what was the nature of his religious experience?"

As to parental influence, Fjellstedt was ambiguous regarding the religious influence of his parents. On the one hand, he recalled that in spite of poverty and work which often took him away from home, his father was a faithful attendant at church. "If it were at all possible, [my father] went to church every Sunday although the church was about a [Swedish] mile away."[1]

His mother attended church irregularly due to the severe injury she sustained at the time of the fire which destroyed the family home when Peter was five years old. Even so, she faithfully carried on the religious nurture of her children. "My mother . . . instructed me and my little sister [Marta] at home on Sunday, reading together with us God's Word."[2] His parents taught him many prayers and urged him to employ them morning and evening.

On the other hand, he wrote: "My parents were pious and God-fearing even though they did not truly know themselves or their Savior."[3] Of his father, Fjellstedt wrote that even though his father talked with joy about Christ's suffering and death for us sinners, "he was by no means a slave to the law. Yet, it was also true that at that time, he was not fully enlightened regarding the new life, born of God's Spirit and hidden with Christ in God."[4] No doubt this remark can be taken as a sign of the different direction from that of his parents which Fjellstedt's own religious experience took—a warm-hearted conversion with a deep emphasis on the freedom of the Christian in Christ as proclaimed in the liberating power of the Gospel.

Not only practices and habits bear the stamp of parental influence on Fjellstedt, but also certain episodes such as the fire had their effect. The impairment of his mother's health as she saved Peter and his sister was never forgotten by Fjellstedt. The impression of costly sacrifice on his behalf was strong. The religious significance of that event was apparently less dramatic than in the case of John Wesley who went through a similar experience at the age of five or six. "This deliverance [of Wesley] was taken

---

[1]"Autobiography," p. 580.

[2]*Ibid.*

[3]*Ibid.*

[4]*Ibid.*, pp. 580-81.

thereafter, both by mother and son, as a sign of special providence for him."[5]

A more convincing evidence of parental impression upon the young Peter occurred in another event. When as a young boy he was forced to become a tender of cattle and sheep, he one day found himself in the company of a little shepherdess. She had picked some wild strawberries. Peter was so hungry that he stole the berries. In what he later termed "a wicked work," he told how his conscience bothered him. Years later when he heard the person from whom he had stolen the strawberries was suffering from poverty, he sent her one crown for the berries. He further noted that in other situations, he found himself helping others because of his memory of the "wicked work he had done."

This reminds one of the agony which Augustine in a similar way recounted in his *Confessions* when with a group of young boys, he stole some green pears and fed them to swine. Augustine later concluded his action was an expression of original sin.[6] In both instances, young boys had been made sensitive in their consciences by concerned parents. In spite of criticism of his parents' religious experience, Fjellstedt owed much to them for his moral discernment.

Often persons in their adolescent years have significant religious experiences. Such people nurtured in churches where confirmation and the first communion come together look upon these events as crucial. They have high expectations.

So it was with Fjellstedt. "When I arrived at my fifteenth year, I prepared myself for my first communion . . . On the day I was to celebrate the holy supper, I cast myself down before the God whom I did not yet know and prayed from my heart for grace and help that I wanted to be his child." Still, his expectations did not issue in a satisfying conclusion. "I knew that something was lacking, but I did not know what and even less did I know how to win what was absent. I knew no teacher who could counsel me in whom I could trust."[7]

Yet, the event of confirmation and first communion was not without significance. The desire and felt need to read the Bible were greatly intensified but the opportunities to do so were limited. He wrote: "Since the Bible which my parents had owned was destroyed when the house burned down, they had not the means to purchase a new one. The Bible in my home region at that time was quite uncommon. It was expensive to buy."[8] Fjellstedt further stated that Bible Societies were not yet found in his land. That statement was not quite true since the first Swedish Bible Society had been founded in Stockholm under royal auspices in 1815. Practically,

---

[5]Albert C. Outler, ed., *John Wesley*, A Library of Protestant Thought Series (New York: Oxford University Press, 1964), p. 6.

[6]Robert M. Hutchins, ed., *Great Books of the Western World* (Chicago: Encyclopedia Britannica, Inc., 1952), 28:11-12.

[7]"Autobiography," pp. 584-85.

[8]*Ibid.*

however, Fjellstedt was right. He was confirmed in 1816 or 1817. The impact of a young society located in Stockholm could scarcely yet have been felt in a remote parish in interior Sweden.

He inaugurated another exercise in order to satisfy his spiritual hunger— the keeping of a diary. He kept a close account of his manner of life on a day to day basis. The enterprise turned out to be disappointing. "In my spiritual blindness, I found no other sin in myself except I was negligent in my prayers." He saw himself as guilty of a pharisaical attitude. "In this ignorance I remained for many years until it pleased the Lord in his grace to open my eyes."[9]

When Peter was fifteen, his mother died. Following her death, Peter wrote: "Peace be with you, beloved soul! O, that I might meet you again one time and thank you for your motherly tenderness." His feelings toward his departed mother were remorseful because of his lack of true appreciation for her and all she had done for him. He continued: "I have caused you much worry. You have lavished many tears of love upon me, and these I shall always esteem higher than costly pearls."[10]

Some years later, Fjellstedt was with a number of people from Dalarna, many of them youth. They were returning from Stockholm by boat after having spent the summer in the Stockholm area working as gardeners or boatmen. Fjellstedt spent some of the time during what he called a glorious day singing with the group. Many of the songs were folk melodies. Of that experience, Fjellstedt wrote: "My deceased mother, who had a good voice, sang them often in my childhood by the spinning wheel during the long winter nights whenever she was well enough to do so and we children sat along side her by the hearth and eagerly listened to her." The memory of these childhood evenings drew from Fjellstedt a deep emotional response: "When again I heard those mellow, beloved and elegaic tunes, then began the strings of my soul, long slumbering, to vibrate and I could have wept to the full if only I would have had a corner to myself."[11]

Later in his life, he remembered his parting from his father when he left for school in Karlstad. His father walked with him for two Swedish miles. Fjellstedt remembered: "He gave me the warmest and sincerest encouragement and admonition. The parting was difficult." This separation must have had a spiritual impact upon Fjellstedt for he wrote that after his father had left him, he turned in to the woods and fell down

> "before the Father in heaven and prayed many sighs and tears that his grace and blessing might escort me and his fatherly hand preserve me and make my way prosperous. That was my desire, to be a useful person and I prayed God to help me be that. I realized my helplessness."[12]

[9]*Ibid.*, p. 585.

[10]*Ibid.*, p. 586.

[11]Anshelm, 2: 68.

[12]"Autobiography," p. 587.

He must have felt a similarity between his father who had followed him the first stage of that "long and unknown way" and God whom he had learned to know as Father.

Fjellstedt's experiences at Karlstad have been recounted including the serious illness in the barn on the completion of his first term at Karlstad. Of that event, he related: "I sighed to the Lord with the resolution and promise that if the Lord would help me, I would be his obedient child. Alas, I did not yet know the life or essence of Christianity."[13] That Peter Fjellstedt remembered this vow to be an obedient child of God in exchange for divine aid in the recovery of health must be regarded as significant in his religious development.

Though his studies at Karlstad went well, it was otherwise with his spiritual life. That period was the beginning of the nadir in his religious development.

> During all this time, my heart grew more and more cold. My Bible in which I formerly did much searching became for me unimportant, and I lived in such spiritual darkness, that I yet today must marvel over God's grace which preserved me so that I did not sink completely into the character of a pagan.[14]

He did not, however, sink into immoral habits. For that he gave credit to two forces: the grace of God and his own bashfulness. Otherwise, it would have been easy for him to adopt that manner of life since he felt many students at Karlstad practiced questionable habits.

In spite of this negative evaluation of Karlstad, his years there likely played a greater role in shaping his religious experience than he realized. Certainly the presence of the cathedral and worship in that edifice were in striking contrast with the very much simpler church structure and worship atmosphere of the country parishes where he had lived. The much more impressive cathedral services in Karlstad must have been important in the development of Fjellstedt's later growing appreciation of the Church and its worship life.

The spiritual coldness of which he complained continued into the first period of his residence in Lund beginning in the autumn of 1823. During an interlude of a year and eight months when Fjellstedt lived in the homes of the boys he tutored, his economic condition greatly improved. During that time, life for Fjellstedt was pleasant. "I came to be regarded as a member of the family. My salary was sufficient so that I was able to purchase for myself respectable clothing and save some for my future needs at school." The contrast of that new kind of life with the poverty which he had suffered deeply impressed the young student. "After such a long time of need and denial, these changed conditions raised my depressed courage."[15]

Perhaps there is a time when one needs to withdraw from life which has been under intense pressures such as poverty or zealous studying. Fjellstedt

---

[13]*Ibid.*, p. 589.

[14]*Ibid.*, p. 592.

[15]*Ibid.*, p. 594.

had experienced both. He wrote: "I soon experienced that days of prosperity are less good for our inmost being than those of adversity. My former zeal for serious study was crippled so that I instead turned my ardent imagination in my free time to such activities as reading poetry which had no worth and was an occasion for a waste of time."[16] The works of his adviser at Lund, Tegnér, especially interested him and he was drawn to read romantic literature. As he looked back on those activities in later years, he was prompted to write: "I lived neither in heaven nor on earth but in a dream world which I had created for myself."[17]

According to his standards, he later judged the young people with whom he associated as worldly. This is additional evidence of his tendency to be judgmental. For example, Fjellstedt remembered that though the young people attended the Christmas morning services, in the evening of that day, they celebrated with a dance which lasted long into the next day. Although Fjellstedt had not participated, he looked upon that time of his life as outwardly correct in churchly form but lacking in inward religious faith.

In 1824 three events occurred which were crucial in the development of a deeper religious faith. One day when Fjellstedt was swimming with his students, after the swim he entered into play and laughter with the boys. For this, he was reproached by a peasant who said to him: "How can you who want to become a preacher lead the young in such frivolous living?"[18] The incident left an unforgettable impression on the young student-tutor.

A second experience also affected him. He wanted to preach: during the summer of 1824, he was given that opportunity. He immediately showed great gifts. After his third sermon, a peasant approached him. He thanked Fjellstedt for the sermon he had heard. He indicated that he had been shown his ruined condition but he had not been told how he could be saved. Fjellstedt related he tried to help the man with the "little dogmatic knowledge that I owned." From the young preacher, the peasant had received more law than gospel. Fjellstedt admitted that he was shown the inadequacy of his counsel. "[The peasant] set forth the truth of Christianity so clearly and distinctly that I was amazed. I was rather his pupil than his teacher. I talked further with him. His word was not in vain for it was God's word."[19]

Finally, a third event deepened his religious life and helped lead him to the mission field. Of these three events, it was this one which he considered crucial in his vocational decision.

During the summer of 1824, he had a dream. He found himself in the forefront of a large mass of people rushing forward toward a steep cliff. Fjellstedt was carried along toward certain ruin. He tried in vain to warn the people of danger. Suddenly he heard a voice. He looked up and saw a radiant figure clothed in a white mantle. From the garment hung red threads upon which Fjellstedt laid hold and thereby was saved.[20]

[16]*Ibid.*

[17]Anshelm, 2:52.

[18]*Ibid.*, p. 55.

[19]*Ibid.*

[20]*Ibid.*, p. 66.

The dream had a two-fold meaning for him. First, he marvelled that he had been saved by the grace of God. In his own experience, he could identify the wonder of grace with the dream. Secondly, he could not forget all those who had perished. For him, it was similar to the vision Saul had received on the road to Damascus. Fjellstedt knew he must go to the heathen to bring the word of salvation. His fellow countrymen had that word but hundreds and thousands in pagan lands were without the Gospel. The dream constituted an important part of his religious experience.

Fjellstedt showed the impatience of a new convert. Paul the Apostle was his model. His desire to become a minister took a new direction; he would go to the heathen. He asked himself why should they be denied the glorious Gospel which had so changed his life. He also wondered why he could not earn his living as Paul had earned his livelihood as a tentmaker. So Fjellstedt, equipped to earn money either as a carpenter or a tailor, could likewise be independent of financial support from others. He was so filled with the thought of missions that had he been able, he would have left immediately.

It was fortunate that he did not have the money to leave for a foreign country. He soon realized the need to further his education. He was given more opportunities for preaching and people came in large numbers to hear him. Later reflection on his preaching caused him great dissatisfaction. "I preached often although certainly with little biblical or solid basis. Yet numerous people came to the churches. But I was only a weak beginner. If God's grace would not have protected me, it would have been easy for me to have become a fool."[21]

He realized his need to deepen his spiritual life and enrich his intellectual resources. He returned to Lund in the autumn of 1825 to pursue and complete his theological studies. Eventually, he completed his work and was ordained in 1828.

What then were the influences in his life which brought Fjellstedt to his spiritual crisis and consummated in his committed and rich ministry? In addition to the influence of his parents and the three events of the summer of 1824, was the time of unusual spiritual revival in Sweden. Among the principal persons in this movement were J. O. Hoof from Svenljunga and Per Nyman from Burseryd who were very influential especially upon the people of Västergötland, Småland, Blekinge and Halland. Of a different type was the influence of Henric Schartau who was more dogmatic and at the same time dynamic. The revival began in the third decade of the nineteenth century. "From these various sources came the influence of a type of ascetic piety with which Fjellstedt now became acquainted and which was decisive for him the rest of his life."[22]

As a young man, J. O. Hoof was married to a woman described as an "old widow." The marriage was not happy. Hoof attempted to find solace in card playing, dancing and drinking. He came to a crisis sometime during 1808 and 1809 when, in a vision, he saw himself in the power of the devil

---

[21]"Autobiography," p. 596.

[22]Anshelm, I, 54.

and living in hell. From this emerged his religious viewpoint which drew from two types of pietism: the older which stemmed from Halle (of which more will be written later) with its emphasis on the law and ascetic living and the Moravian which emphasized the reconciling power of the blood of Christ. As an outer sign of his religious viewpoint, he adopted drab clothing and taught zealously the doctrine of self-denial. His preaching and example were powerful. Many came from long distances to hear him at his church in Svenljunga.

What influence Hoof had on Fjellstedt is not entirely clear. In his early preaching, Fjellstedt's emphasis upon law may have come from Hoof's sermons. More likely, Hoof's contribution to Fjellstedt's religious experience was the general religious climate which Hoof helped develop.

A more direct influence seemed to come from Per Nyman. Of Fjellstedt's early preaching in the summer of 1824, it was said: "They who had been awakened by Nyman's preaching a couple of years earlier rejoiced because they seemed to perceive something of the same life and warmth in Fjell-stedt's preaching."[23]

Nyman's was a troubled career. He was influenced by Halle pietism and in that respect was similar to Hoof. He also drew both from the Moravians and Schartau. He enthusiastically studied the Bible and Luther. At one time, he became so involved with the temperance movement and carried on his activities in such an unreasonable manner, in the minds of many, that he came into conflict with others in the Lund diocese. At Växjö, he became extremely enthusiastic in the pulpit. Some felt that he became so wild and careless that for a while he was suspended from that parish. He moved to Hälleberga where he was very popular. The church was filled with large crowds. Later he returned to Växjö and then moved to Stockholm. In each place, many were attracted to his sermons. In later years, he moved more and more toward the Schartaun position with its emphasis upon the Church and the confessions. Interestingly, he became an opponent of the evangelism represented in the preaching of Fjellstedt and Rosenius.

Although Fjellstedt's early preaching was likened to that of Nyman, it is difficult to ascertain what the direct relationship was. Perhaps it was the style of a rather free type of preaching with a good measure of enthusiasm which led the hearers of the young Fjellstedt to compare him to Nyman.

A significant observation about Nyman is that he brought together important forces in his life and thought which contributed most significantly to the changed religious climate in Sweden. Three of these forces were: the old pietism of Halle as represented in Hoof, Moravianism and Schartauism. The influence of the old pietism on Fjellstedt has been observed. The questions arises what influence, if any, did the Moravians and the Schartauian teaching have upon Fjellstedt's religious life?

No doubt the Moravians had a great impact upon him. He always referred to this movement as "Herrnhutism." The Moravians, spiritual

[23]Hjalmar Holmquist, *Handbok i Svensk Krykohistoria: från romantiken till första världskriget* [*Handbook of Swedish Church History: from the Romantic Period to the First World War*] (2d ed., Stockholm: Svenska Kyrkans Diakonistyreles Bokförlag, 1952), III, pt. 3, 39-40.

descendants of John Hus, were later generously patronized by the eighteenth century Nicholas Ludwig Count von Zinzendorf at his estate, Herrnhut. They had come to Sweden in their characteristic missionary zeal during the first third of the 1700's. A significant contact for Sweden with the Moravians was through a Swedish layman, Sven Rosén, who had encountered them on his travels to Riga, Russia. Sometime between 1731 and 1734 Rosén brought back to Sweden the Moravian influence. Thereafter, the Moravians were a continuous force in the development of pietism in Sweden.[24] They travelled through the country as "diaspora workers." Not only laymen but a number of clergymen were influenced by them. It was felt the Moravians were similar to Lutherans in their Christocentric emphasis and their stress upon the atonement. Moreover, Zinzendorf himself claimed to be a Lutheran and Fjellstedt was attracted to them because of their subscription to the Augsburg Confession. Finally, the Moravians, unlike more radical pietists, did not counsel separation from the Church. Like Würtemberg pietism, Moravianism tended toward a churchly position.

Fjellstedt came into contact with the Moravians when he was engaged as a teacher in a Moravian school in Göteborg in early 1826. He remained in that position until September 1827. He was greatly influenced by the head of the school, Efraim Stare. He later expressed his gratitude for the benefits he had received there: "I learned to better understand my inner condition of ruin and received a clear, evangelical perception of the great biblical truths."[25] In fact, so impressed was he that on November 13, 1826, he became a member of the Society of the Moravian Brethren.

He may well have remained a Moravian except for a close friend of his, Carl Wilhelm Lilliecrona. An able man, Lilliecrona had served in the Swedish army. Later, he went to America where he came in contact with the Moravians and was impressed with their gentle innocence and fear of God. He became a member of that community. Upon his return to Sweden, Lilliecrona associated himself with the school over which Stare presided. He spent a short time at a Moravian community in Christiansfeld where his enthusiasm for the Moravian faith and life began to fade. He also began to have doubts about the sincerity of Stare and came to regard him as guilty of self-interest and hypocrisy. The disenchantment with the Moravians of his good friend no doubt influenced Fjellstedt in his decision not to remain a Moravian.

Although Fjellstedt did not remain a member of the community, he continued to think warmly of its members. After his residence in Basel, he returned to Sweden in December 1828 to awaken interest in missions. In his judgment, the tour fell short of the results he had desired. The one successful accomplishment was the establishment of the Swedish Missionary Society of Göteborg in early 1830, the first of its kind in Sweden. Stare, was the moving force of the new association. The new Society was established on the pattern of Moravian organizations: one division for men, one, for women, and one, for children. The Society met

---

[24]Karl A. Olsson, *By One Spirit* (Chicago: Covenant Press, 1962), pp. 29-30.

[25]Anshelm, I, 73.

the first Sunday of every month and began a library with more than 200 articles and works on missions. In subsequent years, Fjellstedt visited his Moravian associates in Göteborg and continued to do so even after the death of Stare in the early 1840's.

Sympathy for Moravian expression and view of the Christian faith continued to the end of his life. This was symbolized by the way in which he planned the chapel at the Fjellstedt School in Uppsala. While he resided at the School during the four years prior to his death, a new building, dedicated in 1880, was erected. Fjellstedt was responsible for the design of the chapel. He followed the Moravian plan of architecture. The large auditorium with its flat ceiling was furnished with benches on three sides but grouped very closely together near the front where, at the center of that wall, were the altar and pulpit. Two doors, one on each side of the wall opposite the altar and pulpit, followed the custom of separate entries for men and women. This corresponded to the Moravian custom that the men and boys sat on one side of the building while the ladies and girls sat on the other. This design was in stark contrast with Lutheran architecture not only in its greater simplicity but also in its rejection of the long and narrow nave so typical of Lutheran congregations.[26] The style and seating arrangement emphasized what their congregations were often called: "brödra-församlingen"—"Congregation of Brothers." Obviously, the views of the Moravians were highly valued by Fjellstedt to the end of his life.[27]

One other aspect of the relationship between Fjellstedt and the Moravians must be explored. Certainly it would seem that their missionary zeal strongly nurtured Fjellstedt's determination to serve on mission fields. He did express his desire to Stare to become a missionary who encouraged Fjellstedt in that direction. It is strange that neither in his autobiography nor in Anshelm's work is much made of this factor. Still, Fjellstedt could scarcely have lived in Göteborg from early 1826 to September 1827 and been unaware of another Swede, Hans P. Hallbeck (1784-1840), who had been associated with herrnhutism and its educational work in that city. Hallbeck later in 1810 was teacher and leader of herrnhut congregations in Ireland and England. In 1817, he went as a missionary to Gnadenthal, South Africa and became Africa's first bishop.[28]

---

[26]Goran Lindahl, *Högkyrkligt läfkyrkligt frikyrkligt i Svensk arkitektur 1800-1950* [*The High Churchly, the Low Churchly, and the Free Churchly in Swedish Architecture*] (Stockholm: Svenska Kyrkans Diakonistryrelses Bokförlag, 1955), p. 30.

[27]I am indebted to the kindness of Allan Parkman, Rector of the Fjellstedt School, for this interesting information about Peter Fjellstedt. Rector Parkman shared this with me in a conference in August 1979. Two other features of the Chapel might be noted. One, the Moravians built their chapels with two sets of windows so that from the outside, the structure gave the appearance of a two-story edifice. On the inside, however, no dividing ceiling-floor was built. A second feature, which may have been Fjellstedt's innovation, was the twelve upper windows each with a star of David design. It is Rector Parkman's belief that for Fjellstedt those represented the twelve tribes of Israel and also the twelve apostles. That may well be. Certainly the emphasis of the Moravians on brotherhood would thus be expressed.

[28]*Svensk Uppslagbok*, 12 (1955), 766.

In addition to the influence of the Halle pietism and Moravianism, the question remains whether Henric Schartau was important in Fjellstedt's religious development. The great influence Schartau had upon the religious life in both the Göteborg and Lund areas left an imprint on Fjellstedt also. When he entered the University of Lund in 1825, Schartau had just died earlier that same year but his strong influence continued to live in the Church.

Early in his life, Schartau, like Fjellstedt, had been attracted to the Moravians. It may have been their sincerity and warmth in contrast to the cold rationalism and dead formalism which characterized the Church of his day that drew him to them. His break with the Moravians was more radical than that of Fjellstedt. After having considered himself a Moravian from 1781-1787, he became a severe critic and accused them of a lack of moral earnestness, too much stress upon feelings and too great a divergence from scripture and the Lutheran faith.[29]

Henric Schartau, a complex man, was a diligent student of the Bible. Next to the Bible, Luther was his chief source of inspiration. He did not hesitate to employ the resources of the Enlightenment for the sake of clarity in his teaching and preaching. All this was brought to bear upon a most effective ministry which began in Lund in 1785 and continued there until his death in 1825. During his long ministry, the interesting amalgamation within him of the "old churchly piety, Moravian Christocentrism, pietism, biblicism, asceticism and mysticism" issued into an influence which especially after his death was felt for a long time particularly in western and southern Sweden.[30]

In relation to Fjellstedt, what may have been the most important contribution of Schartau was the latter's churchliness. He saw the Church as the center from which the saving work of the Gospel should go forth. He held to an orthodox view of pure teaching but combined this with a strong ethical emphasis and so avoided a dry, rigid dogmatism. Schartau saw salvation as progressing in five steps: God's call, the illumination through the law, the illumination through the Gospel, justification or new birth, and sanctification or new awakening. The process was accomplished through the preaching and teaching in the Church. Schartau's order represented a coming together of conservative orthodoxy and moderate pietism. For Schartau, those five steps showed the normal way in which the human being experienced his encounter with God. Consequently, he was critical of the revivalistic methods of the new evangelism to which Fjellstedt was more friendly. Yet, at a very important point, Fjellstedt and Schartau were in agreement: both held high the place of the Church. Whether Schartau's high view of the Church was directly communicated to Fjellstedt is not known. It may be conjectured, however, that from the religious climate created by Schartau who so strongly emphasized the Church, Fjellstedt was inclined toward a similar position.

[29]Arthur B. Carlson, "Pastoral Care in the Faith and Practice of Four Selected Swedish Churchmen" (Ph.D. diss., Boston University, 1962), p. 35.

[30]Holmquist, p. 33.

Another influence Schartau may have had on the religious experience of Fjellstedt was the warmth of piety Schartau had. It is too easy to assume that because one is churchly one cannot therefore have the warmth of spirit associated with pietism. That is not true. Pietism with its biblicism had a deep effect upon Schartau. In his teaching—and he was a most effective catechist—"Schartau spoke of a certainty of faith grounded in the promises of the Word and a witnessing certainty of faith evidenced in human feelings and experiences."[31] Quite plainly, the emphasis on "feelings and experiences" belongs to the nature of pietism.

One Schartauan influence on Fjellstedt was direct. With one of his teachers at Lund, B. J. Bergquist, professor of dogmatics, Fjellstedt had a close association. Bergquist was a follower of Schartau. From him, Fjellstedt received an insight into Schartau's theology. The relation between professor and student was good. "For Bergquist, Fjellstedt always held the greatest respect."[32]

In addition to Halle pietism, Moravianism and Schartauism, one more important factor in Fjellstedt's spiritual growth as well as his theological development was Würtemberg pietism. Fjellstedt became acquainted with this type of pietism when he became associated with the Basel Mission Society in 1830. The contrast between the religious coldness of Sweden and the warm spirit in Basel created an indelible impression upon him. In subsequent years, partly because of Fjellstedt's deep spiritual attachment to Basel and partly because of Mrs. Fjellstedt's fondness for her home in Kornthal, Würtemberg, the Fjellstedts made frequent visits there. To Peter Fjellstedt, Basel was truly his spiritual home, "the home of his heart."

Würtemberg pietism is of interest to students of American Church history because it is a piety somewhat different from that of American Christianity. The latter has been characterized by strong tendencies toward separatism and anti-churchly sentiments. By anti-churchly is meant opposition to, or at least a downgrading of, confessions, ordained ministry, and the sacraments with a corresponding heightening in importance of the Bible ("The Bible is our creed"), laity and religious experience.

Fjellstedt was quite clear in his positive regard for the Church even though he was highly critical of the coldness of the Church in Sweden especially in his earlier years. This forms no contradiction. What Fjellstedt was doing was to compare the Church he knew in his native land with the "one, holy, catholic, apostolic Church" and by that norm, he made his criticism. Even so, he did not support separation from the Church.

> Beloved brothers, do not separate yourselves from the Christian establishment which has brought and brings much blessing for our people . . . . It is necessary for Christians to separate from the wicked ones who are out in the world but not to go out of the Church in our land in which God's word is adequately present and the sacraments administered according to biblical teaching.[33]

[31] Arthur Carlson, p. 43.

[32] Anshelm, 1: 70.

[33] "Eder skäliga gudstjenst" ["Your Reasonable Service"], *Dr. P. Fjellstedt's samlade*

The churchly pietism of Würtemberg was very important in the religious formation of the Swedish Lutheran immigrants in America to which Fjellstedt contributed greatly. Though critical of the Lutheran Church in Sweden, the immigrants remained loyal to the confessions and the worship tradition of their religious heritage.

Würtemberg pietism, while inspired by Spener, took a direction different from that of Halle pietism which had influenced apparently the younger Fjellsted through Hoff and Nyman. A comparison between the two shows four distinctive differences. First, the adherents to Würtemberg pietism were predominately among the clergy, the middle classes in the town and rural areas. Halle pietism in northern Germany was centered in the nobility.

Secondly, Halle pietism tended to downgrade intellectual pursuit in theological studies; Würtemberg pietism was sympathetic to scientific theology. The latter was largely due to the influence of the noted New Testament critic and exegete, Johann Albrecht Bengel (1687-1752). He ably combined the warmth and feeling of pietism with the discipline and scholarship of the mind.

In a more specific manner, Bengel contributed to the shaping of Fjellstedt's religious outlook. This was especially true of his apocalyptic view. Fjellstedt was drawn to the noted New Testament scholar and read his works. This most certainly must have included Bengel's well-known *Gnomen Novi Testamenti.* He was not solely inspired, however, by Bengel. His ideas about both Roman Catholicism and Islam helped create his personal interpreation on this aspect of his theology. A more detailed statement of this issue will be made at a later point.[34]

Thirdly, Würtemberg pietism was characterized by a range and diversity of religious expression and life much more varied than that of Halle pietism. The latter type tended to be rigid with an authoritarian cast. It was taught by Halle pietists that authentic religious experience must be known within a narrow kind of conversion event. The subsequent life was also interpreted in a rigid pattern of behavior which tolerated little variation from a legalistic norm. Conversion "was not viewed in the light of an individual phenomenon, but as the normal way to salvation, regardless of other experiences taught by the history of the religious life."[35] Halle pietism became judgmental, certain of its ability to distinguish between the "saved" and the "unsaved."

Finally, and most importantly for Fjellstedt, was the higher value Würtemberg pietism placed upon the Church. The difference lay in that it preserved the Church ideal because of "the moderate and reasonable course adopted by the ecclesiastical authorities as well as by the absence of a contentious type of orthodoxy."[36]

---

skrifter, Vol. 2, *Bibliska betraktelser och uppsatser* [*Collected Writings: Biblical Meditations and Essays*], p. 576.

[34]See below, pp. 145 ff.

[35]Carl Mirbt, "Pietism," *The New Schaff-Herzog Encyclopedia of Religious Knowledge,* 9: 59.

[36]*Ibid.*

There may have been a point of contact in Würtemberg pietism between Fjellstedt and Schartau. Anshelm suggested a relationship of spirit. He wrote: "During his [Fjellstedt's] residence in Basel, he was fully won over to the Würtemberg pietism with which Schartau was spiritually related."[37]

The religious experiences described in this chapter were of a decisive character. The period from 1822-27 marked a watershed point in his life. So greatly different was his perception of Christian experience and faith after those years than it had been before that one may doubt whether his judgments of the spiritual well-being of others was always accurate or just. At least in his early ministry, he did not hesitate to pass judgment on the validity or lack of authentic Christian faith in the lives of others. It will be recalled how negatively he felt toward the Church in Turkey. Admittedly, the Greek Orthodox Church was scarcely a model of Christian spirituality. Still, Fjellstedt too may have lacked the virtues of charity and patience appropriate in difficult situations. Other instances of his tendency to be censorious can be recounted. For example, following his return from Turkey, he undertook a tour into Alsace in 1843 as a representative of the Basel Mission Society. Of one of the congregations he stated:

> There were only a few awakened souls in Cernay and these were surprised to see their pastor attend the meeting and his remarkable friendliness. I afterwards said to them that they should pray zealously for him. He is a gifted man and if he would come to the new life, he would be a blessed worker in the Lord's vineyard. May God grant that.[38]

One can scarcely admire such action both on the grounds of judging a fellow human being and the ethical implication from such an act that involved the relationship between a congregation and its pastor.

Another example of this tendency toward censoriousness was seen in his relation to his parents. On the one hand, he expressed appreciation for their piety. On the other hand, looking from the vantage point of his decisive religious experience, he deplored the fact that they never talked to him seriously about repentance or about the new birth through the Holy Spirit. Anshelm was correct when he wrote: "Fjellstedt employed a later won, richer experience as a measuring rod against a more simple and unreflective Christianity." Even on one of his final visits with his aged father, Fjellstedt wrote: "It is not easy to understand how it is with father in regard to his Savior. Yet one hopes for the best. One certainly finds no clear light but yet there is a fairly warm heart and at least an outer pious life and love to the Savior and his word."[39]

In spite of this rather unattractive feature of his religious attitudes, the authenticity and power of his Christian faith are obvious. The commitment and accomplishments of Fjellstedt were large indeed. He remains one of the giants of the nineteenth century religious life in Sweden. The source of that

[37]Anshelm, 1:122.

[38]*Ibid.*, p. 354.

[39]*Ibid.*

life-work was inspired by God with its character endowed by his Christian experience. The years 1822-27 remain something of a kairos event—that time in which a watershed mark occurs in a life and from which the subsequent character of that life is shaped. That includes the theology of Peter Fjellstedt to which attention is now turned.

Fjellstedt's Church in Överum, built around 1820, as garden pavilion in the estate park, later used for church service until 1872, now used as a doctor's reception office.

Chapter III
His Theology: Its Formation And Expression

Theologically, Peter Fjellstedt was a moderate confessional Lutheran. In his preaching, he stood between rigid Lutheran orthodoxy and the ecstatic fanatics. He did not find easy fellowship with strict orthodoxy. His differences with the orthodox Reuterdahl-Faxe faction were dramatized at the organization of the Lund Missionary Society. By that group, Fjellstedt was held suspect. In 1849, King Oscar I had wanted to confer upon him the Order of the North Star. Paul Genberg, then the Minister of Ecclesiastical Affairs and later bishop of Kalmar (1852-1875), refused that action on the basis of his doubt regarding Fjellstedt's theology.

Neither did he find identification with ecstatic preachers. He did, however, take a favorable view toward colporteurs. One instance was the case of the Norwegian Johannes Andersson. He came to Sweden and began to preach. Although uneducated, he was an impressive preacher. His utterances were shaped by the religious conversion he had experienced under Haugeanism in Norway. Andersson suffered the wrath of some pastors who accused him of disobeying the Conventicle Act which forbade the gathering of laity in private homes for religious services.

Fjellstedt defended and guided Andersson. Their relationship became so close that the latter came to be known as "Fjellstedt's Johannes."[1] Fjellstedt took him into his school which was then located in Stockholm where Andersson was taught the rudiments of literacy.[2] He accompanied Fjellstedt on preaching tours. As a colporteur, Andersson was advised by his mentor to "read God's word to his assembled friends but not to make an interpretation. . . . Instead read to them . . . from a book of sermons as a devotional book."[3]

Andersson did not follow Fjellstedt's counsel; he continued to do some preaching. The relation between Andersson and Fjellstedt illustrates the temporizing influence the latter had on what came to be known in its more ecstatic forms as "preaching fever." "Dr. Fjellstedt exerted a healthy influence upon the layman's movement in our land."[4]

Ecclesiastically and theologically Fjellstedt was a moderate. His openness and friendship with the lay and revival movements and his close association with the Moravians not surprisingly brought upon him suspicion by the strict orthodox Lutherans. Yet, his faithfulness to the Lutheran Church,

---

[1]"Fjellstedt's Johannes," *Augustana och missionären*, 26 (February 9, 1881), 153.

[2]Andrew Kinell, "Memoirs," trans. Marie Kinell, typewritten (n.d.), Archives, Denkmann Library, Augustana College, Rock Island, Illinois, pp. 18-19.

[3]Anshelm, 3:107.

[4]"Fjellstedt's Johannes," p. 154.

especially after 1857, could not be doubted. Although he supported the free movements within the Church, he consistently counselled against zealotism and separatism.

1. Fjellstedt's View of God

Fjellstedt's view of the deity was trinitarian. In his catechism was a closing section, an appendix, in which he employed the scheme of the order of the church year. For Trinity Sunday, he affirmed the Holy Trinity according to the revelation in God's Word. The doctrine is beyond human understanding. Through God's Word by the leading of the Holy Spirit and the right use of the sacraments, the Christian accepts this truth by faith.[5] Here, as throughout his theological thought, the Bible was his chief source. He also employed the confessional books of the Lutheran Church.

i. God, the Father, and the Atonement

Fjellstedt's theology became more precise and extended as he set forth his views on the persons of the Godhead. God, the Father, from a biblical point of view, centers on the text from Exodus 3:14: "I am who I am." Skilled in the use of the Hebrew language, Fjellstedt extended his range of thought to two Old Testament names for God. The first of these was "Elohim" which means "the Almighty." This is the universal name for deity, the name under which God makes himself known to all humankind.

Fjellstedt did not follow the traditional treatment of God, the Father, by concentrating on the creation and providence themes as set forth in the first article of the Apostles' and Nicene creeds and Luther's explanations. To be sure he did not neglect that theological view. "Whenever we see the name "God" in the Bible, we must think of the Almighty who created everything and with his power sustains all creation."[6] Yet, Fjellstedt was so concerned with soteriology (the doctrine of salvation through Jesus Christ) that the emphasis on God's creation was secondary. For one thing, the vivid nature of his religious experience led him to emphasize the theme of salvation. Also, his concern for missions and the interpretation of his vocation in that context strongly inclined him to make that emphasis central. Finally, Würtemberg pietism with its stress upon the apocalyptic element led him in that direction. All these factors shaped his theology to make central the doctrines of salvation and redemptive love rather than those of creation and providence.

Fjellstedt included soteriology in his treatment of the name "Elohim." Because God has revealed himself to all of humankind through his

---

[5]*Guds swar på menniskan frågor: biblisk cateches med ett bihang af frågor och swar rörande den christna kyrkans största högtider* [*God's Answers to Human Questions: A Biblical Catechism with an Appendix of Questions and Answers About the Main Holy Days of the Church*], trans. from German, 2d ed. (Stockholm: P. Palmquists förlag, 1855), pp. 14-18.

[6]"Herren-Gud, *Samlade Skrifter*, Vol. 1, i ordnadt urwal: *Bibliska betrakelser och uppsatser* [*Biblical Meditations and Articles*] (Stockholm: Tryckt hos Nya Tryckeri-Aktiebolaget, 1883), p. 312.

creation, none can be excused for denying the deity. The Almighty God had revealed his will to all humankind and his will requires that he be obeyed. Yet, humankind has chosen to deny him and follow other gods. Only as the wonder of God's grace comes to humanity do some members of the race respond in faith and obedience.

Fjellstedt did not, however, assume that simply the revelation of God as Almighty is sufficient to save the non-Israelite (or non-Christian). All must be confronted with Christ. Of this, more will be noted in his treatment of the second Person in the Godhead.

The second divine name with which Fjellstedt dealt was "Yahweh." It was under that designation that God had revealed himself to Israel. Fjellstedt taught that from "I am who I am," the name "Yahweh" takes its substance. The name denotes the following traits: the holy, Lordship, trustworthiness, truth.[7]

Two of those characteristics Fjellstedt treated in some depth. The holy has a two-fold character. First, there is the holiness of God through his law. Thus holiness as seen in God's righteousness is expressed in God's wrath against all humanity for its disobedience against him. Secondly, God's holiness is disclosed in the Gospel. The benefit of that expression of holiness is salvation by grace to all who believe in God's righteousness.

Fjellstedt also described the meaning of Lordship. As Lord, God claims Israel for his own people. Within the scope of the name of Lord, there is a relation to Christology. In Christ, the fullness of God's Lordship is shown. The actuality of this truth was declared by Thomas when, looking upon the wounds of the risen Christ, he exulted: "My Lord and my God!" It is to this Lordship Christians are called to be servants even as Christ, the Lord, came to serve humankind.

Although the central importance of soteriology was developed early in Fjellstedt's theological development, he was led to define it more sharply in the Waldenströmian controversy. He met that challenge in the last decade of his life. That controversy shook both the Lutheran Church in Sweden and the Augustana Lutheran Church in America. The conflict produced the most serious schism in these sectors of world Lutheranism in the nineteenth century and probably in the whole history of Swedish and Swedish-American Lutheranism.

Paul Peter Waldenström (1838-1917) whose theology was the occasion for the disruption was a student at Uppsala University from where he graduated with honors. Ordained into the ministry of the Lutheran Church in Sweden, he was regarded as conservative and a pietist who supported the revival movement. He was considered sufficiently orthodox so that in May 1862, he received a call from Hasselquist to become professor of theology at the fledgling Augustana Seminary. Waldenström declined the call.

Waldenström was a close and younger colleague of Carl Olof Rosenius (1816-1868), the father of the revival movement in Sweden which in large part was the root of the Augustana Lutheran Church. Rosenius' work included the editorship of a paper, *Pietisten*, which exerted great influence

---

[7]*Ibid.*, pp. 314-15.

upon the Swedish Lutherans both in Sweden and America. Upon the death of Rosenius in 1868, Waldenstrom became the principal leader of the revival movement and showed every evidence of continuing along the lines of Rosenius. It was not long, however, before a change in his theology occurred.

In 1872, Waldenström published a sermon for the twentieth Sunday after Trinity in *Pietisten* of which he was then editor, successor to Rosenius. (The sermon was never formally preached). He expounded the five points of his doctrine of the atonement: through our fall no change occurred in the heart of God; neither cruelty nor wrath in the heart of God obstructed humanity's salvation as a result of the fall; that the change which occurred in the fall was in humankind alone in that humanity became sinful and thereby fell away from God and the life which is in God; as a result, an atonement was needed for man's blessedness but not an atonement which appeased God and rendered him once more gracious but an atonement which took away man's sin and again rendered him righteous; this atonement took place in Jesus Christ.[8]

This view of the atonement has strong similarities to that of Abelard (1079-1142) and his moral influence theory. It ran counter at important points with nineteenth century Swedish Lutheran theology which tended to define the atonement along the Anselmic lines of satisfaction, that is, Christ died to satisfy the injured justice of God because of the human fall. First, Waldenström removed the distinction between the redeeming love of God and the holy and righteous justice of God. God is absolute and pure love and no change is required in the divine disposition. Secondly, according to Waldenström, it is humanity which must be changed and this Christ does through his sacrifice by implanting in the human heart a change from willful disobedience to the ability to love God. The change occurs in humankind, not in God.[9]

For Fjellstedt as well as Waldenström, the love of God was primary. One of his students, S. G. Youngert, after completing his course at the Fjellstedt School which he entered in 1882, emigrated to America. He completed his education at Augustana College and Seminary, was ordained and gave distinguished service to the Church. For many years, beginning in 1901, he was professor of Biblical Introduction and Greek at Augustana Theological Seminary. In a letter, his son, Eugene, made the following statement:

> My father talked often of Fjellstedt—always in a deeply grateful way. I am sure it is safe to say that he *was* deeply *influenced* by what he called the "Fjellstedt Skola." Often, when he talked to me, he'd speak of Fjellstedt's emphasis upon *God's love* as an important element in our worship.[10]

In response to the Waldenströmian controversy, Fjellstedt wrote: *Hvad lärer bibeln om försoning? Kort Bidrag till swar på denna fråga med anledning af den på 1870-talet wäckta striden derom* [*What Does the Bible*

[8] Karl Olsson, p. 110.

[9] Arden, *Augustana Heritage*, p. 177.

[10] August 9, 1978.

Teach about the Atonement? A Short Essay in Answer to This Question Aroused by the Lively Controversy on This Question in the 1870's]. After two opening paragraphs of introduction in which he described briefly the occasion for, and nature of, atonement and then proposed to present some of the chief biblical teachings on the nature of God, he wrote:

> In the first place is God's love which is for us the foremost attribute of his unchangeable fullness, his boundless and wonderful glory. God is love. . . . When God created the world, it was his love which laid the foundation. God well knew beforehand that humankind which he would create would fall into sin and thereby draw upon itself the displeasure of his righteousness and the horrible consequences of sin; yet, notwithstanding this, he brought into being the creation for the sake of his only Son who was foreordained before the beginning of the world to be its Redeemer and Savior.[11]

Fjellstedt wrote that an eternal covenant existed between the Father and the Son for our atonement. This convenant rested upon the blood of the Son "which in the fullness of time would be shed on Golgotha for the fallen human race and would be called the blood of the eternal covenant."[12]

In regard to God's love, Fjellstedt would agree with Waldenström that no change took place in the heart of God.

> To this we answer that since God in his essence is love and his essence is unchangeable, His love is therefore not changed and underwent no change by man's fall especially since man as fallen was included in the only-begotten Son as his surety, and God thus regarded man in (the light of) the only-begotten Son as a sacrifice which was to be offered for the sins of the world.[13]

This rather interesting view of Fjellstedt brings humanity into a close identification with Christ who in turn is related to God by an eternal covenant. Also, then, as far as God's love is concerned, it does not change in this relationship which he has with humanity in Christ. As he cannot cease loving his Son, so he cannot cease loving humanity whom he has created.

The relationship because of the fall, however, does change. God is also righteous. Human sin offends that righteousness and at the same time obstructs God from revealing the fullness of his love.

> Sin in humankind hindered God's love from being fully revealed to it; sin evoked and caused the change in God's relation to humanity because he as holy and righteous could not with loving pleasure love humankind because sin was the occasion for his displeasure, his wrath.[14]

In the light of Fjellstedt's insistence that God's love is unchangeable, his

---

[11]*Samlade Skrifter*, 1:508-77.

[12]*Ibid.*, p. 510.

[13]*Ibid.*

[14]*Ibid.*, p. 511.

reference here that God "as holy and righteous could not with loving pleasure love humankind" must mean that although God's love is unchangeable, God's righteousness in its wrath against sin obstructs God's love from flowing into the lives of sinners.

Fjellstedt did not thereby say that God does not love humanity but that because God is righteous, the full measure of his love cannot be poured forth upon humankind because of the latter's sinfulness. "Although God is loving, he can as a consequence of his righteousness and holiness do none other than hate the evil."

Fjellstedt made a sharp distinction between God's love and God's wrath. At this point he clearly separated himself from Waldenström who essentially had eliminated the distinction between these two attributes of God. Also the two men differed in regard to the locus of change which must take place for the sake of reconciliation between God and humanity. Waldenström saw the change occurring in humanity so that now by the example and power of Christ's sacrifice on the cross, persons are enabled to adequately love God.

Not so with Fjellstedt. He employed the nineteenth verse from chapter five of Paul's second letter to the church in Corinth: "God was in Christ reconciling the world to himself, not counting their trespasses against them and entrusting to us the message of reconciliation" Fjellstedt made the following interpretation:

> That God has reconciled the world to himself does not signify that he has changed humanity's fleshly mind, which is in enmity against God, or that he has taken away humanity's hatred for God and instead implanted friendliness and love, devotion and gratitude in the world. No, the word [reconciliation] signifies that through Christ, there reconciliation occurs and he establishes such a relationship of himself with the sinful world of humanity so that now he does not look upon their sins but invites humanity, even though it is sinful, to his fatherly mercy, his eternal life, his saving grace.[15]

For Fjellstedt, God is both loving and righteous. Although persons sin and alter the relationship, God does not cease loving them. Yet, God's righteousness cannot tolerate sin. A change must occur: this is accomplished in Christ. Now humanity is estranged from God not on the basis of sin against the righteousness of the law but against the righteousness which is Christ. "The one who does not believe in the Son, that one shall not see life, but God's wrath remains upon that one."

God the Father is almighty and Lord. He is both loving and righteous. He is sovereign and to God's Lordship humanity must relate on God's terms. For those who would deny the displeasure of God's righteousness to sin, Fjellstedt had the following word:

> An expression which one often hears in our time is that God is so good, he can never punish anyone. This is a witness not only of gross ignorance and thoughtlessness but also bears the imprint of a sorry condition regarding morality.[16]

[15]*Ibid.*, p. 540.

[16]*Ibid.*, p. 515.

Undoubtedly, Fjellstedt was referring to Waldenström in this indictment but he included more.

> This is one of those rationalistic and false philosophical assertions; materialism has already reached its logical conclusion in its concept and assertion that to be punished for evil is an absurdity because everything which humanity does is a work of its unfree nature so that it cannot do other than it does.[17]

ii. God, the Son, and Soteriology

As with God, the Father, so with God, the Son, Fjellstedt's theology was basically within the Lutheran tradition of scriptural authority and the Lutheran confessions. In his Catechism, Fjellstedt affirmed the Person of Christ as truly God and truly human, a great mystery. The name, "Jesus," identifies him as Savior and to the title, "Christ," is related the three offices of priest, prophet and king. He has now ascended and sits at the right hand of God from where he shall come to make final judgment upon the world. On the basis of numerous biblical passages throughout the Catechism, Fjellstedt further asserted that Christ, God's only begotten Son, born of the Virgin Mary, has existed from eternity. His ultimate ministry was his suffering and death for the atonement of the sins of all humanity and his resurrection wherein his victory over sin and death was complete.

Central to Fjellstedt's Christology was the atonement as the reconciling work of Christ. By an eternal covenant between God the Father and God the Son, God the Father has offered reconciliation to the world through Christ. He is the God-Man through whom alone God the Father can accomplish this work whereby through unchangeable divine love humanity can be brought back to God to whom alone it belongs.

Fjellstedt traced the doctrine of the atonement through the Old Testament. He referred to a number of sacrifices which were offered by the priests both for themselves and the Israelites. He dealt, for example, with the paschal lamb offered at the Passover which was to stay the plague excited by Korah's disobedience (Numbers 16: 41-48). He wrote about the sacrifice offered annually on the day of atonement. He saw these as the prototype of Christ's sacrifice.

Christ himself is the ultimate fulfillment of God's atoning work. He quoted from I Peter 3:18: "Christ also died for sins once for all, the righteous for the unrighteous, that he might bring us to God." He observed from this passage that we are thus shown:

> Christ, in order to again unite us with God, as if we were a pleasing offering for God, gave himself and died for the sake of sin. His suffering of sin occurred to take away the guilt of sin before God so that we might once again be reconciled to him. A consequence thereof, a work and fruit of this atoning suffering is that the Lord says: "I will be merciful toward their iniquities, and I will remember their sins no more" (Hebrews 8:12).[18]

[17]*Ibid.*

[18]*Ibid.*, p. 544.

Christ was the one Being through whom alone humanity could be reconciled to God, Christian and non-Christian alike. How then did Fjellstedt confront the problem of those who had never had the opportunity to hear the Gospel? Did God consign all such to eternal condemnation?

The zeal with which Peter Fjellstedt gave his energy to the cause of missions could lead to the belief that for him, apart from Christ, there is no salvation. Nearly ten years of his life had been spent as a missionary in South India and Turkey. Several years were devoted as a representative for missionary societies and his whole ministry was committed to the stimulation and nurture of missionary interest among people in Sweden, Germany, Switzerland and Alsace.

Surprisingly, Fjellstedt did not restrict salvation only to those who had heard the name of Christ in this life. Ruben Josefson, archbishop of Sweden at the time of his death in early 1972, who before his election to the archbishopric was director of the Fjellstedt School wrote: "It is not without interest that a missionary so active as Fjellstedt and with his type of piety should solve this problem so difficult for thought and faith."[19]

The issue of salvation for religious heathen was not, of course, new. Ever since Augustine's formulation of the doctrine of original sin, the Church had taught a rigid foreclosure against salvation for non-Christians. Toward the end of the seventeenth century, the issue was raised around such questions as: "Could Socrates have obtained salvation?" Johann August Eberhard, a German theologian of the Enlightment, in 1772 wrote "Neue Apolologie des Socrates oder Untersuchung von der Lehre von der Seligheit der Heiden" ("New Apology in Behalf of Socrates or an Investigation into the Teaching of Salvation for the Heathen"). Within the spirit of the Enlightment, Eberhard took an optimistic view toward human nature as over against the pessimism about humanity which orthodoxy taught. The image of God was humanized. The conclusion reached was that God who is righteous and loving according to the witness of the Gospel could not deny salvation to one so noble in morals and virtue as Socrates.

The controversy within Lutheranism was joined. On the one side was the orthodox party with its emphasis on original sin. One who had not been exposed to the Gospel could not be saved. On the other side were those who, according to Josefson, were from the Melanchthonian tradition. These Lutherans did not place emphasis upon original sin as the cause for damnation but unbelief in Christ. Theologians of this viewpoint still had to deal with the problem of what happens to those who never hear the Gospel. Persons such as Socrates had what Fjellstedt called a "longing faith." Joined with the conviction that God's love is universal and he desires to save all, Lutheran theologians of this viewpoint still had to face the issue as to how God would accomplish that salvation.

---

[19]"Hedningarna och Saligheten: en studie i Peter Fjellstedts teologi," *Ny Kyrkliga Tidskrift* ["The Heathen and Salvation: a Study of the Theology of Peter Fjellstedt," *The New Churchly Journal*] (Uppsala, 1947), p. 40. To affirm a longing faith was not original with Fjellstedt. In the eighteenth century, pietism often emphasized longing faith. That influenced the Lutheran message: "If you only long after Christ, that longing which is nourished from sorrow for sin, then you can be certain of salvation."

For the Reformed theologians, there was no problem. Since God had predestined some to eternal damnation, that meant no heathen would be saved. The emphasis was upon God's righteous will rather than his universal love.

The theologians who taught as Eberhard elevated the universal love of God above both predestinarian thought and the requirement that only those who believe in Christ can be saved. Moreover, each person can be saved according to the way he or she knows God. Therefore, the heathen who are obedient to the law which God has placed in them may hope to be saved as will Christians who believe in Christ. God saves a person such as Socrates simply on moral grounds on the basis of his works.

How much Fjellstedt was directly influenced by this Enlightenment approach is not clear. Sweden was not isolated from its influence. As noted earlier, Esaias Tegnér (1782-1846) was Fjellstedt's adviser when the latter was studying at Lund from the autumn of 1823 until the spring of 1828 (with some interruptions). Tegnér was greatly influenced by the Berlin professor of theology, Wilhelm M. L. DeWette (1780-1849) who sought to relate religion and Christianity to the general intellectual life, to science and to the science of religion. DeWette was much attracted to the German idealism of Kant and Herder. Tegnér, in turn, had such an impact on his student that for awhile, Fjellstedt, in reflecting upon his adviser's influence, felt that he had been drawn away from his love for the Bible and the influence of pietism. Later, Fjellstedt reacted against whatever influence the Enlightenment might have had upon him and returned to a strong biblical basis which became the mark of his work for the rest of his life. Still, living as he did in the milieu shaped in no small way by the Enlightenment, it may be that some aspects of that humanistic and philosophical movement had an influence on the way he looked at theological issues. Nevertheless, Fjellstedt was governed more by the biblical approach than Enlightenment or other non-biblical assumptions.

To state that Fjellstedt was governed by the biblical approach prompts the question: from what perspective of the Bible? The observations made thus far in this study recognize the central importance of pietism and pietism of a certain type, that of Würtemberg, in Fjellstedt's theological development. It could be added that Fjellstedt's ecumenical spirit disposed him to a sympathetic view toward salvation for those truly religious persons such as Socrates who were outside the ken of the Gospel. Even this sympathy toward religious unity was nurtured in part by the pietism which characterized him.

To recognize apocalypticism as in part the disclosure in the future of that which is now hidden in the mysteries of God also showed Fjellstedt's pietism as well as the ecumenical disposition that pietism nurtured. He was not unfaithful to the biblical approach but the piety which had shaped him gave him the freedom to believe that for noble non-Christians, opportunity for salvation in Christ could be effected. From his apocalyptic perspective, he saw the salvation of heathen as a possibility to be disclosed. This enabled him to have some appreciation for the cultures and values of other than Christian traditions.

Fjellstedt may even have been able to appreciate Islamic culture. During his days in South India, he had considered his missionary efforts among those people to be no more difficult than among the Greek Orthodox. Although his strictures against Islam were severe, Fjellstedt was not as harsh as Bengel. The contrast is shown in their respective interpretations of Revelation 21:24 ("By its [the new Jerusalem] light shall the nations walk; and the kings of the earth shall bring their glory to it."). Fjellstedt expressed his view of possible salvation for non-Christians with longing faith when he wrote: "The city called Jerusalem is to be opened to the faithful of Israel's people and to the redeemed heathen who shall yet be participants in Israel's citizenship and walk in [Jerusalem's] light."[20] Such an interpretation at least allows for Fjellstedt's inclusion of the adherents of the Islamic faith.

Bengel, on the other hand, rejected the view that heathen will be permitted entry to the heavenly city described in the New Testament apocalypse. He wrote: "This reference to the heathen to be blessed is a later addition by Erasmus and, without proof, has been perpetrated. This is not corroborated in the ancient manuscripts." Bengel's general attitude toward the Mohammedans and the Islamic faith was harsher than that of Fjellstedt's.[21]

At times, Fjellstedt was not beyond speculation. For example, he suggested that non-Hebrews were not without knowledge of God since, beginning with Noah, all persons would have heard of God. After the flood, all people descended from Noah from whom the tradition of the faith would have gone forth. Thus it could be explained why certain non-Hebrews such as Melchizedek, the Moabite; Elimelech and his family from the Moabite Ruth, an ancestor of King David; and Jethro, the father-in-law of Moses had knowledge of, and devotion to God. It was because of Noah, Fjellstedt wrote, that there "is found among several heathen people even to this day remarkable stories about the creation, the flood, the ark, the rainbow, etc."[22]

Primarily, Fjellstedt argued from other and more reliable biblical perspectives. On the basis of such passages as Psalm 19, Acts 14:17-18 and Romans 1:18-22, he wrote:

> Partly through the memory of the primordial revelation given to the ancestors of the human race by which knowledge was retained from generation to generation among the people of the earth, partly through the wonder of creation and nature, partly through acts of Providence, and partly through conscience and once in awhile even through extraordinary ways God has revealed himself to the heathen in all times.[23]

[20]*Bibel . . . med Förklaringar,* 3:727.

[21]Johan Albrecht Bengel, *Gnomon: det är handledning vid läsningen af Nya Testamentet* [*A Guide to the Reading of the New Testament*], trans. J. Ternström (Jönköping, Sweden: J. H. Nordström and Sons Förlag, 1878), pp. 1237, 1161-62, 1175, 1210.

[22]"Guds olika sätt att uppenbara sig för menniskor" ["Different Ways in Which God Reveals Himself to Humankind"], *Samlade Skrifter,* 1:33.

[23]*Ibid.,* pp. 32-33.

Fjellstedt stated his position most clearly in an essay entitled: "Finnes någon salighetswäg för de hedningar, some icke få höra evangelium?" ("Is There Any Way to Salvation for the Heathen Who Do not Get to Hear the Gospel?"). In this work, Fjellstedt began with the assertion that Christ had died for all and in his death had reconciled all to himself. He based his conviction on Colossians 1:19-20: "In him all the fulness of God was pleased to dwell, and through him to reconcile to himself all things, whether on earth or in heaven, making peace by the blood of his cross." In Fjellstedt's apocalyptic view he made room for the possibility that in the final judgment, faithful non-Christians could stand with believing Christians as heirs of eternal life. So he interpreted Revelation 7:9: "After this I looked, and behold, a great multitude which no man could number, from every nation, from all tribes and peoples and tongues, standing before the Lamb, clothed in white robes, with palm branches in their hands." Based on the Swedish version, he translated "nation" ("hedningar") as "heathen."

Yet, a problem remained for Fjellstedt. He could not ignore the biblical declaration that only in Christ is there salvation. "There is salvation in no one else for there is "no other name under heaven given among men by which we must be saved" (Acts 4:12). Thus far, Fjellstedt agreed with the orthodox of his time. He refused, however, to accept their solution to the problem as to whether non-Christians who had not heard the Gospel could be saved.

What Josefson called the older orthodoxy argued that the non-Christians had already had the chance, had forfeited it, and were now lost. Josefson wrote:

> This solution to the problem of the heathen and salvation was already developed in the theology of the middle ages in the general notion that the message of Christ had already gone out in early Christianity to all people. It could not be thought otherwise than that the apostles had actually obeyed the Great Commission of the Master and that they also had assembled disciples among all people. Much effort was therefore made to show that the witness (to the Gospel) was made in advance by an early Christian proclamation among different people and cultures. These thoughts naturally restricted missionary interest. The heathen had had their time of visitation. . . . [They] had made their choice and were therefore rightly damned.[24]

Fjellstedt, while declaring with orthodoxy that Christ must be the basis of salvation for all, sought a different solution. He referred first to the writing of Paul to the Romans: [God] will render to every man according to his works: to those who by patience in well-doing seek for glory and honor and immortality, he will give eternal life; but for those who are factious and do not obey the truth, but obey wickedness, there will be wrath and fury."[25] Fjellstedt made this condition universal on the basis of Romans 2: 9-10: "There will be tribulation and distress for every human being who does evil, the Jew first and also the Greek. For God shows no partiality." He made the following interpretation:

[24]"Hedningarna och saligheten . . . ," pp. 37-38.
[25]2:6-8.

Here the Apostle speaks not only about the Jews but also about the
Greeks, namely the heathen, and says to us that God shall give to each
and every one according to his works, namely glory and honor and an
imperishable nature who with good works seeks after eternal life, but
those who are stubborn and will not obey the truth but obey
unrighteousness are rejected and under wrath.[26]

Fjellstedt also took into account Paul's treatment of the role of conscience
and natural law:

When Gentiles who have not the law do by nature what the law
requires, they are a law to themselves, even though they do not have
the law. They show that what the law requires is written in their hearts,
while their conscience also bears witness and their conflicting thoughts
accuse or perhaps excuse them on that day when, according to my
gospel, God judges the secrets of men by Christ Jesus.[27]

Considering this passage as well as Paul's statement on God's
self-disclosure through creation ("Ever since the creation of the world his
invisible nature, namely, his eternal power and deity, has been clearly
perceived in the things that have been made. So they are without excuse"
Romans 2:20), Fjellstedt asserted: "God has laid down much of his holy law
in human conscience, and much of his truth has been revealed in creation
and in the order of the world." Hence for all those non-Christians who are
obedient to the highest that has been revealed to them with their best
efforts, Fjellstedt willingly acknowledged:

They who do such are in some sense admitted to the knowledge of the
Gospel and learn to know Christ and his atonement as it is written
about the pious heathen Cornelius who was godly and godfearing
together with all his house, gave generous alms, and prayed constantly
to God.[28]

Still, unlike those who accepted the Enlightenment viewpoint, Fjellstedt
could not affirm the sufficiency of primordial revelation, creation, natural
law, conscience, acts of providence or extraordinary revelation of God for
ultimate salvation. Christ must be confessed by non-Christian and
Christian alike. So how did Fjellstedt solve the problem? He turned to that
passage which is a chief source for the phrase "descended into hell" in the
Apostles' Creed: "The gospel was preached even to the dead, that though
judged in the flesh like men, they might live in the spirit of God" (I Peter
4:6). From this Fjellstedt mused:

We have here a remarkable hint of the mystery of the unseen world. We
cannot find it impossible that God for the sake of the atoning death of
Christ shall give salvation to those heathen who here in the time of
grace, with patience and good works seek after eternal life and long

---

[26]"Finnes någon salighetswäg för de hedningar, som icke få höra evangelium?"
Samlade Skrifter, 3:284-85.

[27]Romans 2:14-16.

[28]"Finnes någon salightetswäg för de hedningar . . . , *Samlade Skrifter*, 3:285.

Peter Wieselgren
Pen drawing from 1847

> after the greater light so that such heathen after death learn to know
> him [Christ] who is the only ground of salvation.[29]

On the basis of this scripture from I Peter, Fjellstedt built his case to bring together elements similar to the Enlightenment which argued for salvation for noble non-Christians and orthodoxy which insisted upon Jesus Christ as the ground of salvation.

Josefson identified longing faith with trust in the Lutheran scheme of faith which consists of three stages: knowledge, assent, trust. Fjellstedt seemed to incorporate the three when he wrote:

> Those heathen who will be saved although they have not in this life learned to know Jesus, have nevertheless already been converted by God's Spirit as he is shown by the Apostle Paul ["To those who by patience in well-doing seek for glory and honor and immortality, he will give eternal life" Rom. 2:7]. After death for the first time they will learn to know the ground of their salvation. They do not forego a proper conversion upon which their salvation depends: they have already in their lives through their longing hearts turned to Christ even though they did not know him.[30]

Coupling their longing faith with the encounter they had with Christ who preached the saving Gospel to them after death, Fjellstedt believed non-Christians such as Socrates could hope for salvation.

[29]*Ibid.*, p. 287.

[30]*Ibid.*, pp. 287-88.

P. Fjellstedt

A final problem for Fjellstedt remained. Josefson wrote: "A basic motive for mission would be weakened if in every circumstance the heathen could be brought before the message of salvation and obtain the righteousness of Christian faith."[31] In the particular document ("Finnes någon salighetswäg för de hedningar, som icke få höra evangelium?") where Fjellstedt clearly set forth his position, he wrote little to refute the charge that the position he supported might dampen the zeal for missions.

[31]P. 47.

In other utterances, however, Fjellstedt left no doubt as to his conviction that the Church must pursue missions. First, no other option but condemnation could await those who reject the Gospel. "By no means is there found in Scripture any ground to suppose that after death God's grace in Christ invites anyone who has in this life had opportunity to hear the Gospel but has rejected it."[32] This statement related to his central assertion in this whole issue: that Christ is the ground of salvation and that the positive response to the Gospel which declares this truth is necessary in order to gain salvation.

Secondly, in inference, Fjellstedt would likely argue that since the Gospel has the power to create the new birth, non-Christians who lack the nobility of a Socrates may nevertheless be brought to a "longing faith" through the conviction of sin effected by the preaching of the Gospel. From this stance, an adequate concern of missionary activity would emerge.

Finally, Fjellstedt took seriously the Great Commission (Matthew 28:18-20). He quoted those verses from Matthew after the following utterance:

> In many plain words Christ has explicitly set forth what people must do who would follow him. Likewise he gave to his disciples and to his Church before his ascension the Great Commission together with the promise of the certainty of his presence and leading.[33]

On the basis of faith's response in obedience to Christ, no option remained for the Christian Church but to obey.

iii. God, the Holy Spirit, the Gatherer to Salvation

Continuing his theological formulations on the nature of God, Fjellstedt remained within the trinitarian framework in his treatment of the Holy Spirit. He formulated his thought around two foci: the nature of the Holy Spirit and the work of the Holy Spirit. In both instances, the trinitarian formula was central.

(1) *The Nature of the Holy Spirit.* Fjellstedt affirmed that the Holy Spirit is of the same essence as the Father and the Son. He referred to the Great Commission of Jesus when he commanded his disciples to go out to teach and baptize in the name of the Father and the Son and the Holy Spirit.

The disclosure of this oneness of the Godhead did not, however, have its origin in Jesus' pronouncement prior to his ascension. The declared fact of this goes all the way back to creation. Fjellstedt drew from Genesis 1:1-2 ("In the beginning God created the heavens and the earth . . . and the Spirit of God was moving over the face of the waters) and Psalm 33:6 ("By the word of the Lord the heavens were made"). By implication, he identified the

---

[32] "Finnes någon salighetswäg för de hedningar . . . , *Samlade Skrifter,* 3:287.

[33] "Minnesord öfwer missionären C. J. Fast: uttalade i Lunds domkyrka den 3 Mars 1851, wid underrättelsen om hans död ["In Memory of the Missionary C. J. Fast: a Statement in the Lund Cathedral, March 3, 1851 with Information Regarding His Death"], *Samlade Skrifter,* 3:242.

Fjellstedt's grave in Uppsala Cemetery
To the right, stone at Kerfstedt's grave, to the left, stone of
grave for College president Norrmans.

term "word" in the latter reference with the "Word" in the first chapter of
the Gospel of John where the term is equivalent to Christ.[34] Fjellstedt
concluded:

> We see that in the creation the exalted Trinity Father, Word and Holy
> Spirit worked together in that wonderful enterprise to create and

[34]In another writing dated 1857, "Jag tror på den helige Ande, en helig allmännelig
kyrka, de heligas samfund" ["I Believe in the Holy Spirit, the Holy Catholic Church, the
Communion of Saints"], Fjellstedt made the identification explicit: "Before the Fall,
humankind was open to the stream of life from the divine source and stood in fellowship
with its Creator. Also this fellowship was brought about through the second person, the
personal, uncreated Word who was from eternity. Through him, through the Word, and
the Word was with God and the Word was God. The same was in the beginning with
God. Through him all things were made and nothing was made without him." John 1:
1-3. *Samlade Skrifter*, 2:501.

prepare the body of the world which is called earth as a dwelling place for humanity. Here humanity would be raised as the family of God created in His image in fulfillment of its destiny.[35]

This view of the Trinity in relation to the creation of humanity is a richer one than the view which tends to restrict the image of God to God the Father only or perhaps to God the Son. Certainly, the mystery of the human being in its essence is deepened in this trinitarian approach.

Fjellstedt wrote that at various times, preaching had been inadequate because at certain periods, only the first article of the Apostles' and Nicene Creeds had been preached. At other times, only the second article about God the Son had been set forth. In still other periods of Christian preaching, only the third article about the Holy Spirit had been preached. All three of these options must be rejected. "Not for long could hungry souls be satisfied with such dry spiritual food."[36] Thus Fjellstedt asserted that all that is declared in each of the articles must be preached and taught. And he prayed that Christians would be led to read the Bible and the symbolical books of the Lutheran Church.

Finally, Fjellstedt saw the oneness of the Holy Spirit in the Trinity in the Church. "The Church is a living, growing temple for the triune God." He displayed his ecumenical sympathy and, again, his emphasis on love by writing that "if they have love for one another or at least pray to the Lord for such a love and thereafter truly try not to do anything against Jesus' word: 'Judge not that you be not judged,' they all show themselves to be God's children even though they belong to different confessions."[37] How is this unity as God's children in obedience to Christ's command of love accomplished? Through the Holy Spirit. "The Spirit is one, who likewise shows that humanity which is not driven by God's Spirit but by the prince who is powerful in the air, that spirit which works in the children of unbelief (Ephesians 2:2) cannot possibly belong to Christ's true congregation."[38] The unity of the Trinity then, according to Fjellstedt, which abides in the Church is expressed by the unity of believers who are at one among themselves through the love of the triune God.

(2) *The Work of the Holy Spirit in the Lives of Individuals.* In his writing, "Om den Heliga Ande" ("About the Holy Spirit"), Fjellstedt set the substance of his understanding of the work of the Holy Spirit by beginning with a passage from Paul: "No one can say Jesus is Lord except by the Holy Spirit" (I Corinthians 12:3). He made a twofold interpretation of this verse. First, "no person can be personally reconciled to Christ and receive the forgiveness of sins through faith in his name except it occur through the Holy Spirit's work of grace." Secondly, Fjellstedt pointed to his view of

[35]"Den helige Ande och hans werk ["The Holy Spirit and His work"], *Samlade Skrifter,* 3: 111.

[36]"Om den helige Andes wägledanda och tuktande nåd ["On the Guiding and Corrective Grace of the Holy Spirit"], *Samlade Skrifter,* 2:247-52.

[37]"Jag tror på den helige Ande . . . ," *Samlade Skrifter,* 2:513.

[38]*Ibid.*

humanity in that he saw the human inability to effect reconciliation with God. The reason for that condition is the "clear consequence of the ruin of sin and the situation of spiritual death which makes it impossible for a human being to make oneself alive."[39] Into the human situation the Holy Spirit enters to give the person the one thing needed—a living faith.

> It is through the Holy Spirit that the individual person is awakened and enlightened through the law and the Gospel and through the light of grace so that the soul comes to repent and sorrow over sin and becomes aware of its own poverty and hungers and thirsts after the righteousness of Christ; then the Holy Spirit works in the soul a true and living faith in the Lord Jesus.[40]

Subsequent to the gift of faith, the Holy Spirit endows the believer with other gifts. Fjellstedt quoted Galatians 5:22: "But the fruit of the Spirit is love, joy, peace, patience, kindness, goodness, faithfulness, gentleness, self control. Against such there is no law." Fjellstedt affirmed the greatest gift of all as Christ himself. "He offers himself through the Holy Spirit."[41]

In his work as in his nature, the Holy Spirit is one with the Trinity. "The Apostle noted that the heavenly Father gives us strength according to the mystery of his kingdom so that we may be strengthened in our inner being through his Spirit, so that Christ may dwell by faith in our hearts."[42]

Other observations Fjellstedt made regarding the Holy Spirit in the lives of individuals included his work as the giver of new life, the preserver of Christian belief and discipline, the guidance of the believer away from the law as a way of salvation, and protection and victory over sin and the devil. At the center of Fjellstedt's theology of the Holy Spirit is the unity of the Spirit with God the Father and God the Son. Fallen humanity is completely dependent upon the Holy Spirit for a saving and living faith in the loving triune God by whom the human being is saved.

(3) *The Activity of the Holy Spirit in the Life of the Church.* As with the individual person, so with the Church there is complete dependence upon the work of the Holy Spirit. As the individual cannot be a Christian apart from the Spirit's work, neither can a community be the Church except by the activity of the third person in the Trinity. "Apart from the Holy Spirit, there can be no Church, no communion between God and humanity, no light, no life, no righteousness, no salvation.[43]

Here, too, Fjellstedt remained within the tradition of Lutheran biblical and confessional theology. He defined the Church as the community of Christian believers created by the Holy Spirit.

> We read in the Torgau articles issued in 1520: "The Church is none other than those who believe in Christ." The word *ecclesia* or Church

---

[39]"Om den helige Ande ["About the Holy Spirit"], *Samlade Skrifter*, 2:1.

[40]*Ibid.*, p. 22.

[41]*Ibid.*, p. 10.

[42]"Den helige Ande och hans werk," *Samlade Skrifter*, 3:119.

[43]"Jag tror på den helige Ande . . . ," *Samlade Skrifter*, 2:501.

signifies an assembly or a congregation of humankind. In the symbolical books we read: "The Church is not merely an association of outward ties and rites like other civic governments, but it is mainly an association of faith and the Holy Spirit in human hearts. To make it recognizable, this association has outward marks, the pure teaching of the Gospel and the administration of the sacraments in harmony with the Gospel of Christ.[44]

Fjellstedt employed several figures or parables to describe his view of the relation between the Church and the Holy Spirit. One was the model of the lampstand, the lamp and the oil which feeds the lamp.

> The congregation is the lampstand and every individual soul which by faith belongs to the true congregation of Christ is a burning lamp of faith which daily receives the oil of grace from the Holy Spirit and thereby burns in the Spirit.[45]

Fjellstedt's source for this figure was Revalation 1:12, 13, 20, and 2:1. An examination of these passages shows Fjellstedt in error regarding the identification of the Holy Spirit as the giver of the oil of grace (Christ is the giver). Within his view of the oneness of the Trinity, however, Fjellstedt did not hesitate to identify the source of light as the Holy Spirit.

Another model Fjellstedt used was that of the offerings or sacrifices made by the Old Testament individuals, Moses, Aaron and Solomon. The main point was that none of these kindled the fire for the offering. That was supplied from heaven which Fjellstedt saw as the work of the Holy Spirit. Christ's own offering of himself, according to Fjellstedt, was through the Holy Spirit. He based his conviction on Hebrews 9:14: "How much more shall the blood of Christ, who through the eternal Spirit offered himself without blemish to God, purify your conscience from dead works to serve the living God."

Within this context, Fjellstedt described baptism by which persons are made living offerings to God and, by implication, by which the Church is nourished and enlarged as Christ was offered up.

> So are also God's children baptized with the Holy Spirit and fire, spiritually crucified and buried with Christ and raised to a new life in him, Rom. 6 so that afterwards of them it is written: "If anyone is in Christ, one is a new creature (a new creation), the old has passed away, behold, everything has become new. In this new life, they shall

---

[44]*Ibid.*, p. 508. Fjellstedt erred in attributing the date 1520 to the Torgau Articles. They were formed ten years later. When Emperor Charles V summoned the princes and representatives of the cities of Germany to the Diet of Augsburg for April 8, 1530, Elector John summoned his theologians to draw up articles of the Protestant faith to be presented to him at his castle in Torgau by March 20. These articles became the basis for the second part (Articles XXII-XXVII) of the Augsburg Confession. See Conrad Bergendoff, *The Making and Meaning of the Augsburg Confession* (Rock Island, Ill.: Augustana Book Concern, 1930), pp. 8-12 and Theodore G. Tappert (trans. and ed.), *The Book of Concord* (Philadelphia: Fortress Press, 1959), p. 24. Fjellstedt's observation can be identified in Articles VII and VIII of the Apology of the Augsburg Confession. See Tappert, p. 169, sec. 5.

[45]"Om den helige Ande," *Samlade Skrifter*, 2:13.

continuously offer themselves as living sacrifices, the old humanity
shall be constantly crucified and put to death, and the whole nature of
humanity shall be surrendered to the Lord to be cleansed, purged and
sanctified through grace and live not for themselves but for him who for
us and died and is risen.[46]

Other figures and parables Fjellstedt used to illustrate the activity of the
Holy Spirit in the Church were the limbs and the tree, the ten virgins and
the wind. His chief source was the Bible supplemented by the Lutheran
symbolical writings. In every instance the point was the same: as with the
individual, so with the Church, there can be no existence, no life, no godly
activity apart from the ministry of the Holy Spirit in his oneness with the
triune God.

2. Fjellstedt's View of the Church

One cannot adequately understand Fjellstedt's view of the Church by
confining discussion to one area where the Holy Spirit works. His thought
as well as the times in which he lived forced him to give a prominent place
to the nature of the Church in his writings.

Even during a brief time around 1855 when he was most critical of the
condition of the Church in Sweden, Fjellstedt was a loyal churchman. Much
of his view was worked out in conflict with those who wanted to separate
from the Church. He warned against following sectarians and false guides
"who lead them to some particular party instead of to Christ." Rather, he
said: "Oh, how necessary it is that the people receive God's word and be
lifted up in our church's pure teaching before it is too late. . . . With the
greatest of inner joy and with full confidence, seeking souls, turn to such
shepherds who are honest so that above all, the people do not immediately
fall into the hands of some party."[47]

In his attitude toward the visible and invisible Church, Fjellstedt affirmed
classical Lutheranism which refuses to separate out the evil persons from the
good. In the Apology of the Augsburg Confession, it is stated: "That is why
we added the eighth article, to avoid the impression that we separate evil
men and hypocrites from the outward fellowship of the Church or deny
efficacy to the Sacraments which evil men or hypocrites administer."[48] The
reference is to the eighth article which includes a condemnation of the
Donatists who believed they could identify the visible from the invisible,
separate out the "visibly" evil people and thus create a pure church.
Fjellstedt made it clear that it is not for human beings to make the judgment
as to who belongs to the visible Church who alone are the invisible
community of God. That decision belongs to God alone.

The Church is not the Church by virtue of the holiness of the members.
The visible Church includes both evil and good. Fjellstedt made reference to
Jesus' parable of the net and the fish (Matthew 13:47-50). "The net of the

---

[46]*Ibid.*, p. 10.

[47]"Jag tror på den helige Ande . . . ," *Samlade Skrifter*, 2:518.

[48]Tappert, ed., p. 171.

Gospel truly gathers bad and good fish and the bad are not separated and thrown out before the judgment."[49]

In an essay entitled: "Om församlingen och läro-embetet" ("About the Congregation and the Office of Teaching"), he elaborated: "Experience shows that although one Church fellowship can have a purer doctrine and Christian confession of faith than another, yet, notwithstanding teachings and confessions, spiritual death and great ruin can take over." Using the biblical figure of the vine and the branches, he condemned the practices of the Swedish Church. "Members of the communion are discarded and branches are torn off of the vine. . . . Not the whole [visible] Church constitutes a pure congregation of true believers or living members of the body of Christ; but in the visible Church is found a small number of true believers who Christ alone knows and who can be called the invisible Church."[50] To human observation, the number of the faithful who are Christ's real congregation, the true limbs or branches on the vine, must remain hidden and unknown. Only at the judgment can the identity of the invisible Church from the visible be known as revealed by the triune God.

The Church is a mingling of good and evil persons under whom the true Church is hidden. In the Apology, it is further stated: "He [Christ] teaches us that the Church is hidden under a crowd of wicked men so that this stumbling block may not offend the faithful and so that we may know that the Word and the Sacraments are efficacious even when wicked men administer them."[51] Not only from a biblical and confessional point of view but also empirically Fjellstedt supported his view.

> Concerning the Baptists, we have had several opportunities which God's word shows that in regard to teaching, they have by no means represented an advance beyond our Church. Also among them we now know there is no perfect Christian discipline. . . . One finds also among them open sinners. . . . They have separated themselves from our Church and have themselves tried to build pure and better congregations. . . . They who think they have greater biblical insight and more sincerity than the other soon divorce themselves from the small separatist congregation which had withdrawn from the Church.[52]

Fjellstedt was not, however, lax on the matter of discipline. For one thing, he affirmed an orderly ministry. He quoted from the fourteenth article of the Augsburg Confession: "It is taught among us that nobody should preach publicly in the Church or administer the sacraments unless he is regularly called."[53] He strengthened his position by use of scripture that the office of the teaching and preaching should not be delegated to "a new Christian but must be given to one with spiritual experience and maturity."[54]

---

[49]"Jag tror på den helige Ande . . . ," *Samlade Skrifter*, 2:511.

[50]*Bibelvännen*, 9 (June 1856), 84.

[51]Tappert, ed., p. 171.

[52]"Om Separatismen" ["Regarding Separatism"], *Bibelvännen*, 12 (April 1858), 53.

[53]*Ibid.*, p. 518. For the English translation, see Tappert, ed., p. 36.

[54]*Ibid.*, p. 519. The scriptural reference is apparently I Timothy 3: 1-6, especially v. 6.

He was critical of the requirement made by the Church of Sweden that all members were compelled to attend periodically the celebration of the Eucharist. Fjellstedt regarded this practice as a great breach of discipline.

> As soon as a Church is so fallen that all Church discipline ceases, that all the citizens of a land, even the most shameless sinners are included in the Church and are treated as true Christians and all are preached to as if they believed in Christ and are not in need of undergoing a change in order to be saved, no conversion is required, and when the unconverted are compelled to go to the Lord's Supper, then such a church community has broken down the wall of separation between itself and heathendom. It has abolished the difference between Christian and heathen and misused holy baptisms so that thereby humankind is blinded. It is put to sleep. Humankind is kept in this spiritual sleep of death through the lullaby of a Spiritless preaching and through the administration of the Lord's Supper to the human flock, most of whom neither obtain nor desire to receive any cure of souls. At no time is full seriousness given for exhortation to renewal and conversion.[55]

Fjellstedt saw a narrow but precise line between his rejection of the identification of the pure or invisible Church and the indiscriminate mix of Christian and unconverted people under the guise that all these constitute the true Church. He did not, however, surrender to this second condition, the blending of the Christian and the unconverted, as a necessary one. The Church can and must act in a corrective fashion. Although he confessed the inability of any person to know the heart of another, the Church "must nevertheless seek to prevent open sinners to come to the Lord's Supper, if, after instruction and admonition, as Christ prescribes, they show no sign of repentance or improvement."[56]

To identify true believers presented a problem. How does one tell whether a person is truly religious according to the norms of her or his community in which membership is claimed? Fjellstedt said "open sinners" should be excluded. To this, he added three other criteria by which persons should be forbidden access to the Eucharist: those who show gross ignorance of the teaching of salvation, who show little experience of the working of grace, and who show in neither word nor prayer any relation to God.

In the light of his own religious experience and fervent participation in the pietistic revival, one may assume Fjellstedt used rather definite signs dictated by the pietism of his day and place as to who were the true Christians. Such signs included the absence of open sin such as drinking, adultery and the breaking of the Sabbath, and the participation in faithful practice of Church attendance, Bible reading, prayer and meeting with other Christians. Still, he never lost sight of the Church as it is understood according to the Lutheran confessions. When he wrote: "The Church, properly speaking, is that which has the Holy Spirit," he was not thinking of some nebulous entity. Rather, the concreteness of the Church as defined

[55]*Ibid.*, p. 516.

[56]"Ännu några ord om nattvardens begående" ["Yet a Few Words About the Celebration of the Eucharist"], *Samlade Skrifter* (written in 1861), 2:861.

in the seventh article of the Augsburg Confession was the touchstone by which he located the Church:

> It is also taught among us that one holy Christian Church will be and remain forever. This is the assembly of all believers among whom the Gospel is preached in its purity and the holy sacraments are administered according to the Gospel. For it is sufficient for the true unity of the Christian Church that the Gospel be preached in conformity with a pure understanding of it and that the sacraments be administered in accordance with the divine word. It is not necessary for the true unity of the Christian Church that ceremonies instituted by men should be observed uniformly in all places. It is as Paul says in Eph. 4: 4, 5: "There is one body and one Spirit, just as you were called to the one hope that belongs to your call, one Lord, one faith, one baptism."

The Church, then, is the congregation of baptized believers who through the Holy Spirit by the means of word and sacrament are incorporated into the Body of Christ as the people of God. Fjellstedt wrote: "They who are incorporated into Christ are the temple of the holy Trinity; they compose the Church, they are the actual congregation, they are the holy community."[57]

Fjellstedt not surprisingly saw the Church as the priesthood of believers. "In several places Luther tells us that preachers by no means make up the Church. No! The Church is the congregation, the church's faithful disciples who are enlightened by God's Word." To the priesthood of believers belongs the power to forgive sins. In reference to Matthew 16:19 where Jesus gave the keys of the kingdom to Peter with the authority and power to forgive or to bind, Fjellstedt interpreted that as belonging to the congregation. "Our father-teacher, Luther, was far from thinking about a high-handed office for forgiveness. He expressly stated: . . . . "To all Christians is given this power . . . to forgive sins. . . . Every Christian may say to others: 'Your sins are forgiven;' thus you see that the whole Church is full of the forgiveness of sins."[58]

Yet within the concept of the priesthood of believers, Fjellstedt taught that on the basis of the Old Testament priesthood and the order of offices in the New Testament, God has ordained a separate order to serve the congregation. Referring to Bengel, Fjellstedt wrote: "This office is not the product of the congregation." In his doctoral dissertation of 1857, he made this his central thesis. Ephesians 4:11 ff, became the chief source for his argument. The offices identified therein (apostles, prophets, evangelists, pastors and teachers) were given by Christ who had ordained them. This arrangement was not temporary "but should continue in the Church as an institution through which Christ for all time would be present and work in his Church."[59]

[57]"Om församling och läro-embets," *Samlade Skrifter*, 2:527.

[58]*Ibid.*, p. 523.

[59]Peter Fjellstedt, *Några grunddrag af Nya Testamentets lära om det andeliga presterskapet och församlingens embeten* [*Some Essential Features of the New Testament*

These offices later developed into the episcopacy with the three orders of bishops, presbyters and deacons. He wrote:

> It was a natural consequence in the growth of Christian congregations that when a new one, large or small, arose around a mother congregation that the presbyter became like a respected father for the younger congregation and thereby became bishop over other elders [presbyters] or pastors as still happens in the case of new congregations which are organized on the mission field.[60]

Fjellstedt referred to the experience of Luther. After a brief flirtation with a democratic form of Church government, the Reformer reverted to the form of polity which affirms the ministry as instituted by Christ. After the years 1524-25 (the Peasants' Revolt), Luther often set forth: "The office [of the ministry] is ordained by God and is accompanied by a power which is given by Christ himself." Fjellstedt concluded: "This [is the] form which in every age most nearly corresponds to the nature and the requirements of the Church."[61]

Fjellstedt's concern was not with the episcopacy as such—although this was his favorite form of Church government. He was well aware of corruption which had through history been present in the Church under this form of polity. What Fjellstedt wanted to emphasize was that the servants of the Church were a separate institution ordained by God and not the invention of the Church. This view was to have a significant influence upon the doctrine of the ministry (and the Church) in the Augustana Lutheran Church.

Consequently, Fjellstedt believed that the congregation was responsible for obtaining faithful shepherds of souls. He made reference to the tenth article of the Smalcald Articles. In that writing, bishops were accused of being more concerned with their temporal power than with ordaining worthy men. Luther concluded:

> Accordingly, as we are taught by the examples of the ancient churches and Fathers, we shall and ought ourselves ordain suitable persons to this office. The papists have no right to forbid or prevent us, not even according to their own laws, for their laws state that those who are ordained by heretics shall also be regarded as ordained and remain so. St. Jerome, too, wrote concerning priests and preachers in common.[62]

Fjellstedt did not discount the office of the bishop. He believed the office should be respected and honored in relation to the appointment of parish pastors. But neither did he exalt the office to the place it had been elevated by the medieval Church. In agreement with the Smalcald articles, he wrote: "The bishops according to the New Testament, are the same as the

Teaching Regarding the Ministry and the Office of the Congregation], doctoral dissertation utgiven och till offentlig granskning framställes [prepared and delivered for public examination], December 5, 1857 (Uppsala: C. A. Leffler, Kong. Akad. Boktryckare, 1857), p. 15.

[60]*Ibid.*, p. 25.

[61]*Ibid.*, p. 26.

[62]*The Book of Concord* (Tappert, ed.), p. 314.

presbyters and cannot claim undue authority. Above all they are to allow the free preaching of the word of God."[63]

Fjellstedt clearly reflected his adherence to the tenth article of the Smalcald Articles as well as his belief in the Church as the priesthood of believers when he wrote: "In our symbolical books, it is set forth as an altogether necessary duty for a congregation to obtain for itself a true shepherd of souls when the one who has been installed is unrepentant and unspiritual." He counseled order. "The congregations are not to take matters into their own hands but are to continue to pay their money for properly called pastors and do so without wrath or reproach." Rather, the congregation should go "in all humility and in an accommodating manner to the bishop and lay before him what is his duty and ask whether he can give them a true teacher."[64]

Fjellstedt encouraged the employment of laymen in the work of the Church because of "the burden of work which the clergy have both in spiritual and worldy matters." He suggested that they could serve as teachers on Sunday afternoons when there would be no conflict with the regular worship services. Their form of ministry could include Bible reading, prayer, singing, biblical instruction and catechization. Already, Fjellstedt observed, several laymen had begun such ministry. The good fruits of such work were "clear demonstrations that the Lord and King of the Church, Christ himself blesses and furthers such work." He saw this service as one of edification which "cannot and ought not to be forbidden or hindered."[65]

He also encouraged the employment of colporteurs to act as travelling preachers and to hold meetings. Many Swedish persons lived long distances from the parish church in their respective areas. To such, the colporteurs should go "in humility from house to house, admonishing and warning the ignorant, the depraved, and the fallen, comforting the sorrowing, counselling the brothers, distributing the Bible and well-known Christian books and writings." Always Fjellstedt counselled against any separatist efforts to encourage persons to leave the established Church. He advised the colporteurs: "Never encourage them [to whom you go] to separate from the Church."[66]

A wide range of voluntary societies emerged in the 1800's. The issues were many: distribution of Bibles and tracts, temperance, education, missions, prison reform, anti-slavery, women's suffrage. These societies tended to embrace three features: they were concerned with few issues—usually one; they were inter-or non-denominational; and, they were in large measure spawned by the widespread pietistic revival of that century.

[63]"Jag tror på den helige Ande . . . ," *Samlade Skrifter*, 2:522.

[64]*Ibid.*, p. 519.

[65]"Om nödvändighetens af Diakon-verksamheten åter" ["About the Resumption of the Work of Deacons"], *Samlade Skrifter*, 2:582.

[66]"Pröfwen andarne, om de äro af Gud!" ["Prove the Spirits Whether They Are of God!"], *Samlade Skrifter*, 2:582.

Fjellstedt heartily supported those movements. In an article written in 1865, he expressed his joy over the many organizations which had risen in the previous sixty years. He saw that development as the work of the Lord in response to two conditions: the deadness of the Church and God's love revealed in the laity who could no longer wait for the Church to do its work. Among those organizations, none was more highly valued by him than the Bible Societies which had been organized in many Protestant lands. He was exultant that during the sixty years of the work of those societies, 50,000,000 Bibles in approximately 160 languages had been distributed. According to Fjellstedt, 132 of those languages did not even have an alphabet before the Bible was translated into them. Indeed he felt the case could be made for the upbuilding of civilization as the result of such an enterprise.[67]

Other voluntary societies won Fjellstedt's admiration. He wrote appreciatively of the Evangelical Alliance organized in 1846 to work for unity among Protestants. He likewise admired the inner mission societies in their efforts "to help the needy, care for the sick, raise the fallen (with special societies for fallen women), gather together the many for Christ, support underpaid evangelical teachers, found and support both Christian elementary and higher schools."[68]

In his view of the Church, Fjellstedt was a moderate. His distinction between the visible and the invisible Church became quite narrow because of his concern with church discipline particularly as it related to who should be allowed admission to the celebration of the Eucharist. His emphasis upon the priesthood of believers as over against unquestioned obedience to church authorities was balanced by his respect for church order. In conclusion, Fjellstedt remained true to the view of the Church as affirmed by the Lutheran confessions.

3. Fjellstedt's Ecumenicity

The ecumenical spirit of Peter Fjellstedt is very evident. His early years together with his temperament inclined him to work for Christian unity. In all likelihood, the first influence upon him came from his contact with the Herrnhut community during his months as a tutor in 1827 and 1828 at Göteborg. Their pronounced ecumenicity together with Fjellstedt's high admiration for them undoubtedly did much to excite his interest in this matter. His many contacts with the Herrnhuters during the rest of his life strengthened and nourished this concern.

Another evidence of his ecumenicity was his contact with Anglicanism during his student days in London which began in the spring of 1829 and continued there until the autumn of 1830. From that date and for several years thereafter, he had a very close association with the Anglican Church. It was under that Church's auspices (Church Missionary Society) that he spent nearly a decade of service on the mission fields of India and Turkey.

---

[67]"Den fria föreningswerksamheten," ["The Work of the Free Societies"], *Lunds Missions-Tidning*, 18 (November 1865), 161-71.

[68]*Ibid.*, pp. 166-67.

For a period of time after his return from that service when it was clear he must devote his future ministry in the homelands of Europe, the Society still contributed to his salary.

During his years as a missionary in Turkey, Fjellstedt expressed a preference for the church government of the Anglican Church. He felt the type of polity of that ecclesiastical body was best suited to deal with the problems posed by the religious conditions in Turkey. In a letter written in 1841 to Wilhelm Hoffman, head of the Basel Institute and successor to Christian Blumhardt, Fjellstedt wrote: "It seems to me that the Anglican Church is the best able to take up the battle against the grim artillery of the Eastern Church and against Mohammedanism."[69] He believed an episcopal polity should be adopted in Constantinople. The choice of an episcopacy was limited to the patterns found in Anglicanism and Swedish Lutheranism. At that point in his life, Fjellstedt, with some justification, saw little missionary strength issuing from his own Church. More than once he expressed his admiration for the appropriateness and the superiority of the Anglican Church for the work of missions among the Eastern Orthodox Churches in Asia Minor. At one point he even wrote that he had often wished he belonged to the English Church and considered the possibility of ordination according to Anglican orders.

The ecumenical spirit of Fjellstedt incorporated a warm rapport not only with the Anglicans and the Moravians. He was also very close, as already noted, to the interdenominational (but Reformed Church oriented) Basel Institute. That "spiritual home" never lost its lure for him. His feeling for the Swiss organization was shown in November 1845 when he received the call to become the Director of the Institute of the newly established Lund Missionary Society. It was not with great enthusiasm that he accepted the strict Lutheran confessional viewpoint at Lund.

As director of the Institute, he did not feel that relationships with other like organizations of different confessional persuasion should be ignored. For example, when two of the students from the Institute, Carl Ouchterlony and Gustav Lundgren, desired to go out under the auspices of the Church Missionary Society, Fjellstedt in no way opposed their desires. As late as 1856, the year the Institute was moved to Stockholm, Fjellstedt wrote to Anders Blomstrand (a student of the Institute who in 1858 began more than a quarter of a century as a missionary to India) that he intended the relationship between the Lund Society and the one in Basel would continue in the working arrangement the two organizations had in working together in India.[70]

Fjellstedt's ecumenical interests can be further described in his relationship to the Evangelical Alliance. The Alliance had as its objective the unification of all Protestants on a nonsectarian basis "who with a living conviction confess their common faith in our Savior, Father, Son and Holy

[69]Anshelm, 1:317.

[70]Gustaf Lindeberg, *Ett sekel i missionens tjänst* [*A Century of Service in Missions*] (Lund: C. W. K. Gleerups Förlag, 1945), p. 88.

Spirit, live in brotherly love and with their lives and deeds glorify that Savior who has bought them with his blood."[71]

Contemporary Christians are well acquainted with the annual January week of prayer for Christian unity now jointly sponsored by Eastern Orthodox, Protestant and Roman Catholics through the World Council of Churches and the Secretariat for Unity. Of less common knowledge is the fact that a similar octave in behalf of Christian ecumenicity was practiced by the Evangelical Alliance. Its first observance of worldwide scope was January 6 to 13 in 1861. In the previous December issue of his *Bibelvännen*, Fjellstedt published the concerns to be prayed for each day in accordance with the suggestions issued by the Alliance. Furthermore, he participated in the celebration of the week itself in *Trefaldighetens kyrkan* (Trinity Church), Uppsala.

In his later years, Fjellstedt was recognized widely as an ecumenical figure. He was nearly seventy when he was urged by Philip Schaff to address the Evangelical Alliance meeting in New York in 1870. Before Schaff's proferred invitation to Fjellstedt, the Alliance, in 1867, had urged him to be a representative of Sweden to its meeting in Amsterdam. At first, he accepted the invitation but in June, declined on the ground that he could not obtain the substitute for preaching upon whom he had depended. So eagerly was his presence desired in Amsterdam that an appeal was made to Wieselgren (with whom Fjellstedt was then adjunct pastor) to intercede but to no avail.[72]

Four years later, in 1871, the Alliance again attempted to engage Peter Fjellstedt. On that occasion, the oppression of Lutherans in the Baltic countries by the Russian Czar raised the advisability of sending a delegation to seek relief for those suffering people. Captain J. C. Berger, spokesman on this matter for the Alliance, appealed to Peter Wieselgren that from Sweden should come both a bishop and "a noble person of mature and good name" and that no better one could be found than "brother Fjellstedt." The proposal to include Fjellstedt apparently did not have the support of the bishops. Of the four Swedish representatives who were included among the thirty-nine persons who went to the Baltic countries, Fjellstedt's name does not appear among them. No reason was given for his absence.

In the instances of the negative responses which Fjellstedt gave to the Evangelical Alliance between 1867 and 1871, an interesting question appears. Were the reasons Fjellstedt gave for his inability to go to Amsterdam or New York adequate? It would appear that certainly had Fjellstedt considered the ecumenical efforts of the Alliance as significant, he would have found ways of overcoming the hindrances to his acceptance. For example, his answer to Schaff that his age prevented him from travelling to New York does not correspond too convincingly with the energy he showed in subsequent years to continue his far-reaching preaching tours.

[71]Quoted in Karl Olsson, p. 81.

[72]Anshelm, 3:328-9.

Fjellstedt's devotion to *Evangeliska fosterlandsstiftelsen* with its strong Lutheran emphasis and the differences which arose between that organization and the Evangelical Alliance in the 1850's cannot be overlooked as having had a decisive influence upon him. Reference to Fjellstedt's close association with the *Fosterlandsstiftelsen* requires an elaboration of the character of that organization. A deeper knowledge of it as well as Fjellstedt's involvement with it work will give a clue as to why his enthusiasm and willingness to relate to the Evangelical Alliance seemed to lessen as he grew older.

Evangeliska fosterlandsstiftelsen was inspired by the revival. It had its beginning with a group of students at Uppsala during the academic year 1851-52. Concerned about their spiritual welfare, they gathered for prayer, the study of God's word and for witness to one another. In this group was a young man from Dalarna, Hans J. Lundborg. He had experienced a spiritual awakening from conversation with a dying cousin. He, together with his companions, chose for their motto, "God's glory, our fatherland's weal."[73]

Following his ordination November 10, 1853, Lundborg served in a number of parishes in the diocese of Västerås. He carried on a zealous ministry. Many people were spiritually awakened but he also met opposition. Because of ill health perhaps due to his strenuous labors and the pressure from adversaries, he was given a leave of absence. In May 1855, he travelled to Scotland. He was much impressed by the Scottish Free Church and its work. The idea of a society for Sweden which might nurture Sunday schools, educational projects, and the printing and distribution of Christian literature took shape in his mind. A similar enterprise had already been a concern for which the students at Uppsala had been praying.

In the spring of 1856, Lundborg returned to Uppsala and from there to Stockholm where he met with a number of evangelically concerned people, both clergy and laity. In the latter group was Rosenius who was among those who on May 7 organized *Fosterlandsstiftelsen för evangelii befrämjande* [The Evangelical National Foundation for the Furtherance of the Gospel]. Later the name was simplified to *Evangeliska fosterlandsstiftelsen*. Among its aims were to print and spread Christian literature and to send out carefully selected colporteurs. Included in the dissemination of Christian teaching was the publication of a paper, *Budbärenen* [*The Messenger*], edited by Bernhard Wadström. The work of the organization was to be "by voluntary association with the organization of our church's fellowship in order to carry the Gospel to our Swedish people in agreement with our Lutheran confessions."[74] This strong confessional character was a distinctive trait of *Fosterlandsstiftelsen*—a factor which was to cause difficulty for some of the less confessional Lutherans who were associated with the Evangelical Alliance with its simple confessional position. At first Fjellstedt belonged to the latter group, but with his growing confes-

[73]Stiftelsen's Styrelse [Directors of the Foundation], *Evang fosterlandsstiftelsens 50-åriga verksamhet 1856-1906* [Fifty Years of Activity of the *Evangelical National Foundation 1856-1906*] (Stockholm: Evang. Fosterlandsstiftelsens Förlag-Expedition, 1906), p. 19.

[74]*Ibid.*, p. 5.

sionalism, he became an increasingly fervent supporter of *Fosterlands-stiftelsen.*

Another reason for his decreasing devotion to the Evangelical Alliance was the controversy which arose in the Alliance between the Baptists and the evangelical Lutherans. At first, ecumenically minded Swedish Lutherans along with others including Baptists joined the Alliance. Primarily, the Lutherans who belonged to that organization were from the *läsare* or pietistic movement. Ultimately, however, the union as it affected the relation between the Baptist and the *läsare* Lutherans unravelled. This was due to two reasons. First, the Baptists drew their inspiration from Anglo-American sources. Their pietism was of a separatist type with its low regard for the institutional church. The *läsare* Lutherans, by contrast, drew their view and practice of pietism in part from the Moravian influence which, with its commitment to the Augsburg Confession, induced them toward non-separatism. This characteristic of the *läsare* Lutherans also showed itself among the Swedish Lutherans in America. Although critical of the Church in Sweden, really the basic issue on which they differed from their fellow Lutherans of the state Church was on the insistence of the former that conversion was essential for salvation. On other major points, the kinship was strong. *Läsare* and state Church members sensed a relation which could not be denied.

Secondly, the inevitable necessity to consider doctrinal differences arose in the Evangelical Alliance. "In witnessing and conversations, controversial matters like baptism were to be avoided. This did not prove to be practicable. It is understandable that newly-won Baptists would seek, in spite of their promise, to inculcate Baptist doctrine [especially adult baptism]." At that point, the *läsare* Lutherans objected and affirmed their own doctrines. "The Lutheran *läsare*, whose convictions on infant baptism were just as strong as the attitudes of their opponents . . . [resented] the Baptists carrying on partisan activities in an ecumenical venture."[75] This endeavor toward Protestant unity by the Evangelical Alliance failed in Sweden and its influence greatly deteriorated.

In his relationship to the clearly Lutheran oriented *Fosterlandsstiftelsen*, Fjellstedt's faithfulness to the Lutheran Church was shown. Sympathetic as he was to the voluntary societies and free Christian movements, he was also concerned that laymen such as colporteurs should be faithful to the teaching of the Lutheran Church. Hence, he counselled that colporteurs should be "proven as experienced, churchly-minded Christians or have references from *Evangeliska fosterlandsstiftelsen* or some other society which stands completely on the teaching, faith and confessions of our Evangelical Lutheran Church."[76]

The fact that, on the one hand in 1865, he wrote in support of the Evangelical Alliance and, on the other hand, gave qualifications for colporteurs which seemed to reject the purpose of the Alliance should not be taken

---

[75]Karl Olsson, p. 86.

[76]"Den der träder i en annans embete" ["As a Mischief-Maker in Another's Office"], *Samlade Skrifter*, 2:590 fn.

as a serious inconsistency. Essentially Fjellstedt was ecumenical. Yet, as a member of the Lutheran Church who was faithful to its confessions, his ecumenism must be brought in line with his Christian faith (at least as he grew older) as interpreted to him through Lutheran teachings.

Fjellstedt's ecumenicity in no small measure grew out of his interpretation of the Bible as it declares God's relation to all of humanity. It was Fjellstedt's belief that God had always provided and would continue to provide for the salvation of all. None would be left without opportunity to respond to God's grace. His interesting view of salvation for non-Christians demonstrated his position on this issue.

Fjellstedt had a similar ecumenical interpretation of primordial and patriarchial history as recorded in the Bible. He taught that from the beginning the Holy Spirit had established communion between God and humankind and among humankind, a condition that not even sin had destroyed completely. Human conscience remained through which the Holy Spirit worked its influence.

Fjellstedt affirmed that all who live in Christ are united in Christ. "We are not to think only of people in the Church but of the Church in the hearts of the people."[77] Christian unity consists of those persons who are incorporated into Christ as branches are grafted into the vine or as the body is related to the head. All who live in Christ are united in him. This basis of unity is the true one and more valid than the unity built on churchly confessions. He wrote:

> Experience teaches that although one Church may have a purer teaching and confession of faith than another, notwithstanding the superiority of its teaching and confessions, spiritual death and great corruption can take the upper hand so that the members of that Church are cut off from the vine and cast away. It is sad to say that in large measure this condition now holds in our Swedish Church.[78]

Fjellstedt concluded that not confessions, important as they are, but the life of love in Christ expresses Christian unity. Because these Christians are found all over the world, the Church is *"allmännelig,"* that is, catholic, universal. He further elaborated this term:

> The word *"allmännelig"* is also expressed by the word "Christian," as Luther said: "One can no better express this basic word in the confession of faith with the word "Christian," i.e., wherever Christians are found throughout the world. . . . An infallible sign of God's children is that they have love for one another even though they belong to different confessions. . . . In this Church, there are many gifts but the Spirit is one.[79]

His ecumenical orientation was strongest up to 1857. Ahnfelt-Laurin dated from that time a stronger movement toward Lutheran confessionalism.[80] The nature and some of the reasons for this change

[77]"Jag tror på den helige Ande . . . ," *Samlade Skrifter,* 2:508.

[78]*Ibid.,* p. 528.

[79]*Ibid.,* p. 513.

[80]P. 289.

included the mellowing of Archbishop Reuterdahl toward the pietists and *läsare* movement and the revocation of the restrictive Conventicle Act in 1858. Other factors played a role in the development of Fjellstedt's confessionalism and changing attitude toward ecumenicity.

First, one may assume that Fjellstedt's assocation for a decade with the Lund Missionary Society tended to make him more sympathetic toward the high church view and its confessional stand. Schartau's influence continued to be strong in southwestern Sweden. If Fjellstedt had not always been enthusiastic toward Lutheran confessionalism, he nevertheless respected it.

This can be shown in an occurrence in 1850. Theodor Hamburg, a talented young man, had been inspired in his missionary zeal by both Fjellstedt and Rosenius. In 1844, he entered the Basel Institute to study. Two years later, under the auspices of the Basel Mission Society, he went to southeast China. There he performed a noteworthy work cut short, unfortunately, by his early death in 1854.[81] In 1850, together with a Lund Society missionary, Anders Elgquist, Hamburg enthusiastically proposed the purchase of an American Baptist mission facility which had become available. The two young men not only wanted to obtain the property. They also proposed that the work from that mission should be conducted on the basis of a simple confession similar to that employed by the Basel Society. Hamburg wrote in a letter:

> In the confession, we do not want to compel anyone's conscience. Yet, it is understood that if only with an upright heart, the Lord Jesus is loved and served, then we can be brothers. Our common goal is to turn Chinese to God by faith in Jesus Christ and be renewed by his Spirit.[82]

Although Fjellstedt, at that time in his life, may not have objected too strenuously to that requirement, he was aware that such a statement of faith would never win approval from "such a strong Lutheran confessionaly [sic] oriented organization as the Lund Missionary Society."[83] Fjellstedt opposed Hamburg and Elgquist's proposal: the enterprise came to naught. Who is to say, however, that Fjellstedt was not also acting by that time out of his own convictions?

Secondly, by 1859, the theological climate had changed both in Stockholm and Lund so that the Lund Missionary Society had a more comfortable feeling toward the group in the Swedish capital city. This had been demonstrated four years earlier when in 1855 the Lund Society had joined with the Swedish Missionary Society in Stockholm. The changed relationship between Lund and Stockholm allowed greater flexibility for differing views. Certainly Stockholm did not become a duplicate of Lund nor Lund, of Stockholm. Now, however, each was able to accept the other and the more interconfessional tradition of Stockholm and Uppsala where Fjellstedt spent much of his life after 1855 was more sympathetic toward Fjellstedt's pietistic and revivalist approach as well as his Lutheran confessionalism. What cannot be overlooked was the significance of

[81]Sundkler, pp. 230-36.

[82]Anshelm, 2:317.

[83]*Ibid.*, p. 319.

Rosenius' activity in Stockholm and his spirit. He was important in bringing together the two societies.

Fjellstedt must have been encouraged by the change which had taken place in the Church in Sweden. For him, it must have justified his hope that the power of the Holy Spirit was still present and working. Hence, the criticisms he had expressed before the 1855-59 period in his life no longer applied or at least to the same degree.

Thirdly, the increasing tension within the *läsare* movement itself forced adherents to the revival to make a choice. Beginning in the late forties, several groups which were seen as threats by many Swedish Lutherans arose and organized work in Sweden. In 1848, the first Baptist congregation was established through the efforts of Fredrik Olaus Nilsson. Four years later, he baptized Anders Wiberg as a Baptist. Wiberg had been a close associate of Rosenius and Wiberg's action shook Rosenius' confidence in an uncontrolled religious revival.

Also, about that time was the disturbing phenomenon of Erik Janson. He abandoned farming in Uppland in 1840 to become a free-lance preacher. His scathing criticism of such honored persons as Luther and Arndt along with his claim that God had given to him alone a special revelation which qualified him to interpret the true message of the Bible exposed him to severe persecution including arrest and jail sentences. He left Sweden in 1846 with a band of followers. During the next two years, about fifteen hundred Swedes left their native land to take up residence in his Illinois colony, Bishop Hill.[84]

About the same time, the Mormons began their work in Sweden. By 1855, there had been 126 Mormon baptisms and the subsequent efforts of its Reorganized Church of Jesus Christ of the Latter Day Saints was to mark Sweden as one of its fertile mission fields.

Within this complex development must also be seen the position of the Evangelical Alliance. Certainly its proponents would have been highly suspicious of such non-traditional groups as the Mormons and the Jansonites. Yet its relatively minimal creedal requirements and its deep concern for Christian unity exposed this organization to deep suspicion.

As with the Evangelical Alliance, so it must be stated that the *läsare* movement as a whole would not have supported either Jansonism or Mormonism. The problem, however, was not so simple as to be solved in relation to those extreme movements. Rather, the issue revolved around such fundamental issues as authentic authority and freedom. A division was taking place within the *läsare* group on the subject of authority. One group wished to remain within the Lutheran Church in Sweden and thus espoused the confessions as reliable guides for the interpretation of scripture. The other group, more affected by Anglo-American revivalism with its casual if not low estimation of creeds, liturgy and traditional parish life, saw authority experientially based solely on the message of the Bible.

[84]For an interesting study of Jansonism, see Paul Elmen, *Wheat Flour Messiah: Eric Janson of Bishop Hill* (Carbondale, Ill.: Southern Illinois University Press, 1976). In Sweden, the movement is called "Erik-Janssonismen;" the followers are referred to as "Erik-Jansarna."

Closely associated with the issue of authority was that of freedom. Fjellstedt himself spoke on this issue when he wrote against episcopacy: "For us as Evangelical Christians, it is impossible that anything human should come between God and human conscience."[85] This is an interesting statement for it shows how Fjellstedt's view of episcopacy had changed from his earlier defense of Anglicanism.

The orientation of the Alliance was symbolic of that group in the *läsare* movement which desired only the authority of the scriptures and freedom from traditional ecclesiastical polity as it operated in Sweden and from Swedish Lutheran confessional theology. Both Fjellstedt and Rosenius supported the policy of *Evangeliska fosterlandsstiftelsen* with its strong Lutheran emphasis. Increasingly, the latter organization became more confessionally restrictive. By 1860, a committee had been organized to examine colporteurs on the soundness of their Lutheran faith. Although the existence of *Fosterlandsstiftelsen* does not in itself explain the change that took place in Fjellstedt's ecumenical attitude, his support of its theological position showed he had moved to a more conservative and confessional stance.

Finally, it must be remembered that even in the early years of his ministry when he seemed to be more ecumenically minded, Fjellstedt showed a deep love for Luther and the Lutheran confessions. He had translated *Luther's Small Catechism*. Even though his *Bibel med Förklaringar* is based on a careful study of the Bible, he did not neglect the Lutheran confessions as a resource. One critic of this work wrote that Fjellstedt showed "a deep appreciation for the word of God and was faithful to the Lutheran confessions in his interpretation."[86] Both of these works had been produced by 1855. During the same period, out of the conviction that the Church needed to be aware of its confessional heritage, he translated in 1854 the *Concordia pia, Evangelisk lutherska kyrkans symboliska böcker* (*Book of Concord*).

The confessional position of Fjellstedt was consistent throughout his ministry. He exalted the confessions as the sign whereby true Christians are known. He wrote that many had suffered and died for the confession of their faith. "It is still true both in the Christian Church and in the kingdom of the world that people know one another by language and that by the confession they recognize one another in spirit. . . . This is a great joy for true Christians, for in the spiritual language they recognize each other and discover that together they are walking the road to heaven."[87]

For Fjellstedt, the ultimate ground of Christian unity lay in Christian experience but Christian experience which was within the context of the Church as it and its ministry were described in the confessions. Herein lay the apparent discrepancy in Fjellstedt's ecumenical spirit. On the one hand, he could join with the Anglicans and the Moravians in an ecumenical spirit.

[85]"Om församlingen och läro-embetet," ["Regarding the Congregation and the Teaching Office"], *Bibelvännen*, 9 (August 1856), 126.

[86]Anshelm, 3: 15.

[87]"Olika slag af bekärmelse," ["Various Kinds of Confessions"], *Samlade Skrifter*, 1:87.

On the other hand, he became increasingly hesitant toward the Evangelical Alliance. The reason for the different positions he took revolved around the nature of the Church. The Anglicans and the Moravians both took the Church seriously, its worship life, its creeds, its confessions. The confessional simplicity of the Evangelical Alliance, by contrast, together with its willingness to harbor such as Baptists who, in Fjellstedt's mind, had an inadequate view of the Church, prevented him from wholeheartedly expressing an ecumenical attitude toward the Alliance. On similar grounds, his disagreement with Waldenström's views led Fjellstedt to oppose him. Waldenström's repeated utterance of the question: "Var står det skrivet?" (Where is it written?) and his insistence upon biblical authority apart from the historical interpretation of scripture as forged in the Lutheran confessions were too simplistic for Fjellstedt. To be ecumenical on those grounds would have been a cheap and insufficient expression of Christian unity.

To Fjellstedt, the confessions were a true statement of Christian faith and experience. If one lacked the true faith and experience, then one, of course, was also guilty of unfaithfulness to the confessions. Of prior importance was the experience of repentance and forgiveness in the believer's heart which was the work of the Holy Spirit.

> To Christ's congregation belong all persons who are in living fellowship with Christ through faith. This union with him depends not upon different confessions and different churches but upon this: that a person through Christ's word and the work of his Spirit comes to a knowledge of sin and grace and allows God's Spirit to work a living faith in Christ so that one takes Christ into one's heart.[88]

That a certain ambiguity existed in Fjellstedt's ecumenical stance is true. Yet, it is interesting to note the similarity between his position and the twentieth century ecumenical movement beginning in 1910 which led to the organization of the World Council of Churches in 1948. Leaders of that movement also took seriously the various confessions. Rejected was the course of watering down confessional differences. Central to the convictions of the leaders has been: "The closer we come to Christ, the closer we come to one another."[89] No doubt Fjellstedt would have agreed with this statement.

---

[88]"Om församlingen och läro-embetet," *Samlade Skrifter*, 2:528.

[89]The message of the Universal Christian Conference on Life and Work in 1925 at Stockholm, so much the creation of the Swedish Archbishop, Nathan Soderblom, was one of several instances when the thought of "the closer we come to Christ, the closer we come to one another" was expressed: "Only as we become inwardly one shall we attain the real unity of mind and spirit. THE NEARER WE DRAW TO THE CRUCIFIED, THE NEARER WE COME TO ONE ANOTHER, in however varied colours the Light of the World may be reflected in our faith. Under the Cross of Jesus Christ we reach out hands to one another. The Good Shepherd had to die in order that He might gather together the scattered children of God." (emphasis mine). Quoted in Ruth Rouse and Stephen Neill, eds., *A History of the Ecumenical Movement 1517-1948* (London: S.P.C.K., published in behalf of the Ecumenical Institute Château de Bossey, 1954), p. 548.

4. Fjellstedt's Views on Church and State

As a churchman, Peter Fjellstedt, for his time, was somewhat liberal. His support of the *läsare* and his criticism of the established Church placed him in the forefront of those who were moving toward religious change.

The same cannot be said for his view of the state. He represented that interesting although not unfamiliar paradox of a person who in one area of human activity is a liberal, in another, conservative or even reactionary. At best, he was ambiguous.

He expressed himself on a variety of subjects: separation of Church and State, types of government, duties of citizens to the state and the revolution of 1848. His views were scarcely helpful in a time of needed change in political affairs. He had been shaped by previous history and could not accommodate his thought to the new age which was appearing on the horizon.

i. Separation of Church and State

Fjellstedt's view of separation of Church and State was ambiguous. He was adamant against any encroachment of the state upon the sacramental life of the Church. A sore point was the requirement of the state that every person must show civic loyalty by periodical participation in the celebration of the Eucharist. Persons could not be married legally until they had been baptized and confirmed and had communed. Against the law which required compulsory Eucharistic attendance he wrote in 1861:

> When people now in our Church are required for the sake of marriage or for any other reasons to misuse this precious means of grace and eat and drink to their own condemnation, that law wreaks an anwarranted coercion against human souls and the most horrible violence against Christ and the congregation. Each and every one who has a heart for the truth ought to thus seek in all lawful ways possible to promote the abolition of such unreasonable coercion.[90]

In another area, he was not completely opposed to the use of state power over Church affairs. He was not entirely at odds with the Conventicle Act of 1726 which forbade, among other activities, the assembly of people "under the pretext to practice their piety and particularly to worship and that in those places [e.g., private homes] there should be no preaching and exposition of the pericopic texts nor the explication of prayers or novel practices."[91]

It seems strange that Fjellstedt did not oppose the law as such. The Act had been preceded by two others (December 1, 1713 and December 8, 1721) for the purpose of prohibiting religious activity of "*katteri* and *Swärmeri*" [heresy and fanaticism].[92] Fjellstedt also approved of other

[90]"Ännu några ord om nattvardens begående," *Samlade Skrifter*, 2:853.

[91]*Konglig placater resolutions och påbud: 1726-27* [*The Royal Edicts, Resolutions, and Decrees: 1726-27*] (Stockholm: John Henry Werner, director of all printing in the Kingdom: n.d., presumably 1728), no page numbers but the equivalent of pp. 9-16.

[92]"Hwilka sammankomster äro förbjudna?" ["Which Assemblies Are Forbidden?"], *Lunds Missions-Tidning*, 4 (March 1851), 43-44.

provisions of the Conventicle Act such as the admonition that parents, heads of households and pastors should be faithful to their offices. No doubt he agreed too with the prohibition of ungodly behavior on Sundays and Holy Days.

The inconsistency of Fjellstedt lay in his disapproval of the exercise of state force on the one hand and his approval of it on the other. In regard to the Eucharist, he was forceful in support of separation of Church and State. The Church was to be the ruler over matters spiritual. Nevertheless, he approved the use of state power to protect the Church from fanaticism and heresy. One must ask the question: "Was the latter not also a spiritual matter?" Plainly, Fjellstedt was not clear on the issue.

Fjellstedt's ambiguity may well have been a reflection of the view of the Lutheran Church on the issue of Church and State. In one of his articles, Fjellstedt at the same time condemned enforced celebration of the Eucharist as a state requirement and approved the employment of the state to counteract heresy. He wrote:

> Truly Luther urged kings and princes to remove unworthy and fake priests and to replace them with true teachers. He wrote to his elector that as a Christian prince he was obligated to hinder the wolves from ruining the flock and he urged the Count of Schwarzenburg to take the pastorate away from such pastors who would not preach the pure teaching of the Gospel. Hence, the princes began to act in agreement with this counsel. Had not our King Gustaf I acted according to his duty as king, our country would likely be under the Pope to this present day.[93]

Immediately following this statement, Fjellstedt condemned the Eucharistic law. His ambiguity was obvious. His consistency lay only in his respect for law but the application of law in relation to freedom of conscience in matters of religious faith is a matter of confusion which remains unclear.[94]

[93]"Jag tror på den Helige Ande . . . ," *Samlade Skrifter*, 2:524-25.

[94]In the end, Fjellstedt took a firm position against the Conventicle Act, not on the ground of its unlawful character, but on the way in which it had been enforced and the bad consequences of the law. Even at the time of its abolition, he was not entirely sure of the just enforcement of the new law. It contained a clause that private gatherings "considered to lead to schism in the Church or to be contemptuous of the public worship or which could otherwise disturb religious sanctity" were forbidden. Fjellstedt was concerned as to how such meetings would be identified and hoped those decisions would not be arrived at subjectively. But he could only rejoice over the abolition in 1858 of the hated Conventicle Act of 1726. He listed the bad consequences which had flowed from the law: (1) it led to lawlessness—and thus, for Fjellstedt, it was a serious fault against his whole view of the sanctity of law—in that serious minded Christians felt compelled to break the law for their conventicles and some law officers broke the law by not preventing such gatherings; (2) it had created distrust of, and hatred for, authorities; (3) it had encouraged ruffian type behavior on the part of some to injure people who held conventicles and to damage their property; (4) it had made the word "*läsare*" a scandal so that people had become ashamed and/or afraid to read God's Word for fear of being called a *läsare* and ministers were afraid to support the *läsare* for fear of being called "*läsare* preacher;" (5) it had created a negative attitude toward the ministry and the Church by shutting up God's Word behind the walls of the Church since people feared

ii. Types of Government

Another area of the Church and State relationship on which Fjellstedt expressed his view was the type of government he preferred. Here, too, there was ambiguity. Ideologically he declared himself to be neutral. He wrote that it would be most fortunate for any society in which all lived according to the commandment of love. Then it would make little difference whatever form society would take.

> If they have this inner life and this noble mind, then the constitution of communities and their whole character may be very dissimilar, each according to the character, disposition, customs, employment, habits of life, and behavior of its people. Their different organizations and outer forms will not hinder the essential welfare and development toward the enlightenment and ennoblement of their way. So the relationship between sovereign and subject, between master and servant in addition to the special relationship among the classes of the community may be very different but upon the whole fortune and existence and upon the contentment and welfare of the individuals, this has little essential influence. Hence, Holy Scriptures contain no laws or prescriptions regarding the outer organization of the life of a society but they rather treat of the human spirit and insight that humanity should be enabled, of itself, according to the true freedom of the full law, to create the organization and take the measures which are reckoned to be the best for all according to the true commandment of love for humanity. It is thus a great heresy to believe that the ruin of a whole people is the consequence of inadequate laws and prescriptions although laws and prescriptions certainly can significantly bring about good or evil according to their character.[95]

Fjellstedt's naiveté is clearly shown in this romantic statement. For one who took sin seriously, as he did, this utterance is highly inconsistent. His belief that if love rules, human relationships will be good and healthy whatever the outer organization may be simply was not in keeping with his view of humanity as sinful. He was highly unrealistic as well as ambiguous in the belief that love could create those structures in which society could best operate.

In spite of his assertion that he was neutral, for him, the most satisfactory form of government was the monarchy. In this belief he was typical of conservative Swedish opinion at that time. He wrote: "It [monarchy] is the highest image both of the kingdom of God and of the best organizations on earth which have been derived from the noblest rulers."[96] He made a distinction between the absolute type and the constitutional type of

studying it in their homes. He concluded: "It has been a cancerous ulcer not only in the State but also in the Church." It has created a gulf between pastors and people, "a gulf which will not be easy to fill." Upphäfwandet af 1726 års konventikelplakat" ["Abolition of the Conventicle Act"], *Lunds Missions-Tidning*, 12 (January 1859), 8-13.

[95]"Samhallslifwets grundval," ["The Foundation of Community Life"], *Bibelvännen* 2 (March 1849), 41.

[96]"Hura kan den bästa statsförfattningen åstadkommar?" ["How Can the Best State Constitution be Produced?"], *Bibelvännen*, 1 (October 1848), 152; Anshelm, 3:41.

monarchy. During Fjellstedt's time, absolute monarchies were found in
China, Persia and Turkey. Those he rejected. "Such a king, Caesar or
prince has the power over the life and death of his subjects to do what he
pleases without having to give an account."[97] Persons such as absolute
monarchs who were a law unto themselves could not be trusted.
Theologically, human sin made such people dangerous. Here Fjellstedt was
inconsistent with his view that love was capable of overcoming the destructive forces of sin.

Fjellstedt accepted the constitutional monarchy which was based on law
apart from and beyond the king. His example was his own country of
Sweden. "Such a form is a good organization and is the most fortunate type
of government. Its power is shared. Such a balance sets a barrier so that
power cannot be misused by any sector."[98] According to Fjellstedt, many of
the lands of Christendom had that form of government. Those he saw as
based on the strongest foundation of all, the law of God. If God's law were
kept, those countries would have a sure defense against all other
powers—another example of his naiveté.

He showed his conservative political view by his rejection of
representative type of government. In his doctoral dissertation, he wrote
that the democratic form of government as far as the Church was concerned
had been found wanting. He cited Luther's experience in the Peasants'
Revolt of 1524-25, which turned Luther against a democratically shaped
congregational life. Not only on the basis of his understanding of the
scriptures but also as he viewed democracy in the Church, Fjellstedt felt it
was inadequate.

> In every congregation which we have known, where the conditions
> have been completely democratic, there has ruled spiritual death and
> self-will. There, whoever is the pastor or the teacher is usually a lonely
> cypher. He must learn the will of the congregation even when the
> congregation will not endure the word of the Bible.[99]

The date of this statement is significant. It was made in 1857. By that
time, Fjellstedt had moved somewhat away from the more extreme
free-church position. The following year, 1858, he wrote "On Separatism."
It was then he noted that the Baptists who separated from the Church in
Sweden in order to form a pure and democratic community soon separated
from it in order to attain an even higher degree of purity.

Of all forms of government, socialism and communism were the least
acceptable to Fjellstedt. They were, in fact, reprehensible.

> This monstrous delusion has shown itself time and again from ancient
> days and even more in our time. It roves like a wandering Jew from land
> to land and seeks rest but finds none. If it were to be a great success,
> then it must have the power to recreate human nature and make all
> children equally gifted and at the same time make the minds of angels

[97]"Socialism och kommunism," *Bibelvännen*, 3 (May 1850), 67.

[98]*Ibid.*

[99]*Några grunddrag af Nya Testamentets . . .* , p. 25.

prevail in humanity. However, this cannot be. *As soon as Christianity is denied,* and as soon as all private property is abolished, the whole land becomes a poorhouse where all need help and there is none who can help. But no lasting success for communism is possible as has already been shown. It brings misfortune to countless people. It has in these last years cost many thousand lives and many hundreds and thousands of people have been brought into misfortune and misery.[100]

Even here Fjellstedt was illogical. He found communism as recorded in the book of Acts as ideal. This was due to the naive way in which he looked upon love as adequate to create governmental structures. He tried to unite law and the Christian commandment of love as the *sine qua non* for good government. He wrote:

> In the highest meaning of the term community, all gifts and all property belong to all because they are from the Lord. There is only one owner and they who enjoy these gifts, power and possessions do so as a loan from God. They have the command from God that they are to love one another as brothers and are not to look only upon that which is best for them but also what is best for others. The spirit of love works continuously upon them who belong to the Lord and makes its command a living law in every heart.[101]

So central was this conviction to Fjellstedt that he could actually accept a communistic or communitarian form of society which held all possessions in common if Christ and his love permeated the whole of the community. He wrote: "Such a condition must be an indescribable blessing, a heaven upon earth which expresses itself willingly through an overflowing pure and holy love under the mighty flow of high spiritual power and the richness of heaven."[102] Basically, if the foundation of a society were Christian, then the outer form of government made little difference to Fjellstedt. Still, on the practical level, he preferred a constitutional monarchy. Fjellstedt was scarcely a reliable guide in the area of political forms.

iii. Citizen's Duty to the State

In an article entitled "Om staten och wåra pligter emot densamma" ("About the State and Our Duty to It"), Fjellstedt expressed his position on the citizen's duty to the state. He quoted Philippians 2:4: "And look out for one another's interests, not just your own." People are to work for their mutual benefit. "Each member is for the sake of the whole and the whole is for the sake of each other."[103] He demonstrated his conviction that a Christian bears a responsibility for the welfare of fellow human beings in his active participation in relief of human suffering through inner mission work.

---

[100]"Socialism och kommunism," *Samlade Skrifter,* 1:218-19. (A more complete version of this article is in *Samlade Skrifter* than in *Bibelvännen* (May 1850). Hence both versions have been used.

[101]*Ibid.,* pp. 222-23.

[102]*Ibid.,* p. 223.

[103]*Samlade Skrifter,* 1:192.

Fjellstedt affirmed that the mature citizens know how to be obedient and what their place is as subjects. In an article, "Om kristnas underdånighet under öfwerheten och den borgerliga lagen" ("About Christian Obedience to Rulers and Civil Law"), he used Romans 13: 1-2: "Everyone must obey state authorities because no authority exists without God's permission and the existing authorities have been put there by God. Whoever opposes the existing authority opposes what God has ordered: and anyone who does so will bring judgment on himself." There is no exception to this dictum. "To be subject is the order for all of humanity according to the Lord's will whether it be to a king as the authority or the representatives which may be sent by the king to punish the evil and praise the good."[104] Fjellstedt concluded that the mature citizen is the one who obeys: the immature is the one who resists lawful authority.

Fjellstedt thought that the presence of an unjust ruler did not give ground for resistance or revolution. The citizen must decide between the commands of the ruler whether they are of an earthly, temporal nature or if they are of a spiritual character. If the former, then obedience must be rendered no matter how unjust the demand may be. "If a Christian lives in a land such as Russia where there is an authority of another kind from ours, or in Turkey, or in a heathen land, it is still the unconditional duty to be obedient to worldy authority even if one is treated by the greatest injustice and unreasonableness."[105]

Only if one should be ordered by a civil ruler to disobey the commands of God can one resist through suffering. His model was that of the apostles who proclaimed to the rulers in Jerusalem: "You yourselves judge what is right in God's sight—to obey you or to obey God. For we cannot stop speaking of what we ourselves have seen and heard."[106] Yet, even here, resistance was not to be active. The ruler was not to be destroyed or displaced. Rather, the pattern of martyrs and especially that of Jesus must prevail. The counsel from I Peter 2: 19-21 was to be followed:

> God will bless you for this, if you endure the pain of undeserved suffering because you are conscious of his will. For what credit is there if you endure the beatings you deserve for having done wrong? But if you endure suffering even when you have done right, God will bless you for it. It was to this that God called you, for Christ himself suffered for you and left you an example, so that you would follow in his steps.[107]

In general, for the Christian two avenues were open: obedience to the ruler no matter how unjust that authority might be as long as those demands involved civil matters; passive resistance which could involve suffering if

[104]*Ibid.*, p. 200.

[105]"Om kristens underdånighet under öfwerheten och den borgerliga lagen," ["Regarding the Christian's Obedience to Authority and Civil Law"], *Lunds Missions-Tidning,* 9 (September 1856), 141.

[106]Acts 4: 19-20.

[107]"Om kristens underdånighet . . . ," *Lunds Missions-Tidning,* 9 (September 1856), 142.

the government required activities contrary to the Christian faith. These options constituted the vocation of the Christian in his relation to the state.

To state Fjellstedt's position so categorically is, however, unjust. He had deep compassion. He recognized human rights and objected to gross violation of them. He wrote often and in unqualified condemnation against the institution of slavery in America as well as its treatment of the Native Americans. On these subjects more will be written later. On these issues he displayed a highly sensitive humanism.

The central belief of Fjellstedt regarding Church and State was obedience to the commandment of love which included a genuine regard for human rights. How wonderful it would be "if the nation's people with the love of Christ and noble altruism would be compassionate not only for individuals but for the welfare of all and exert the effort in the power of the Lord to follow the highest Christian law."[108] Here again Fjellstedt showed his unreal expectation of human society.

iv. Revolution and Freedom

Obviously Fjellstedt was politically conservative. He was greatly disturbed by the revolution of 1848 which had repercussions also in Sweden. During that year, several articles appeared in *Bibelvännen* and *Folkskolan* under his authorship.

He did not deny the validity of the people's complaints against their governments. France was the main object of his criticism but he also applied his view generally. In behalf of the working people throughout Europe, he wrote: "To this point, the people have in many respects been slighted. The powerful have regarded too lightly the welfare of the people and too much their own power and glory. . . . The working classes have been greatly downtrodden and no concern has been shown to alleviate their burdens."[109]

What Fjellstedt protested against was the way in which better conditions were being sought. He recognized the right of people to have freedom but he saw freedom as of two kinds. In its lesser meaning, freedom meant "natural free will and the liberty to exercise that will without hindrance." This was the freedom which belonged to the creature as creature. He feared the extension of this kind of freedom to license. "Some want to go farther," he wrote. "All bonds should be loosed: from Christianity, authority, masters, marriage. All should be torn asunder."[110]

Of particular concern to Fjellstedt was the state of marriage. He deplored what he saw happening in his own time. For him, the integrity of human relationships was at the very heart of healthy community life. At the base of all community institutions was the family. "Such it is in family life that upon this small community, the family, branches of the larger communities

---

[108]"Om staten och wåra pligter emot densamma," ["Regarding the State and Our Duties to It"], *Samlade Skrifter*, 1:197.

[109]"Blick på Christenhetens närvarande politiska tillstånd" ["A Glance at Christendom's Present political Authority"], *Folkskolan*, 1 (February 1848), 17-18.

[110]"Friheten," ["Freedom"], *Bibelvännen*, 1 (May 1848), 72.

are shaped and built."[111] Among the bonds he saw the revolution loosening, none caused him greater concern than its effects on marriage.

The other freedom which humankind has is the freedom which comes from God as a gift by his grace. It is the freedom "which is kindled by God's Spirit, which sanctifies the will through the believing heart . . . which liberates from grave errors and from oppression which some persons on the ground of the old self-assumed power of the sinful nature impose on others."[112]

God himself is perfect freedom. His free will corresponds with his power by which he has created humanity in his own image. That very fact allows the human being to also rebel against God. This has occurred. But God would not have it otherwise. He wants free obedience out of love, not out of compulsion. But humanity had abused this freedom and the consequences of this centuries-old error seemed to be coming to a head, in Fjellstedt's view, in the 1848 revolution. He believed it might well be the time of the final judgment.

Fjellstedt disliked the use of force against established order. "It is entirely against the commandment of Christianity to rise up against authority."[113] Here he reflected a typically Lutheran view which interprets Romans 13: 1 in this light: "Everyone must obey state authorities, because no authority exists without God's permission, and the existing authorities have been put there by God."

Fjellstedt believed the troublesome times of 1848 had resulted because of the failure of the Christian Church to be zealous in its teaching. On that count, he felt no Church had been more delinquent than the Church in France. Among the sins of that country, according to Fjellstedt, had been the failure "to implant freedom's holy teaching." Of France, he wrote:

> A glance at the chief city of France with its permissive attitude toward the inner life of the community speaks more powerfully than the most powerful preacher could talk of the situation which has occurred there. During the year 1847 in Paris a third of all children born or 25,268 children drew the first breaths of their unfortunate lives in a public house of obstetrics. In the hospitals that same year 49,100 persons died who were without house or home.[114]

Plainly, Fjellstedt did not probe deeply enough into the social causes of the conditions of which he wrote. Although he mentioned the oppression which brought about the revolution, for him, it was the lack of Christian knowledge that was the chief source of the human misery. This was a simplistic approach. He feared the rise of some strong figure like Napoleon who would bring a type of peace but would in actuality be the sign of the anti-Christ. For that view he drew upon his interpretation of Revelation 17: 12-13: "The ten horns you saw are ten kings who have not yet begun to rule, but who will be given authority to rule as kings for one hour with the beast

[111]"Samhallslifwets grundval," *Bibelvännen*, 2 (March 1849), 42.

[112]"Friheten," *Bibelvännen*, 1 (May 1848), 72.

[113]"Blick på Christenhetens . . . ," *Folkskolan*, 1 (February 1848), 18.

[114]"Samhällslifwets grundval," *Bibelvännen*, 2 (March 1849), 42.

[the anti-Christ]. These ten will have the same purpose, and they give their power and authority to the beast." He associated this apocalyptic view, a mark of this theology, with the French activities especially. Fjellstedt's strong anti-Catholic bias is evident here. It is difficult if not impossible for him to be objective because of his prejudice against Roman Catholicism.

He supported his anti-revolutionary position by pointing to such figures as the French Socialist author, Pierre-Joseph Proudhon (1809-1865), who supported the Mutualist position. This view was held by those who thought that factories should be operated by associations of workers. Proudhon had as party slogans: "God is evil;" "Property is theft;" "Deny God." Fjellstedt took the opportunity to warn his Swedish countrymen against this position which he felt was making an impressive impact in the revolution and was creating and nurturing a strong anti-religious climate.

> No one should think that our own fatherland is not in danger of being gripped by this pestilence. There is already a harbinger, a terrible harbinger of . . . Proudhon's words . . . which are nothing other than the ripened form of unbelief which is so very general in our fatherland . . . This is the Spirit of the anti-Christ.[115]

It is not fair, however, to state that Fjellstedt was insensitive to the misery of people. Of the hardships which many of the Swedish people were suffering in the mid-nineteenth century, he wrote:

> In many places a base self-interest causes persons to manage their property, which is often far away, through the exploitation of menservants and lady-servants. These poor creatures are left to themselves without proper care, protection and oversight. As servants they ought to enjoy life in the ordinary course of the employer's home as the subordinate members of the family or in their own house, a home life as is found in a cotter's cottage.[116]

Fjellstedt was not sufficiently perceptive to see the need for political action to effect social change. Consistent with his personal view of salvation, he believed that social betterment must come through personal regeneration of all individuals. Once again he fell back on the premise that love could solve social problems.

He also believed eleemosynary work could adequately relieve human suffering. He was much influenced in the expression of Christian outreach by the German pastor and creator of inner mission work in Germany, J. H. Wichern. The alleviation of human suffering should be an extension of the Church's ministry. Fjellstedt did not propose that the building of healthy societal structures should be the responsibility of the State. He saw this task as a part of the two-pronged obligation of the Church. Through its

---

[115]"Huru . . . statsförfattningen åstadkommar?" *Bibelvännen* 1 (November 1848), 171, 173, 174.

[116]"Samhällslifwets grundval," *Bibelvännen* 2 (March 1849), 45. Fjellstedt described the deplorable social conditions which existed in Sweden at that time. The men-servants (drängar) and lady-servants (pigor) were of the lowest strata in Swedish society, below that of the cotters or statare, without land, and subject to the meanest living conditions and the whims of his/her employer.

preaching and teaching ministry, individual lives were to be re-created so
that the commandment of love would be practiced. Upon this foundation
humane communities would be created. The second prong of the Church's
responsibility was its charitable service through the development of inner
mission work. The separation of Church and State in the area of
community regeneration was obvious.

5. Eschatology

In light of Fjellstedt's views of the sinfulness of human nature, of the state
and of the revolution of 1848, it is easy to infer he did not have great hopes
for the building of a new world. He saw the task of the Christian largely in
terms of "ambulance" work. That is, those who were injured by the
economic, political and social systems of a community were to be bandaged
and patched. That was the task of the Church. Any hope to reconstruct the
systems of society was regarded as near hopeless.

His eschatological view was basically apocalyptic. By that is meant that
one looked forward to the better world after death, that this world tends to
be a miserable place and that one's hope lies in the life beyond this one. In
addition, apocalypticism attempts to interpret the signs of the times. This is
in relation to the culmination of history in a final judgment in which the old
order is violently destroyed. A new order is divinely given and ruled by
God. The secrets of history are disclosed. The belief in a millenial rule is
affirmed.

Fjellstedt's eschatological view was movingly portrayed at the time of the
death of their second child, Selma Natalia. Born in South India, she was ten
months old when the family left for England. The little girl became ill
aboard ship, died, and was buried at sea. His thoughts were reflected some
years later when he wrote:

> Now I think with thanksgiving and praise upon God's grace which was
> sent to this child who so early in life was plucked away from the
> dangers, sins, and miseries of this world and of whom one can say that
> she has gone to a beautiful inheritance.[117]

He expressed a similar view at the death of his son, nine year old Joel, of
whom he thought so much. Fjellstedt was in Lund at the time of Joel's last
sickness in Stuttgart where the little boy died in January 1854. He wrote in a
letter in the English language dated February 20, 1854 to his friend, Pauline
Westerdahl:

> My sweet little youngest boy, Joel Elisama, 9 years old was gathered to
> the Lord's eternal rest on the 29th day of January after 3 days illness
> with scarlet fever. He was buried at half past three o'clock the afternoon
> on the 19th just at the time I was standing in the pulpit in the afternoon
> in Jönköping preaching on I John 4:10. My heart is bleeding from this
> painful blow but I praise the Lord my Saviour with all my heart and
> soul, that he has saved and delivered my beloved children from all
> temptations and dangers and sufferings in this evil world.[118]

[117]Anshelm, 1:189.

[118]*Kjerfstedtska Deposition*, a collection of correspondence to and from Johannes

The dim view Fjellstedt had of this world at the time of the deaths of his two children is clear. At the same time one cannot affirm simply on the basis of these instances that his eschatology was apocalyptic. His hope in the heavenly life was so different in beauty and so much greater by contrast that earthly existence appeared bleak.

In a sense, his lack of confidence for the betterment of social conditions in the world except by the renewal of individual lives by the grace of God bore a relationship to apocalypticism. He did not deny that good government can be a help. Still, "If a true fear of God and true piety are lacking in a people, there will be a disintegration and deterioration and no successful change through any kind of government or any type of improvement in the organization of society can occur."[119]

Since Fjellstedt was not very sanguine about a sufficient conquest by God's word of human hearts, he was not hopeful that the world would become better. It is true that from around 1850, he did take with greater seriousness the work of social missions. Still, for Fjellstedt, the Church's ministry included service to those injured by economic misfortunes, political injustice and social inequities with little hope of rectifying these conditions.

His fear of the 1848 revolution deepened his apocalypticism. In March, a riot broke out in Stockholm. Although liberalization in inheritance laws, better provisions for the poor, restrictions of the power of the trade guilds and public education had occurred, there was still much restlessness. Universal suffrage and even abolition of the monarchy were advocated. Windows of the homes of some of the conservative political leaders were broken. The troops were called out and about thirty people were killed.

These events greatly affected Fjellstedt. He wrote:

> I am both troubled and glad. Troubled for I know the indescribable trials it imposes but glad because when "the figtree blooms" then the summer is approaching. Yet, nothing can be said in respect of the signs of the time. The chief signs are still lacking, but we are included in His faithful custody. He rules heaven and earth so that all is well and we can be confident in all storms[120].

His understanding of the events led him to interpret them in the light of apocalyptic passages from the scriptures.[121] He wrote:

Kerfstedt, rector of the Fjellstedt School from 1870 to 1920, Carolina Redivivi, Uppsala University, Uppsala, Sweden, T 260: aa:1, pp. 357-58.

[119]"Om staten och wåra pligter . . . ," *Samlade Skrifter*, 1:195.

[120]"Autobiography," p. 599.

[121]Daniel 7: 23: "This is the explanation I was given: 'The fourth beast is a fourth empire that will be on the earth and will be different from all other empires. It will crush the whole earth and trample it down.' " Revelation 13: 1, 12: "Then I saw the beast come out of the sea. It had ten horns and seven heads; on each of its horns there was a crown, and on each of its heads there was a name that was insulting to God. . . . It used the vast authority of the first beast in its presence. It forced the earth and all who live on it to worship the first beast, whose wound had healed." II Thess. 2: 7: "The Mysterious Wickedness is already at work, but what is going to happen will not happen until the one

Should not this falling away from God develop and bear ripe fruit, so
must humanity necessarily embark in as great freedom as they desire
and nothing will hinder the principle of unbelief to show itself in all
life's activities. So long as the right time had not yet come, God's
Providence set obstacles in the way and evil's power worked more in
secret. But now it appears that the time has arrived that the storm
should begin to rouse up the world's sea and then there awaits the great
general persecution upon all who deny Christ. As the power of darkness
hated Christ, so it also hates his followers. The Jews sought several
opportunities to slay him but so long as God decreed the hour had not
yet come, all their efforts were in vain. . . . When he allowed their
hostile spirits free room to develop and express themselves [Christ] said:
"This is the hour of the power of darkness."[122]

Fjellstedt was not, however, a wild-eyed apocalypticist who predicted
time and place when the consummation of history would take place. A later
commentator on his life wrote: "His conscientious spirit and his sense of
reverence for God's majesty kept him from the error which so many modern
prophets make who recklessly pretend to be authorities and claim to understand and interpret the whole depth of the book of the apocalypse
[Revelation]."[123] In this sense, he was like Rosenius. The latter, however,
also no revolutionary, did not theologize regarding the revolution as
Fjellstedt did. The influence of Würtemberg pietism led Fjellstedt to view
revolutions in an apocalyptic context.

In his interpretation of the scriptures, Fjellstedt followed closely biblical
and historical principles. For example, from a biblical hermeneutical
approach, he followed the view that scripture should interpret scripture. In
his commentary on the thirty-eighth chapter of Ezekiel with its reference to
Gog and Magog, he made a comparison with the use of those terms in the
twentieth chapter of Revelation. He thus protected himself from making
questionable historical assumptions. He went no farther than to suggest that
reference to the mighty armies of the north mentioned in Ezekiel 38: 5-6
bore a similarity to the situation of his day as it applied to "Persia, Turkey
and much of Europe."[124] In no sense, however, did Fjellstedt attempt to
make specific contemporary conditions the fulfillment of biblical prophecy.

He did make application of his apocalyptic studies to some of his chief
concerns but not in a predictive and ultimate manner. For him, Revelation
18: 8-19 with its description of the fall of Babylon could refer to the Roman
Catholic Church. His deep bias against papal ecclesiasticism was indicated
here. Yet, he also included other possibilities. Wherever the souls of people
were sold, there was Babylon. He indicted certain Protestant churches,

who holds it back is taken out of the way." Fjellstedt also used passages from the Gospel
of John to illustrate in what fashion God's power over wickedness was demonstrated in
Christ's life.

[122]"Friheten," *Bibelvännen* (May 1848), 76.

[123]Emil Lund, "Peter Fjellstedt," *Korsbaneret: Kristlig Kalander För Året 1932* [*The
Banner of the Cross: The Christian Calendar for the Year 1932*] (Rock Island, Ill.:
Augustana Book Concern, 1932), p. 25.

[124]*Biblia . . . med Förklaringar*, 2:623.

slave-traders, and those who used alcoholic beverages excessively—all of them signs of the last times. Even here, in faithfulness to biblical interpretation, he was not guilty of distortions so that he made certain present situations the literal fulfillment of apocalyptical utterances in the Bible.

His apocalypticism was related to the Church and its relation to Christ. "The same way Christ has gone through suffering to glory so must Christ's Church go."[125] The revolution of 1848 was seen by him as ending in chaos which would be significant for the suffering of the Church. He likened the life of the Church to the life of Christ in three stages. First, was the stage of unfulfilled hope when Christ suffered ostracism and was a refugee in Egypt. So, the Church in her earliest years knew similar treatment. Early Christians were ostracized and even martyred. Then, as in Christ's life, there was a relative period of peace and quiet, so the Church in its second stage for centuries had enjoyed similar absence of persecution and strife. Finally, in his last stage, Christ suffered and died. So the Church, in Fjellstedt's view, may have arrived at that point in God's design for it.

Fjellstedt did not say the revolution would be the end of history. He wrote: "Whether the time is near or yet delayed, it is not possible for it to occur so long as no stirring shows itself among Israel's people who are the actual fig tree for whose buds we must watch."[126] His figure of the fig tree is based on Matthew 24: 32-34 and II Thessalonians 3. From Matthew he drew upon Jesus' reference to the fig tree how when its branches become green and tender, one knows that the time for summer is near. So, when certain signs appear, it will be known that Christ's coming is near. In the passage from II Thessalonians no fig tree is mentioned. What drew his attention to this passage was its portrayal of the coming conflict between Christ and the Wicked One and the subsequent defeat of the latter.

His was not an apocalypticism that sought flight from the world. Life required a battle against evil and a preparation of as many as possible to be nurtured in a life that would be pleasing to the Lord in the final judgment. Against the background of the French Revolution, he wrote: "No king ever exercised such a tryanny as the tyrants who claimed to be for freedom but murdered both the king and several thousand of the most sober minded and wise among the country's subjects."[127] Fjellstedt urged that Sweden must avoid a similar tragedy by carefully educating its children and youth. He reminded his fellow Swedes that the signs of the times were such that the days must be anticipated when the Lord's favors and promises to the faithful must be taken to heart. He quoted from Jeremiah 45: 5: "Are you looking for special treatment for yourself? Don't do it. I am bringing disaster on all mankind, but you will at least escape with your life; wherever you go. I, the Lord, have spoken."

Fjellstedt accepted the apocalyptic view that this world's order does not hold the ultimate hope for those who fear God; the only option for

---

[125]"Friheten," *Bibelvännen*, 1 (May 1848), 76.

[126]*Ibid.*

[127]"Förord," *Folkskolan*, 1 (January 1848), 4.

Christians is faith in God. But Christians are not thereby immune from making preprations for the day of judgment. Fjellstedt wrote:

> This is not a question as to how near or far the time is of which Revelation 16 and other portions of scripture speak. Be this as it may, it is clear to every thinking person that a worthy education, good ways of thinking, clean morals, in addition to sound insights and an educated understanding, are in all life's circumstances of much higher worth than gold or pearls.[128]

In his apocalypticism, Fjellstedt struck a balance between the refusal to predict a definite date and the expectation that the history of humanity had moved into its final period. This conviction he held for at least the last thirty years of his life. His final work which was not published until after his death was an apocalyptic treatment of certain passages from the Bible, especially the book of Revelation. The two emphases—refusal to predict a specific date and the assumption humankind was in its last days—were as clear as they had been thirty years earlier.

Fjellstedt took his clue as to the biblical "intimations" of the future not from nature but from history. It is true that he made references to the "bowls of wrath" with their disturbances of nature (Rev. 16), but he looked to no unusual behavior of the heavenly bodies for his apocalyptic interpretations. It was to history that he looked.

At the end of his life as he had thirty years earlier, he viewed with anxiety both France and the Roman Church. He saw them as signs of the last times. Of the latter, he wrote that for thousands of years, the Church of the Pope had been the greatest danger to true Christianity. He saw it as a counterfeit of the true bride of Christ. For Fjellstedt, the Church of Rome was the spirit of the antichrist which "has set itself against the Church of Christ through all time until the present day with power and cunning."[129]

The other point of reference was France and the French Revolution.

> The unfortunate, scattered people, bloodied under the guillotine needed a strong ruler. Napoleon came. Without a doubt this was the first act of the final great drama which began as now seen in the contemporary rejection of Christ and the denial of him in life and confession.[130]

Fjellstedt had suspicions about government by the people. He saw popular rule developing in two stages. The first was that each one wanted to rule. Before long, that resulted in chaos, a time in which Christians would suffer. Then would come the second stage: the desire for a person who would be a strong ruler. He would be the antichrist. "Since all his imagina-

---

[128]*Ibid.*, p. 5. Revelation 16 refers to the sequence of plagues (seas turning to blood, fire, earthquakes, etc.) which the Lord brought upon the evil people who in spite of those punishments did not repent. This is the beginning of the final condemnation according to the book of Revelation.

[129]Peter Fjellstedt, *Bibliska Framtidswinkar* [*Biblical Signs of the Future*] (Uppsala: Esaias Edquists boktrycheri, 1881), p. 69.

[130]*Ibid.*

tion and object is toward one high aim he cannot love in any significant sense of that word. He will only rule. He will be God!"[131]

Another sign of the last times for Fjellstedt was a materialism which "claims that nothing of a spiritual nature exists, no God, no immortal soul, no angels, no evil spirit, no life after death, no responsibility for any evil work because what a human being does one does as an animal after its own nature."[132] This observation of Fjellstedt had significant moral implications. If there were no sense of responsibility, then, of course, there could be neither right nor wrong.

To this condition was joined Fjellstedt's rejection of evolution. He could not accept the view that a person "is a thing, which from a worm or an insect little by little after millions of years was elevated to an ape and then to a human being." He interpreted evolution in terms of the moral irresponsibility of the times. He associated this with certain philosophical and political viewpoints of his days. He especially attacked materialism and social democracy. They deny the realm of the spiritual (existence of God, immortality, etc.). Because he believed materialism and social democracy espoused evolution, Fjellstedt wrote that to them:

> No future accountability is to be feared, neither should any deed be called crime or bring on punishment. For, they say, the human being has no power to do other than what one does for such follows after one's own inclination and according to one's inner character which one cannot oppose even as when a wolf tears apart a lamb, it thereby follows its own nature. Just as it would not be reasonable to talk about the wolf's responsibility since it follows its nature, so it would also be preposterous to talk about human responsibility for crime and violence.[133]

What appeared to Fjellstedt as the wholesale rejection of the past with its moral and religious counsels and traditions by the proponents of materialism and social democracy were, he believed, signs of the latter days.

Other signs he saw as indications of the approaching apocalypse were: the preparation for war among the Christian nations; the growing friendship between Jewish and Christian people which he saw as a turning of both groups to a new heathendom may also have pointed to the conversion of the Jew to Christianity which he saw as a sign of the last days; great changes taking place in the Roman Catholic Church and the impending fall of the Mohammedan world. "These and many other signs of the time which could be named are but a period of the final sowing of the harvest which now continues to ripen and which no human being can prevent."[134]

[131]*Ibid.*, p. 66.

[132]*Ibid.*, p. 7.

[133]*Ibid.*, p. 59.

[134]*Ibid.*, pp. 8-9. He did not give historical examples of these signs. It is difficult to reconcile his view of Christian friendship with the Jews in terms of what was happening at that time. True, toleration for the Jews was growing in such places as England, Germany and the United States of America. On the other hand, beginning about 1870,

On the basis of Revelation 20: 1-39, Fjellstedt accepted the coming of a millenial period when the devil would be chained for a thousand years. He had a vivid picture of how all peoples will live together each contributing their unique gifts for the benefit of all as a part of this apocalyptic view. The Chinese, who made up nearly a third of the world's population, would come with their genius, their unusual zeal for work and their unusual ability for self-denial; to the common good, the Hindus would contribute their power of will, the Jews, their rich gifts. Gifted individuals too, then freed from the spirit of falsehood, would be able to serve with their genius, persons such as Cain and Nebuchadnezzar, the Greeks and the Romans, Voltaire, Napoleon, and Hegel. Threats of storms, earthquakes, and war and the curses of drunkenness, vice, fighting, violence, thievery, cheating and lying would be extremely rare. This transformation would occur because since the devil would be restricted, the Spirit of God would be able to work freely and powerfully in the lives of human beings as well as in nature when as Isaiah wrote in 11: 6-9: "The wolf shall dwell with the lamb, . . . and the lion shall eat a straw like the ox. . . . They shall not hurt or destroy in all my holy mountain."

What influenced Fjellstedt's apocalyptic views? One source may well have been the areas of Basel and Kornthal where Fjellstedt frequently visited and stayed for long periods of time. The Würtemberg pietism with its apocalyptic view was strong there.

Most certainly, Bengel, who greatly shaped Würtemberg pietism, was an influence. Johann Albrecht Bengel (1687-1752), the noted German scholar, is perhaps best remembered for his commentary, *Gnomen Novi Testamenti* (1742). One student in writing about this eighteenth century scholar said:

pogroms were occurring in Russia, the Ukraine, Poland and Rumania. As a consequence, many emigrated. During the 1880's, thousands of Jews came to the United States. As to Fjellstedt's view of the growing friendship of Jews and Christians and its consequence of the rise of a new heathendom, he was probably referring to Reformed Judaism which established its first synagogue in Hamburg in 1818. Throughout the nineteenth century in no small measure because of Protestantism which encroached upon it in England and Germany where Judaism enjoyed adequate toleration to develop, Reformed Judaism took on such Christian practices as the replacement of Bar Mitzvah by confirmation not only for boys but girls as well, substitution of the language of the vernacular (e.g., German in Germany) for Hebrew in liturgy and preaching, displacement of the Jewish Sabbath for Sunday as the time of worship, desegreation of the sexes and emphasis upon family seating, elimination of belief in the coming Messiah and rebuilding of Zion, and the leaving of caps and shawls in the place of worship.

Finally, Fjellstedt's reference to Roman Catholicism may have been prompted by the ascendency of Leo XIII (1876-1903) to the papal throne. No flaming liberal, he, nevertheless, set a different tone from his archconservative predecessor, Pius IX. Skilled in the classics and interested in the humanities, in 1879 (*Aeternis Patria*) he encouraged education, established the Aquinas Academy in Rome and, having established the scholastic discipline, he opened the Vatican archives and library to qualified scholars in the belief the Church would not suffer from the publication of documents. He encouraged the clergy to unite the humanities with their theological studies. His action may well have been the first important step to the *Divino afflanti spiritu* (1943) issued by Pius XII which gave impetus and encouragement to the scholarly study of the scriptures in the context of their historical setting.

Over Europe impends a complete change in the relation between Church and State. Before the Roman papacy shall be proven antichrist, unbelief, mysticism and perhaps Islamism will blend together. Upon the overthrow of the personal antichrist, the better millenial days will ensue. These, Bengel thought, would be seen less in temporal prosperity than in an undisturbed, joyous increase of the kingdom of Christ upon the earth.[135]

Fjellstedt was drawn to Bengel in a number of ways. He read Bengel's works. When the former was teaching at the Basel Institute, he wrote to a missionary student named Weitbrecht in London to send some of his books which he had left there. Among those he requested was one written by Bengel entitled *Ordo temporum* [*The Order of Time*] published in 1741. Fjellstedt's letter was sent in 1830 which means that very early in his career he was reading this German scholar. Of significance is the nature of the work. A. Hauck noted that in both his work and *Cyclus sive de anno magno consideratio* [*The Cycle: or Consideration About the Great Year*] which was written in 1745 Bengel endeavored to fix "the number of the beast" and the date of the millenium which he placed in the year 1836.[136]

When he was a missionary in Asia Minor (1836-1840), Fjellstedt may well have shown the apocalyptic influence of Bengel upon him. On one occasion when his missionary companion, Pastor Jetter, attempted to buy a building for their educational purposes and failed to do so, Fjellstedt interpreted it apocalyptically as the last of a long series of obstructions to their work. He concluded:

> It strikes me emphatically that we live in a time that is not suitable for long, certain and expensive preparations for the missionary enterprise. Wherever a missionary comes, let him work as well as he can without any permanent dwelling and soon as he has learned the language, let him preach the Gospel as long as he can. . . . If now they drive him [the missionary] from there, he has lost nothing. He simply shakes the dust from his feet and the witness is all that he leaves. I am very glad that we have not invested in buildings and the like. This is an act of Providence."[137]

Apparently, he compared their situation with the charge given by Jesus to his disciples as recorded in March 6: 11: "If you come to a town where people do not welcome you or will not listen to you, leave it and shake the dust off your feet." This statement may have been prompted in part by the fact that Fjellstedt was living in the area of the sites of the seven ancient churches which are described in the first three chapters of Revelation. The fate which was described for many of those congregations had been fulfilled dramatically. Nevertheless, the likely effect of Bengel cannot be overlooked.

[135]Revere F. Weidner, "John Albert Bengel," *Lutersk Kvartalskrift* [*Lutheran Quarterly Review*], 1 (April 1887), 90.

[136]*The New Schaff-Herzog Encyclopedia of Religious Knowledge*, 2:171.

[137]Anshelm, 1:216.

Fjellstedt wrote apocalyptically: "Many Christians waited according to Bengel's calculation for the imminent return of the Lord. Before that could happen, the Gospel must as soon as possible be preached in the whole world. It now appeared this mission must be done in short order."[138] It is highly likely that although Fjellstedt would not predict a date in his own writings, he was, nevertheless, much influenced by the apocalyptic climate to which Bengel contributed so greatly.

About ten years later, in 1845, Fjellstedt had an interesting meeting with Per Nyman, the revivalist preacher. Both participated in a temperance meeting. For three days the two men held conversations on the teachings of the apocalyptic works, Daniel and Revelation. Nyman was described as an "unusual questioner" and like a "schoolboy" in relation to Fjellstedt who occupied the role of teacher. "Both stood under the influence of Bengel whose chiliastic meditations and calculations during that time occupied many serious Christians."[139]

Fjellstedt's admiration for Bengel was impressive. This was shown in an article he published in 1850 in *Folkskolan*. Fjellstedt wrote that Bengel's apocalyptic interpretations must be taken seriously. He also stressed that as an educator, Bengel had valuable counsel to give.[140]

Important as the influence of Bengel may have been, it is scarcely possible to identify him as the sole influence upon Fjellstedt's apocalypticism. Fjellstedt was himself a diligent student of the Bible and was fully capable of coming to his own interpretations. That he shared the apocalyptic thoughts so prevalent in his day is evident.

In summary, Peter Fjellstedt's theology can be quite clearly delineated. He was trinitarian and confessionally Lutheran. He was not rigidly orthodox for he could appreciate and associate with non-Lutherans, especially with the Moravians and the Anglicans; yet, for his own faith, the Bible and the Lutheran confessions were the objective norms. At the center of his faith was the experience of the indwelling God, Father, Son and Holy

---

[138]*Ibid.*, p. 217.

[139]Anshelm, 2:138.

[140]In *Folkskolan* which Fjellstedt edited and published for four years (1848-1851), he published a short article on Bengel's view of education. This German scholar's approach was moral, religious and temperate. He saw the importance to educate youth to be able to distinguish between right and wrong. Also, "Teachers should keep themselves from becoming angry. They should not attempt to enforce respect upon themselves from their students. Neither should they attempt to break the spirits of those whom they teach. This arouses wrath in them and generally evokes opposition thus hardening and ruining them. The objective must only be to help them to do the right. . . . One has the opportunity to acquaint the children with the Word of God; even if not all is retained, some nevertheless is retained. One should begin to teach them by story and not by speech; example rather than commandments creates the desire [for the Word]." Bengel advised that it is good to leave children and youth more to their own discretion than to overload them with "many expositions and exhortations. . . . One should have prayers with the children at least morning and evening when one may either pray for them and thus give them a pattern or allow them to pray themselves." ("Något af Dr. J. A. Bengel's uppfastringsgrundsatser" ["Some of Dr. J. A. Bengel's Basic Educational Principles"], 3 (December 1850), 178-80.

Spirit and the central power and expression of life was love. He saw no inconsistency between a deep personal experience and subscription to the Lutheran confessions. They were in harmony with each other. He was loyal too, though critical of, the Lutheran Church in Sweden and thus was consistent with his loyalty to its confessions.[141] These statements became the touchstone together with the Bible by which he sought to call back the Lutheran Church in Sweden to its true character.

Politically, he was a conservative, even a reactionary. He favored monarchy and opposed revolution. He never overcame his fear of the revolution of 1848. He had a high view of law and believed changes should come through orderly process. Christians should disobey laws they believed contrary to the commandments of God but their protest must be by way of suffering. He was apocalyptic in his eschatology and, therefore, had little hope for the improvement of political conditions.

Above all, Peter Fjellstedt was theocentric. On the basis of God's sovereignty of love, he made his decisions and formed his theology on the central issues of faith and life.

[141]It will be recalled Fjellstedt produced a Swedish version of the *Book of Concord*. He thus played an important role in modern Swedish Church history. Dick Helander, editor of *Svenska kyrkans bekännelseskrifter* [*The Confessions of the Swedish Church*] (Stockholm: Svenska kyrkans diakonistyrelses bokförlag, 1944), wrote: "Peter Fjellstedt in 1854 revised a new edition which was reprinted in 1880" (p. 7). This was only the third edition of this important work in the history of the Swedish Lutheran Church, the first having been produced in 1732, the second, in 1842.

Chapter IV
Fjellstedt's Relation To The Augustana Lutheran Church[1]

Central to Peter Fjellstedt's concern was missions. His religious development, shaped by personal experiences, contacts with Moravians, mission-minded persons such as the Rappe family and Rosenius, and the Basel Mission Society with its Würtemberg pietism, oriented him toward a world-wide view for the propagation of the Gospel. He devoted all of his ministry to that end: the first decade in basically non-Christian lands (India and Asia Minor), the rest in Switzerland, Germany, and especially after 1845, in his native Sweden to awaken interest in the missionary enterprise.

Elements of his theology were also mission related. His Christology with its provision for the possibility of the salvation of the heathen by their "longing faith" expressed a universal outlook as did his ecumenical sympathies.

But there was also the quality of the particular in his theology. This was evident in his doctrine of the Church. He was a child of the Lutheran Church in Sweden with its folk-character. He saw that Church as responsible for all Swedes whether they remained in the homeland or sought their livelihood and vocation outside its borders.

During Fjellstedt's most active years, thousands of his fellow Swedes emigrated, mostly to North America. Of the 1,153,545 who left Sweden between 1850 and 1930, 1,122,292 or nearly 97.3% went to the United States.[2] For these countrymen in a foreign land, he was impelled not only by ethnic kinship but by his concern for missions and his doctrine of the Church to active participation in the establishment of the Lutheran Church among Swedish immigrants in America.

Emigration from Sweden to America during the nineteenth century was immense especially when compared with Sweden's population. A country of six million inhabitants, Sweden "lost one million through emigration [beginning with 1850], one from every seven of her population."[3] If one takes the longer period from 1820 to 1930, a million and a quarter Swedes emigrated to America.[4]

In general, emigration to America was caused by similar factors in all European countries. The chief motivation was economic but also were

---

[1]See p. 34, fn. 1.

[2]Harold Runblom and Hans Norman, eds., *From Sweden to America: A History of the Migration* (Minneapolis: University of Minnesota Press, 1976), pp. 117-19.

[3]Florence E. Janson, *The Background of Swedish Immigration 1840-1930* (Chicago: The University of Chicago Press, 1931), p. 1.

[4]Franklin D. Scott, *Sweden: The Nation's History* (Minneapolis: University of Minnesota Press, 1977;, p. 369.

involved social, political and religious conditions. In addition was the lure of America. Had there not been the promise—in some respects, not a little inflated—of something better than what they already had, the Swedes would have remained at home.

America was the land of promise. To the agrarian class—and the largest percentage of Swedish emigrants were of that class—the Homestead Act of 1863 which promised one hundred and sixty acres of land to those who would live on it for five years was indeed a bright prospect when measured against the lot of many farmers in Sweden. Because of adverse inheritance laws and economic reversals such as those effected by the disastrous crop failures of 1867-69, America was attractive. Many of the agrarian class had inadequate landholdings; others experienced tenancy with its faint promise of rising above severe poverty; some were day laborers with grave uncertainty about employment. To the ones who chafed under the humiliating customs of paying homage to the upper classes of clergy and nobility, the promise of equality in America described in literature and in letters from fellow Swedes who were in America was bright. America became a place to go where life could be lived with greater hope for the future. To the politically dissatisfied, American democracy appeared very attractive. And to the religiously concerned, especially those who had been stirred by the nineteenth century religious revival, America with its freedom from a state church where all religious persuasions were free and equal beckoned.

1. Attitudes Toward Emigration

Franklin Scott wrote: "Four revolutions marked the beginnings of the nineteenth century in Sweden. . . . In agriculture, constitution, dynasty and foreign policy the country swung off in new paths."[5] The agricultural revolution was the earliest. It was one of the few achievements of the ill-starred Gustavus IV Adolphus (1778-1837; King, 1792-1809), the last of the Vasa line. Economically, Swedish agriculture benefitted greatly by land reforms so that by the forties and fifties, Sweden had become an exporter of agricultural products and the number of farmers increased who were able to own their own land.[6] However, the opportunity to own their own farms was limited in comparison with the ease with which they could obtain land in America; hence, many were drawn to America.

The second revolution was constitutional. If there are watershed dates in modern Swedish history, 1809 must be one of them. In that year, a constitutional monarchy was established. Sufficient power was given to the legislature so that the balance of power shifted more and more to that branch of government in subsequent years. That spirit of independence so important to emigration was nourished.

[5]*Ibid.*, p. 301.

[6]Janson, p. 75: Scott, p. 292.

Thirdly, also in 1809, there was the dynastic revolution. On March 29, Gustavus IV Adolphus abdicated. He was succeeded by the unusual choice of a French General, Jean Baptiste Jules Bernadotte, who became Charles John XIV.

Finally, there was the foreign policy revolution. With the loss of Finland, Sweden was exposed to Russia without a buffer state. She was in some sense forced to cooperate with Russia. This had the advantage of putting to an end the frequent wars fought between the two countries over Finland. It may also have contributed to the policy of neutrality which has kept Sweden from direct involvement in war for nearly one and three quarters centuries. The significance of these four revolutions was that an independent spirit was nourished and increased in Sweden.

The sense of independence was also reflected in the religious life in Sweden. This has been noted in the rise of the *läsare* movement. Increasing criticism of the restrictive Conventicle Act and the reduction, in the minds of such men as Fjellstedt, of the Eucharist to a citizen's duty rather than the expression of free obedience to the Christian faith led eventually to political actions for greater religious freedom.

While not the major cause for Swedish emigration to America, the attractiveness of American religious freedom drew some.[7] The appeal of the prospect for greater religious freedom was described by Stephenson:

> The American pastor portrayed in the letters was a friendly, democratic individual who held religious meetings in homes and on highways and byways and took a personal interest in his fellow men. To the Swedes who visualized the American clergymen through the medium of these letters, the parish pastor appeared stiffer and more indifferent than ever; and it is a fair inference that when at the Sunday morning service he read the names of those who had applied for permission to emigrate to America, many sighed and laid plans for the day when their names would also be read. In the mind of the pietist, America was a land where the pastor was one of the people; he worked with his hands, preached without a manuscript, sought the sheep, and was full of the spirit, light and perfection. Moreover, there was no *konventikelplakat* "contrary to the plain teaching of the Word of God which prohibited believing souls from meeting for edification in the sacred truth of our Lord Jesus Christ." There were no blustering officials to intrude and to disperse meetings of "true believers" and to forbid laymen to spread the "healing salvation of the Gospel."[8]

America was seen as the place where churches could be formed according to people's own convictions. Many went so far as to believe a pure church would become a reality. For example, in the mind of Olof Olsson and his group who came to found the Lindsborg, Kansas community in 1869, "the religious interest was uppermost . . . in whose plans entered the founding of a "pure" congregation."[9]

[7]Runblom and Norman, p. 155.

[8]Stephenson, p. 142 (extracts from several letters).

[9]Ernest W. Olson, *Olof Olsson: The Man, His Work, and His Thought* (Rock Island, Ill.: Augustana Book Concern, 1941), p. 55.

Not only letters and reports from America but sources in Sweden helped paint a picture of unusual religious vitality nourished by religious freedom. Articles in the *Pietisten* written by Rosenius contributed to the bright picture. Typical also was the journalistic contribution of Fjellstedt. In *Bibelvännen* for October, 1858 (one example of many such articles) he described the revival going on in America. After listing several cities where the revival was found, Fjellstedt concluded: "It is in so many places that it is futile to count the cities and the places, the congregations and the societies of every name which rejoice over the outpouring of the Holy Spirit. . . . It is a new Pentecost wonder which shows itself to our eyes.[10]

Lars Paul Esbjörn became the first ordained Swedish Lutheran minister to come to America in the mid-nineteenth century. Esbjörn had read a book by the American Presbyterian minister, Robert Baird, entitled *Religious Freedom in the United States*. Of Baird's influence upon himself, Esbjörn wrote:

> In this book was described in very light colors the religious conditions in the United States. All that a *läsare* minister could wish for appeared to be possible there. There was no mixing of the spiritual and the worldly. Only true born again Christians were members of the church. [At this point, Esbjörn, too, seemed to have had notions of a pure church]. Pastors examine carefully every application for membership. Before anyone can take that important step, such must show oneself to have begun the action to repent and be born again. The free will system for financial support of the church functions in a fully satisfactory manner. An honest preacher does not need to have any worries about his livelihood, not even in a newly built area because there are found home mission societies which support the weak congregations especially in such areas. The free will system applies also with the same good results in the matter of schools and all kinds of social work. Hardly does a need appear before the money streams in. Only good results have shown themselves by the full application of the principle of religious freedom.[11]

Not all Swedes saw America on such terms. Attempts were made in Sweden to discourage emigration. J. S. Haldeman, of the American legation in Stockholm, wrote to the American Consul on August 10, 1862. He expressed the feeling of Sweden (as well as Norway since Sweden and Norway were ruled by the same king until 1905):

> Although Sweden and Norway are but sparsely settled, many of the rich peasants are selling out to emigrate to the United States. *This government* [Sweden] *is opposed to the emigration and does all in its power to discourage and prevent this loss of its subjects,* offering crown lands on better conditions than ever before. Whatever occurs in the United States to check or interrupt this emigration has the approbation

---

[10]"Underrättelser från Nord-Amerika" ["report from North America"], 11: 155-58. Interestingly, eight years before, Fjellstedt wrote an article discouraging emigration.

[11]Sam Rönnegård, *Lars Paul Esbjörn och Augustana-Synodens Uppkomst* [*Lars Paul Esbjörn and the Origin of the Augustana Synod*] (Stockholm: Svenska Kyrkans Diakonistyrelses, 1949), pp. 75-76.

of this government, and as the difficulties in the United States affect and retard this movement of the Swedes and Norwegians "Westward ho," their interests (as they think) conflict with their natural and strong sympathy with our government in the present contest. *It is well known that the King and his brother Oscar are violently and bitterly hostile to all who recommend or encourage emigration,* and I find that if I wish to stand well with the King and his Ministers, the less said for the present on the subject the better. The above I have gathered from frequent conversations with Count Manderström (foreign minister), the diplomatic corps, and others.[12]

Churchmen, too, added their negative note. Peter Fjellstedt warned prospective emigrants not to be deceived by reports that figs and raisins were as easy and free to obtain in America as lingon and blueberries in the woods of Sweden. In the *Lunds Missions-Tidning* for April 1850, he stressed that America required much work—so much, in fact, that only the young, the healthy and the single should emigrate. There were also moral and spiritual enemies in America. Two classes of emigrants Fjellstedt viewed as enemies. There were the Irish who, according to him, under the bondage of the teaching of the Roman Catholic Church, were addicted to liquor and drunkenness and abject poverty. The other group, the German emigrants, had confused notions regarding the Christian faith: they were opportunists who, unfortunate in their homeland, hoped to be lucky in America; and, they wanted freedom according to their own design. By contrast, Fjellstedt wrote that even though Sweden had its faults, it was not without opportunity. Religiously, there was, to be sure, the restrictive act of the Conventicle Law but there were also many faithful pastors to serve the people. Sweden was not crowded as some other countries were. There was plenty of room. Finally, in America with all its space, there may be no churches or pastors or at best, too few churches and pastors to serve the people.[13]

The contrast between the views of Esbjörn and Fjellstedt at mid-century was interesting. Whereas Esbjörn exalted the principle of religious freedom—a position which he would later greatly modify—Fjellstedt showed doubts about the American religious situation. Perhaps Fjellstedt was thinking of those who he said wanted freedom according to their own design.

Just a few months earlier, Fjellstedt had written of ships on their way to America, one of which carried none other than Lars Paul Esbjörn and his company of 147 fellow emigrants including forty-seven persons from his parish in Hille. Two other ships also left at that time with emigrants mostly from Gästrikland and Hälsingland "the main number of whom had been lured by a teacher of another *freedom of religion—a freedom from religion* which is a meaningless expression in many parts of their community." Fjellstedt was referring to the Jansonists who were followers of "Erik

---

[12]*U. S. Consular Letters, 1857-1863*, Stockholm, consul, Charles A. Leas, quoted in Janson, p. 154. Emphasis mine.

[13]"Några ord om utwandring" ["Some Words About Emigration"], *Lunds Missions-Tidning*, 3 (April 1850), 59-64 *passim*.

Janson's horrid and foolish interpretation of Bible reading and prayer which is given to those in need of upbuilding and spiritual food. These are easily deluded. They are denied bread for the soul." In a similarly critical mood he charged the Swedish Church and State for their neglect of the Swedish Lutheran immigrants in America. "We wonder what the Church and State will do to win such immigrants. We have much to complain about, much to pray about, the need for much help. God alone can help."[14]

Obstructions were placed in the way of some of the pastors who decided to leave Sweden for America. When Esbjörn's intention to emigrate came to the attention of Archbishop Wingård, Esbjörn received a strongly worded letter. Wingård's chief complaint was the belief that the pastor from Hille was attempting to "persuade others, and among them easily stirred by lacking in understanding, women, who would exchange their calling, their fatherland and their opportunity to worship God for a dangerous journey and an uncertain habitation in a foreign part of the world." What especially disturbed the Archbishop was the recent departure of many Swedish people for America under the influence of Janson. Wingård challenged Esbjörn: "What assurance can you give that the security of your settlement will not be encroached upon and what assurance have you that the care of souls and the opportunity to worship God will be uninterrupted?"[15]

In a response, Esbjörn told the Archbishop that his intentions were not of a Jansonist type and those going with him were doing so not from persuasive efforts on his part. Apparently Archbishop Wingård was convinced and sent a later letter. He indicated that he did not want to be found opposing the goodness of the Swedish Missionary Society which was to give Esbjörn 300 *riksdaler* for his journey and work. He closed the letter: "Now God be with Esbjörn, his wife and children on the journey and all the future."[16]

Hindrances or not, the Swedish immigrants came to America in increasing numbers. In 1860, eleven years after Esbjörn's arrival in America, there were in America 18,627 immigrants born in Sweden; in 1870, 97,332; in 1880, 194,337; in 1890, 478,041; and by 1900, 665,183.[17] Fjellstedt had not encouraged his fellow Swedes to emigrate but when he realized the numbers that were leaving, he was moved by another motive to encourage help for those many immigrants living in a new land—the concern for their spiritual welfare. In 1859, he wrote:

> It may have been better and wise for them to have stayed home. Perhaps many of them now also think so and would return if they

---

[14]*Lunds Missions-Tidning,* 2 (October 1849), 151-52.

[15]Westin, p. 37, letter written from Uppsala, March 8, 1849.

[16]*Ibid.,* letter written from Uppsala, March 26, 1849.

[17]*Protokoll Hållet vid Augustana Synodens Årsmöte* [*Minutes of the Augustana Synod*], 1861, 1871, 1881, 1891, 1901, 1911 quoted in Hugo Söderström, *Confession and Cooperation: The Policy of the Augustana Synod in Confessional Matters and the Synod's Relations With Other Churches Up to the Beginning of the Twentieth Century* (Bibliotheca Historico-Ecclesiastica Lundensis IV; Lund: CWK Gleerup Bokförlag, 1973), p. 94.

could. Even if most of them went in order to gain temporal benefits, can this be a pretext for us that we leave them without help if we allow our souls to perish out of need for the bread of life? Are not these souls precious? Yes, and now they come to us. Neither can it be said that they can find God's word out there. They cannot find it everyplace as pure and unfalsified as we have it among us.[18]

Fjellstedt's plea came in part as a response to an article in *Hemlandet*, a paper published by Hasselquist. "The harvest is great but the workers are few." In order to meet the religious needs of the burgeoning Swedish immigrant population, the Mississippi Conference had appealed to the authorities in Sweden to take up a collection in their churches but the appeal was refused. Money was needed for the Scandinavian Professorship at the struggling Illinois State University, for help to needy students and especially for pastors who traveled to various places.[19] Fjellstedt concluded his article:

When the world obtains help for some temporal need, it understands and talks often about compassion and how one should be responsible and it never makes its appeals in vain. Can then cries to Christian love be in vain for the sake of the spiritual needs of brethren? O, no![20]

2. Changing Views of the New World

America in the 1840's, 1850's and 1860's, when the Swedish immigration was growing modestly, still had a vast frontier west of the Appalachians. The frontier itself was important not simply as a geographical phenomenon but as a state of mind. It encouraged experimentation, freedom and mobility, features which worked contrary to the established order and traditions of the land from whence the immigrants had come. Heterogeneity rather than homogeneity characterized the new America and this, too, was a threat to the settled institutions of Europe which the immigrants inevitably brought with them.

Politically, America presented an ambiguous picture. On the one hand, America had a political philosophy of equality and freedom expressed by its Bill of Rights. The first amendment of the Bill of Rights of the American Constitution guaranteed not only freedom of religion but also other freedoms: "Congress shall make no law . . . abridging the freedom of speech, or of the press; or the right of the people peaceably to assemble, and to petition the government for a redress of grievances."

On the other hand, there were negative factors in America. The issues of slavery and of the treatment of Native Americans carried with them deep moral implications. These troubled Swedes, both those who remained in Sweden and those who emigrated. Fjellstedt wrote several articles about

---

[18]"Skall jag taga wara på min bröder?" ["Shall I Look After My Brother?"] *Bibelvännen*, 12 (October 1859), p. 156.

[19]An organization of the Swedish Lutheran immigrants within the larger American Lutheran organization to which they belonged, the Synod of Northern Illinois. See Stephenson, p. 183.

[20]Fjellstedt, "Skall jag taga wara . . .," p. 158.

slavery.[21] T. N. Hasselquist was adamant against the practice. Typical of his thought on the issue was his utterance: "It is ungodly in its very foundation and cannot stand the test of Christianity or be defended by a clean conscience, which has been cleansed in the blood that was shed for the people regardless of race."[22]

Another negative issue was America's treatment of the Native Americans. These Native Americans became the object of the mission concern to Swedish people who were concerned with the spread of the Gospel. At least one of the early leaders of the Augustana Church, Olof Olsson, came to America with the intention of doing mission work among the Native Americans.[23] From Sweden, too, came deep criticism of the treatment of the Native Americans. Several articles were written by Peter Fjellstedt on that moral issue.[24]

Religiously, America offered opportunities not present in Europe. Of this something has already been noted. The opportunities which the emigrants believed America gave for the establishment of the Church free from the State drew them to this land. They hoped something akin to a restoration of the Church in accordance with their interpretation of the Lutheran Confessions might be possible.

The questions to raise then are: did these immigrants find in America the answer they had expected as they had looked from Sweden to America? Was the actual America the place they had hoped to find?

In partial answer to these questions, attention must be turned in another direction: to Scotland. In 1843 the Free Church of Scotland came into being. Under the leadership of men such as Thomas Chalmers, the new Church grew impressively. By the end of the century, it could claim 1068 congregations or over forty-three percent of the 2445 congregations in Scotland. The Established Church claimed 1377.[25]

Before the immigrant pastors had left Sweden, enthusiastic reports were filtering back to Sweden about the remarkable Christian community expressed in the Free Church. A typical statement of admiration came from Carl Axel Torén who was later professor and dean at Uppsala University. He made a study tour of Germany, England and Scotland in 1848 and 1849 but it was the Free Church of Scotland which received his accolade. From two letters, one from London (May 20, 1849) and one from Leipzig (November 1849), Nils Rodén has excerpted the following statement:

> No place did I find such a widespread participation on the part of individuals as here, no place such an awakened churchly community,

[21]E. g., in the *Lunds Missions-Tidning*, May and July 1847 and May 1859 and *Bibelvännen*, July and December, 1855.

[22]*Hemlandet* (June 2, 1855), quoted in Ander, p. 153.

[23]Emory Lindquist, *Smoky Valley People, A History of Lindsborg, Kansas* (Lindsborg, Kansas: Bethany Press, 1953), p. 54.

[24]E. g., *Lunds Missions-Tidning*, June 1854, June 1857, October 1860 and December 1867.

[25]"Scotland," *The New Schaff-Herzog Encyclopedia of Religious Knowledge* (Grand Rapids, Michigan; Baker Book House, 1951-57;), 10:299.

such a spirit of brotherhood. And under what form has a zealous pastor greater opportunity to awaken and work in his congregation than here where he is so richly supported by the foremost of the congregation itself, that is the best and most serious men? These elders, *episcopoi*, who are called Lay-Elders, Ruling Elders as distinct from Clergy-Elders, pastors, work together with the pastor for the welfare of the congregation. They are not only ruling as administrative personnel; they are spiritual. They receive a kind of ordination. Special importance is placed in the Scottish Church on that office as a necessary adherence to the example of the apostolic order of the Church.[26]

Fjellstedt in a long article in *Bibelvännen* wrote favorably: "The Free Church in Scotland is truly the Church in which more Christian life is found, more heavenly Spirit, and more power in faith and love than in any church in the whole world.[27] The wide audience Fjellstedt enjoyed both through his journalism and preaching almost certainly had its impact upon many including the Swedish pastors who came to America.

Tuve Nilsson Hasselquist, one of the early leaders of the Augustana Lutheran Church, during his pastorate in Önnestad parish became acquainted with a group of ministers who favored a free, independent Lutheran Church in Sweden. These men had been inspired by the Free Church of Scotland. Hasselquist cooperated with one these men, H. B. Hammar, in publishing *Evangelisk-Kyrko Wän* (*Evangelical Church friend*).[28] After Hasselquist left Onnestad and moved to Åkarp, he maintained his friendly relations with that group of pastors.

It is interesting to discover that in T. N. Hasselquist's possessions was a copy of a book entitled *Den Fria Skottska Kyrkans Grundsatser och Grund-förgattning i Frågor och Svar* (*Catechism on the Principles and Constituion of the Free Church of Scotland*).[29] Two features about this book are deserving of notice. In the foreword of the translation is a quotation from Fjellstedt. Secondly, the copy of the Catechism has on it the following inscription: "Till Pastor T. Hasselquist i Galesburg, från din gamla vännen, C. Bergman, Vinslöf." ("To Pastor T. Hasselquist in Galesburg from your old friend, C. Bergman, Vinslöf"). Dr. C. A. Bergman was one of the foremost proponents for the Free Church of Scotland model. The book was published in 1853. Apparently, not too much time elapsed before Bergman, the "radical from Vinslöf,"[30] sent the book to Hasselquist. This episode illustrates Hasselquist's early interest in the Free Church of Scotland.

When the early leaders of the Swedish Lutherans came to America, however, their attitude changed and changed quickly. Within three years

---

[26]"Skotska frikyrkens inflytande på Svenska fromhetsliv vid mitten af 1800-talet" ["The Influence of the Scottish Free Church upon Swedish Piety in the Mid-Nineteenth Century], *Krykohistorisk Årsskrift* [*Annual Journal of Church History*] (Uppsala and Stockholm: Almquist and Wiksell Boktryckeri ab., 1957, 56 (1956), 140.

[27]"Om den Svenska Kyrkan" ["About the Swedish Church"], 5 (July 1952), p. 105.

[28]Soderstrom, p. 18.

[29]In the archives of the Denkmann Library, Augustana College, Rock Island, Illinois.

[30]Stephenson, p. 44.

after his arrival in America, Esbjörn had second thoughts about the virtues of a free church model. Never as articulate on the subject as Hasselquist, nevertheless, when he arrived in America in 1849, Esbjörn shared Hasselquist's interest in the Scottish Free Church model. By 1852, he wrote a letter which was published in Fjellstedt's *Bibelvännen*. In that letter Esbjörn wrote at length on the advantages and disadvantages of constitutional religious freedom and its practice in America. The disadvantages, in his judgment, far outweighed the benefits. He was not entirely negative. On the one side, he saw two positive benefits in the American situation of separation of Church and State. First, if people are truly like-minded Christians, their religious freedom gives them an opportunity to practice Christian discipline, build up one another and develop a healthy life of faith which "allows light to shine." If, however, a congregation has a majority of unspiritual people, "then this freedom is absent: then it is not one bit better than the State Church."[31]

The second advantage of religious freedom arose from the competition among the various denominations. Esbjörn seemed to view the rivalry which existed among the denominations as including the component of love and respect. Instead of an aggressive competition, the denominations wished to show a brotherly love at least by addressing each other as such. Also this competition had another ingredient, that of discipline. If, for example, a pastor committed a wrong and his denomination attempted to conceal the wrongdoer and his deed, it would be difficult to do so because "they had around them such a 'great cloud of witnesses.' "[32] Esbjörn concluded, however, that the discipline of the "witnesses" may not always be from the highest motives. Quite plainly, the advantages Esbjörn cited regarding religious freedom were severely qualified. The disadvantages were both numerous and clear-cut.

First, Esbjörn saw competition also as a disadvantage in that it led to sectarianism such as Sweden could only dimly understand. What Sweden had seen in the Eric Janson strife was nothing compared to what went on in America. He wrote of a Congregational congregation which had built a beautiful church edifice. Within a short time, there had been a separation and another Congregational group to which a "shoemaker was preaching 'free religion' had built another building just one-quarter of a mile away."

A second drawback of freedom of religion allowed the spread of all kinds of "teaching, opinions and foolishness" which often resulted in more "lies and delusions than truth." These he saw not as the result of American foolishness for "they were otherwise a wise and not an easily deluded people." Rather, the "foolishness" was the consequence of religious freedom.

Thirdly, Esbjörn argued that freedom of religion actually encouraged crime. He did not deny the existence of drunkenness and unchastity in Sweden, but the situation was compounded in America. In Sweden,

---

[31]"Bref från en Svensk Prest i Nord-Amerika" ["Letter from a Swedish Pastor in North America"] 6 (September 1852), p. 139.

[32]*Ibid.*

indifference was primarily against the Church whereas in America, freedom of religion bred indifference to all religion and morality in general. Not only were drunkenness and unchastity present in America but all kinds of false money floated around in the United States. Esbjörn observed that in a recent issue of *Thomsons Bank-Note-Reports*, no less than 2288 kinds of false currency were listed. Esbjörn apparently concluded that to be a member of the Church by law as in Sweden even though one be indifferent in that relationship formed a hedge against crime such as freedom of religion as established by the Constitution in the United States did not.

Fourthly, religious freedom made church discipline difficult. If a member were disciplined in one congregation, it was not difficult to find another group which would recieve such a one with "open arms."

In the same letter published by Fjellstedt, Esbjörn continued with a fifth disadvantage in the horrible waste of time and human resources which resulted from freedom of religion. In one place could be found five small congregations all of different confessions. Each pastor probably had four other places and was consequently required to travel fifty miles, "wasting his time, money and strength." If there were one faith, then there could be five instead of twenty-five churches and each pastor could be responsible for one church of adequate size in one place.

Sixth, Esbjörn criticized freedom of religion because it did not care for an adequate number of the citizens in America. The folk-church system such as Sweden had felt itself responsible for all people. Not so in America. On the basis of population and church membership figures, only 4,597,202 Americans belonged to churches out of a national population (according to Esbjörn's figures) of 23,267,498. Even that figure of 4,597,202 was unreliable. If one subtracted the false faiths of Mormonism, Swedenborgianism and Unitarianism, then there were only 3,265,812 and "how many of these are upright and know God alone? It would be good if it were half as many as these."

Esbjörn's seventh criticism was on the issue of slavery. He stated that there were about as many slaves (3,176,589) as there were Protestants. The churches participated in the horrible business of buying and selling their human brothers consigning them to a life of bondage and often "treating them like cattle." That Esbjörn found totally inconsistent with the principle of freedom. "America with its religious freedom is not cleansed from the blood of its sons who from the earth cry to God."

His eighth criticism of religious freedom stemmed from his view of Roman Catholicism as heresy and its growth in America. According to his statistics, that community comprised more than one fourth of all the church members in America (1,233,350 out of a total of 4,597,202). "This does not say much for the power of religious freedom to oppose heresy and create a living Christianity."

Finally, he was critical of the American scene because the churches were not growing in the same proportion as the population of the country. In the decade of 1840 to 1850, the number of pastors increased thirty-one percent, congregations, thirty-two percent, members, twenty percent and theological students decreased by twenty-two percent. By contrast Americans increased in number thirty-six percent.[33]

On the basis of his observations, Esbjörn warned his brothers and sisters in Sweden against the principle of separation of Church and State. He ended his letter with these words: "Think well and seek better reasons than hereto have been given before religious freedom is introduced into Sweden."[34]

Esbjörn drew a contrast between Jefferson, on the one hand, and a number of religious leaders on the other hand—all pietists—(Arndt, Spener, Francke, Pontopiddan, Nohrborg, Schartau, Sellergren, Wesley and Hauge). "Watch the signs of the times, my dear Swedish brothers in the Lord Jesus Christ and mark well how the whole host of unbelievers stems from this novelty [American freedom of religion]. So, Thomas Jefferson, president of the United States, worked with zeal and drove through complete religious freedom: yet, he was one of the most resolute of unbelievers."[35] (With Jefferson, he included Methodists and Baptists of whom he warned: "They want to open the gates also in Sweden for fellow sects.") All those groups Esbjörn associated with the evil of religious liberty. "On the other hand," he wrote, "we are the most successful of God's people who have desired neither religious freedom nor separation from the established Church in which the chief articles are pure." His solution for Sweden was not religious freedom. Since the Church's confessions and order were good and were only to be followed, what was really required was to "unite your efforts to enliven and purify the Swedish Lutheran Zion from its impurity."[36]

---

[33] According to Esbjörn's letter, the source of these figures was *The Home Missionary*, publication of the American Home Missionary Society which subsidized Esbjorn's work for several years.

[34] Ten years later, when he was about to return to Sweden and began to seek for a parish there, Esbjörn wrote to his friend, Eric Norelius on November 28, 1861: "It seems to me, that we, who have gained experience here, could benefit our homeland considerably by warning against the danger of the American system (i.e., a free church and separation of Church and State)." (Oscar N. Olson, *Olof Christian Telemak Andrén: Ambassador of Good Will* (Rock Island, Ill.: Augustana Historical Society, 1957), p. 49.

[35] "Bref från en Svensk Prest . . . ", p. 144. Jefferson, however, was not opposed to religion, deist though he was. It was the favored situation given to one religion or one confessional group over others in the State Church arrangement which was a centuries old tradition at the time when the American constitution was formed which he opposed. He would have rejected Esbjörn's third argument—that freedom of religion encouraged crime. In the early days of the republic, he "exhibited a pragmatic concern for church or private religion, being convinced of its utility in inculcating morality among the citizens." It is true as he grew older, he did express the confidence that people would some day be able to act for the common good on the basis of natural reason alone. Winthrop Hudson, *Religion in America* (New York: Charles Scribner's Sons, 1973), p. 115.

[36] In a later issue of *Bibelvännen* (5 [November 1852]), Esbjörn was answered by one who called himself "a fervent Lutheran." He upheld the arrangement whereby because of religious freedom, several Christian groups could live and work together. He supported the idea of a visible Christian faith and life for church members. If they did not show such, then they could not belong to a religious organization. If one church could not lead persons to repentance, religious freedom allowed other churches to work on them. If

Although Esbjörn was the most articulate and precise in his criticism of the religious situation in America as well as his defense of the Church in Sweden, other leaders of Augustana also developed a different view of the ecclesiastical conditions in America. T. N. Hasselquist who believed in separation of Church and State did not, however, continue his enthusiasm for the Scottish Free Church model. O. Fritiof Ander in his biography of Hasselquist quoted:

> His [Hasselquist] friends who were supporters of the Free Church Movement [in Sweden] expected much of him, believing that he would test out their ideas in the new country. After arriving in America, however, he severed all connections with them, as he discovered that even the Free Church plan was beset with difficulties.[37]

In his statement that Hasselquist "severed all connections" with his Swedish friends who advocated the Free Church, Ander was in error. There is no record of correspondence between Hasselquist and Hammar who died in 1862. However, in a letter written May 29, 1857, Bergman responded to a previous communication (April 1857) from Hasselquist in which Hammar was prominently mentioned. Bergman concluded his letter by stating the possibility of a visit to Hasselquist and expressed gratitude to his friends in America for what the latter had done for his own spiritual life. The exchange of letters continued between Bergman and Hasselquist until a year before Bergman's death in 1882.

Though he still showed no great enthusiasm for the State Church as found in Sweden, his writings began to reveal a tendency toward conservatism and uncompromising orthodoxy. Hasselquist had visited Sweden in 1870 and while there he had observed colporteurs who for the most part, he felt, "were possessed of a fanatical hatred of ministers and of the office of the ministry." He saw many changes had occurred in the Church in Sweden and he could no longer maintain that Sweden should follow the free church model. Rather, he wrote that for them an "abrupt separation of Church and State would be unfortunate."[38]

Sweden were to excommunicate all its members who live in open sin, drink, break the Sabbath, etc. "how many would be left?" Even though it may have been true as Esbjörn wrote that less than 5,000,000 of some 23,000,000 Americans belonged to Church, that was still better than Sweden because those 5,000,000 were committed Christians. The awful error Sweden committed was to give the impression that all Swedes were right with God simply because they were members of the Church. What was important in that interchange was the conflict of two views of the Church: one was to see the Church as folk Church and that it was both visible and invisible (Esbjörn). This meant that no individual or group could judge where the true Church is. The other was to see the Church pure and visible; the true Church could be identified (Esbjörn's adversary). This is, of course, an old conflict in the Church. It was noticeably present between the Augustana Lutherans and many of their opponents (e.g., Eric Jansonists, Baptists, Methodists) in America. ["An Extract from a Letter Concerning the Condition of Christianity in the United States of North America"], pp. 176-78.

[37] *Korsbaneret*, 13:80. Quoted in Ander, pp. 10-11.

[38] Stephenson, p. 235, fn. 25; E. W. Olson, p. 69.

Anders Richard Cervin, the brother-in-law of Hasselquist, developed a similar view of religious freedom as he saw it operate in America. He first came to the new land in 1856 with Fjellstedt's two sons (Viktor and Richard) in his custodial care. He went back to Sweden but returned in 1864 to become associated with Hasselquist in the latter's journalistic work. In 1868, he became professor at the Augustana Seminary. After his stay in Sweden from 1858 to 1864, he wrote to Peter Wieselgren that he was more than ever a convinced Lutheran and, in the complete context of his remarks in Sweden, spoke of his low estimation of the principle of freedom as expressed in the separation of Church and State in America. In an article in *Väktaren* (*The Watchman*), he expressed the judgment that religious freedom "waits for better and more beautiful fruits" that many who had been favorably disposed to that arrangement thought it best "not to have to live under that system." It had resulted in politics, a formal Christianity and the existence of eccentric sectarians.[39]

In the early glow of idealism upon their arrival in America, these leaders believed they could more than test out their ideas in the new country. They anticipated success. Very quickly, they saw they had been mistaken. The primary criteria of Christian experience based on the Bible apart from any confessional standards proved inadequate for them. They moved instead to a renewed defense of, and devotion to, not only the Bible but the Lutheran confessions. This change was represented in Esbjörn's statement:

> For some time I have found it necessary to read once more through the symbolical books because of the manifold opinions and the conflict here. This reading has at the same time made the Gospel clearer and more alive to me and confirmed my conviction about the purity and the accord with the *Scriptures*, which the Confession of our Church possesses. I have found especially in the *Formula of Concord* that this leaning toward antinomianism, which some who claim to be the strictest Lutherans, is *not* the doctrine of the Lutheran Church. . . . For instance, from this repeated study of the symbols of our Church I have got so much joy, benefit and increase of faith and spiritual life that I want to advise you, if you have not recently done so, to do as I have done, beginning with the *Augsburg Confession* and proceeding to the end of the *Formula of Concord*.[40]

The strong contrast between the anticipation of these early pioneers and

---

[39]Nils Runeby, *Den nya världen och den gamla: Americabild och emigrations-uppfattning i Sverige: 1820-1860* [*The Old World and the New: A Swedish Picture of America and a Swedish View of the Emigrants* (Studia Historia Upsaliensia; Uppsala: Almquist and Wiksells Boktrycheri Aktiebolog, 1969), p. 339.

[40]Norelius' collection in "Tidskrift för Svensk evangelisk luthersk kyrkohistoria i N. Amerika" ["Journal of Swedish Evangelical Lutheran Church History in North America"]: 1898-99 (Rock Island, Ill.) quoted in Söderström, p. 43. His reference to "strictest Lutherans" shows the battle was not only against Baptists, Episcopalians and Methodists but also against fellow Lutherans especially represented by the General Synod which early Augustana leaders thought had become too Americanized and Reformed.

how they interpreted their actual experiences within the American religious scene requires an attempt to understand why the disillusionment occurred.

Several factors were present. For one thing, their model of the Free Church of Scotland was not appropriate for America. The first amendment of the American Constitution stated that the Church and State must be separated. In America, the actual separation occurred as a pragmatic event, not the result of conviction about a principle as was the case with the Free Church of Scotland.

Secondly, the Swedish Lutheran immigrants faced a highly heterogeneous and pluralistic religious life in America. This pattern had been set early. In 1664 there were in New Amsterdam (later New York) fourteen different languages spoken, eighteen nationalities and at least eleven different religious groups.[41] During the last half of the nineteenth century when Swedish immigration reached its highest point, this diversity actually increased. A large number of Orientals and Eastern Europeans, many of the latter from the Eastern Orthodox Church, compounded the American heterogeneity.[42] Neither Scotland nor Sweden presented such variety. Their highly homogeneous religious community in Sweden in no small sense created by the state church relationship ill prepared the Swedish Lutheran Church leaders in America for the sometimes fierce competition they faced under the order of separation of Church and State.

Thirdly, the contrast between the centuries old settled traditions of Europe which created a definite order and the fluid frontier in America was great. Karl Olsson wrote:

> They came to America and they found freedom, but the effect was not all they had anticipated. In America, it is true, they found freedom to worship as they pleased, but here they also found the inevitable concomitants of freedom: disorder, dizziness, heedlessness. . . . In Sweden, freedom had been set over against an ordered society. In America, freedom had no such enriching contrary. Hence both Esbjörn and Hasselquist, as well as a number of other Augustana leaders, relinquished the search for freedom and strove with all their talent and energy to fashion a new and meaningful order in the midst of religious chaos.[43]

To create this order, only one of the two options familiar to them in Sweden was open to them in America. The one, church order insured by a protective state, was closed by the guaranteed constitutional principle of separation of Church and State. The other, the order of the Lutheran liturgy and especially the confessions, remained open. Both against the plurality of the churches and the fluidity the frontier they returned to the classical confessional writings of the Lutheran Church. "They longed for a renewed church. However, while they were working in the New World with its

---

[41]William Warren Sweet, *The Story of Religion in America* (New York: Harper and Brothers Publishers, 1930), pp. 122-23.

[42]Hudson, pp. 261-62.

[43]P. 175

many churches, they were forced to study the Lutheran doctrines more closely."[44]

The competition with other religious groups, while not unknown in Sweden, was less threatening to the Lutherans there both because of the protection they had as the state church and the lesser number of non-Lutherans who challenged the Lutheran position. Erland Carlsson expressed his dissatisfaction:

> America is not the wonderful land either spiritually or materially as it is presented to be. . . . The religious climate is wholly Calvinistic or at least closely associated with it. The Sacraments are generally regarded only as representations and signs. In their preaching and talks of edification one hears much about duty, morality, and reward but very little about Christ, the righteousness of faith and eternal life. . . . Even our Lutheran Church is not wholly true. In the Lutheran Synod [the General Synod] which has not entirely accepted the Augsburg Confession . . . one hears in public and private talk and writing a denial of the presence of Christ's body and blood in the Eucharist.[45]

Carlsson, the pastor of the Immanuel Lutheran Church in Chicago for over two decades (1853-1875), like the other early leaders of the Augustana Lutheran Church, was responsible for other geographical areas. On the basis of a trip to Minnesota, he reported that the condition of the Swedes there was not good. Either they had no church or were the victims of proselytism. Many Swedes had forgotten God and his Word. He wrote that the children were growing up in crudity and ignorance "without schools or in schools where the only teaching is worldly."

An unsigned earlier report, almost certainly from Esbjörn, gave a similarly dismal picture. "Only a few know the living power of Christianity which shows itself in the life of faith, in prayer to God, and in holy behavior."[46] The writer faulted the bad habits formed from the influence of the State Church in Sweden in that many of the immigrants had only a formal Christianity. They assumed that because they had been in church in the morning, they could spend Sunday afternoon in rowdiness and drinking. Also, their familiarity with the tax supported Church in Sweden made them unwilling to adopt the "free-will system"—an arrangement which appeared so laudable to Esbjörn when he had viewed America from the land of Sweden. Hence, voluntary support for the building of churches, establishment of schools and the support of pastors and teachers was not satisfactory. Congregations which had pastors reimbursed them with gifts for ministerial services at baptisms, confirmation and funerals instead of providing them with a fixed salary. Pastors, consequently, could not give full time to their ministry. The writer concluded his dreary account by

---

[44]Söderström, p. 21.

[45]"Utdrag af ett bref från America" ["Extracts of a Letter from America"] *Lunds Missions-Tidning*, 7 (April 1854), 51. Actually this article included extracts from two letters, one dated September 28, 1853 and one, December 1853.

[46]"Ett omdöme från Nord-Amerika om den som invandra" [A Judgment from North America about Those Who Immigrate"], *Bibelvännen*, 3 (August 1850), 128.

saying some churches had services only once a month while others worshipped only four times a year.

Materially as well as spiritually, the leaders of Augustana felt the immigrants had not found America to be a land of "figs and raisins" just as Fjellstedt had warned. Representative of this view but also found in the writings of others was Carlsson's feeling that America was not the wonderful land . . . materially as it was generally presented to be. He wrote that he had spared his fellow immigrants from being the "outrageous prey" of the Germans who had tried to cheat the Swedes out of their money. After two years in Chicago, Carlsson wrote: "Some had prospered but others remained poor. The group of Swedish Lutherans who suffered the most were those who had owned a farm or a home in Sweden. Now they have nothing. They are ashamed that they left but their embarrassment keeps them silent. Now they are only day laborers."[47]

Such was the perspective of those early Augustana Lutherans in America. Not all was despair. In "Utdrag af ett bref från Amerika," Carlsson could also tell of the accomplishment that his own congregation in Chicago numbered 200 and in a few short years, some of the churches would boast remarkable progress in a very fertile part of the world's area.[48]

But that was in the future. Now was the threatening frontier large and quite empty and they were but a few people. They needed aid but to whom should they turn? Could help have been solicited from Lutherans of non-Swedish background in America? The opportunity for that approach was not lacking. On August 7, 1849, Dr. William R. Reynolds wrote a letter which was published in the December issue of the *Lunds Missions-Tidning* 1849. This American Lutheran professor at the Lutheran Theological Seminary in Gettysburg, Pennsylvania, urged that missionary work should be done among the Scandinavian immigrants as well as among the Germans. Reynolds could speak Danish, Norwegian, Swedish and German and he promised that the Lutherans through the Lutheran Missionary Society would be willing to help support work among the Scandinavians. But, Reynold said, the Scandinavian Lutherans needed more than that: *Swedish pastors should be sent.*[49]

Other American Lutherans showed concern for the Swedish immigrants. Peter Fjellstedt's brother-in-law, Pastor G. Schweitzerbarth of Zelienople, Pennsylvania, wrote to Fjellstedt in 1850:

> We must now have a Scandinavian professorship at the university in Columbus [Capital University]. We believe not only the officials of Sweden and Norway would approve of this but both the church's people and pastors in this country would support it. . . . Ten years

[47]"Utfrag af ett bref . . . , *Lunds Missions-Tidning*, 7 (April 1854), 52.

[48]For example, by contrast to the sacrifice undertaken in the completion of their first small chapel, thirteen years later the Andover congregation completed a magnificent building in 1867 at a cost of $40,000. It was debt free at its dedication. The building with a seating capacity of well over 600 people still stands.

[49]2:187-88. Ironically, as Reynolds wrote this letter, Esbjörn was on his way to Sweden to ask the Swedish Church to send pastors to America.

from now, people from Sweden and Norway will have streamed in by
the thousands. Now is the time to be concerned about their spiritual
needs and educate and prepare a pious and zealous ministry to meet
them on their arrival in the new land and talk to them of the heavenly
truth. . . . It is good that our immigrants should be associated with the
Church.[50]

The early leaders did not neglect the possibility of asking for and
receiving help from fellow American Lutherans. Esbjörn related to Fjellstedt
that he had travelled from April 29 to July 7, 1851, a total of 3500 miles
through the states of Illinois, Ohio, Pennsylvania, New York and into
Boston, Massachusetts. Wherever he went, he asked for help from fellow
Lutherans. His venture was quite successful. He received a total of about
"8000 *riksdaler*" ($2000 in American money).[51]

But Esbjörn's efforts were not without their dark side. The combination
of disillusion with the principle of separation of Church and State,
competing religious groups, economic disappointment for many and an
alien feeling toward fellow Lutherans whom they met in America caused
uneasiness in Esbjörn. To whom then should the Swedish Lutherans in
America turn?

It was to those with whom they felt most at home not only spiritually but
ethnically. It is true that tension had existed between the Augustana leaders
and the Church in Sweden. Still, they felt much closer to that communion
with its liturgy and adherence to the Lutheran confessions than they did to
any Lutheran group in America.

So, to the Church in Sweden they turned. However, the response on the
whole was disappointing. No doubt Swedish pastors found the rigorous
demands of frontier living uninviting in comparison with the relatively
comfortable and secure life they enjoyed in their homeland. They attempted
to use more impressive arguments: the spiritual need for pastors was as
great, if not greater, in Sweden as in America; the Swedes in America
already owned the Bible and the knowledge of God's Word and had the
opportunity for spiritual care; as emigrants, they had of their own free will
abandoned their homeland; and, the same degree of responsiblity could not
be felt for the emigrants as for those who remained at home. Furthermore,
economic help was needed in the Swedish Church more than in America.[52]
The Church in Sweden, and its pastors, at least as far as pastoral response
to emigrant need was concerned, supported their rationalizations with
actions. In the first half century of its existence, the Augustana Church
received only seven pastors who had been ordained in Sweden and six of
these came between the years 1849 and 1856 before the Church had been
organized. Of these first six, two returned to Sweden to occupy pulpits in
the Lutheran Church in Sweden: L. P. Esbjörn and O. C. T. Andrén. When

---

[50]"Prestbilding i Amerika för invandrade Swenskar" ["Education of Pastors for the
Swedish Immigrants"], *Bibelvännen*, 3 (September 1850), 144.

[51]Of this sum, $1500 was contributed by a fellow Swede, the "Swedish Nightingale,"
Jenny Lind, who was on concert tour in Boston when Esbjörn contacted her.

[52]Runeby, p. 336.

the Augustana Church was organized in 1860, it could claim 4124 members but in the United States there were then 18,625 Swedish immigrants—more than four times as many as the Church had been able to gather into its communion.[53] It is easy to understand why Esbjörn in 1853 made his plea in which he also addressed at least one of the rationalizations used by the pastors in Sweden—that pastors were needed more in Sweden than in America:

> Come over and help us at least for a few years. Do not say that pastors are needed at home [Sweden]. Here the need is greater than there. Just now, the Lutheran Zion must help in this country; otherwise the work here will be undermined for all time. Then at home you will as a consequence experience anxiety and suffering. The host of fanatic one-sided party makers, after they have established themselves here among the Scandinavians will cast themselves over the homeland and uproot truth, pure teaching and work, and deep, living Christianity. Believe me, I have seen how they do. It is fantastic how they make for themselves friends and acquaintances with upright Christians and join with them to complain about the fallen Church and dead Christianity. Then when they have gained the confidence [of these Christians), *they* turn with all their might against the Lutheran teaching. They actually aim to tear down this as a rock of offense. . . . After a few years when we have been able to educate and ordain pious young men here in our country, we shall be more able to do without pastoral assistance from home.[54]

To whom was this letter written? To Peter Fjellstedt. It was to such individuals that the Augustana Lutheran Church looked and from them received significant help.

> With the exception of men like Wieselgren and Fjellstedt, the parish pastors took little or no interest in the immigrants, whom they regarded as black sheep, wanton deserters from their native land, deserving of whatever fate might be in store for them. Moreover, with many pastorates vacant at home, it was not reasonable to expect the authorities to bestir themselves and deplete the man power of the Church even further by sending missionaries to America among countrymen who were looked upon as destined to lose their religious identity in the great crucible of the American population.[55]

There were others in Sweden who shared Wieselgren's and Fjellstedt's concerns. One was C. O. Rosenius who greatly influenced the Swedish immigrants through his paper, *Pietisten*. Still, none interested himself more in the religious needs and welfare of his countrymen in the new land than Peter Fjellstedt.

Before treating specifically the character of Fjellstedt's involvement in the ministry to Swedish emigrants to America, the question arises: did the increasingly negative attitude of the pioneer leaders among the Swedish

---

[53]Söderström, p. 94.

[54]"Brev från en Svensk . . . ," *Bibelvännen*, 7 (September, 1852), pp. 134-35.

[55]Stephenson, pp. 147-48.

immigrants toward separation of Church and State effect a similar view in Fjellstedt and dampen his enthusiasm for the Free Church of Scotland? Apparently not. The unfavorable views from the leaders in America were made known between August 1850 and April 1854. It was later in 1855 that Fjellstedt, fully aware of the views of such a Esbjörn and Carlsson, made his surprising statement that if Swedish Church leaders lacked concern for the kingdom of God, then believers should build a free Lutheran Church on the pattern of Scottish Free Church. His more conservative view on the issue of a free church developed later. To that change, the Swedish American Lutherans seemed to contribute little. The fears Fjellstedt expressed about the spiritual welfare of his fellow Swedes in America were not due to the issue of a free church but to the frontier conditions which severely limited the availability of ministry for Christian nurture and the unwillingness of the Church in Sweden to meet their needs.

3. The Nature of Peter Fjellstedt's Concern and Relationship to the Augustana Lutheran Church

Against the background of Fjellstedt's life, religious experience, theology and ministry it is not difficult to understand why he was concerned about the Swedish Lutheran immigrants in America. Like them, Fjellstedt was critical of the Lutheran Church in Sweden, yet opposed, as they were, to separation from the Lutheran Church—an important factor in the formulation of Augustana. Also, all were alike in that, for awhile, they had been attracted to the Free Church of Scotland.

Important as these factors were, one stood out above all others—Fjellstedt's missionary concern. Here was the unique motivation for his interest in Augustana. America was another foreign land to which those with missionary zeal looked as a place of service. Organizations in Sweden sent money for missionary purposes. One of the projects promoted by Fjellstedt was for the Lund Missionary Society to include among its beneficiaries the Augustana Lutheran Church in America.

In addition to the missionary concern, the Swedish Lutherans in America were of concern to Fjellstedt on an ethnic basis. Consequently, he felt a difference between the Augustana Lutheran Church and that of any other foreign mission field. In a letter to Hasselquist, he communicated the information that the directors of the *Gustaf-Adolf Stiftelsen* at its November 11 meeting had decided to send "three hundred *riksdaler* . . . to the Augustana Synod in Paxton, Illinois, to be used for one or more of the neediest Swedish Lutheran congregations in North America." Fjellstedt further commented: "We want to try to awaken increased interest for our brethren in the new homeland.[56]

It is interesting that America appeared to Fjellstedt as a "new homeland" for his fellow Swedes. Also of significance is the organization which sent the gift. The name indicates that nationalistic concern was important to the *Gustaf-Adolf Stiftelsen*. Undoubtedly the members of the Society viewed the Church in America in terms of their own folk-church model in Sweden.

---

[56]November 20, 1871, Westin, p. 317.

As such, the Church belongs to all the people and unless persons indicate otherwise, they belong to that Church by virture of their birth. In an important sense, the Church and State together assume responsibility for the spiritual welfare of all citizens. Of course such a view of the Church could not be fulfilled in America. And certainly, Sweden had no authority over its emigrants to America. Yet something similar to this folk-church concern was demonstrated in Fjellstedt's attitude toward Augustana. Plainly, the deeper spiritual motivation as a Christian missionary dominated his action, but the folk-church sense of responsibility also seemed to be present. In an impressive manner, Fjellstedt combined the ethnic and the religious dimensions in his relation to the Swedish-American Lutheran immigrants. An example of that combination was expressed in the letter he wrote to Hasselquist from Göteborg (November 20, 1871). He closed with the words: "God's grace and blessing be with your house and with all our Swedish brothers in the new world."[57] The new world seemed to Fjellstedt a place of hope as it was for millions of European emigrants who, by contrast, saw only limited possibilities if not decay and despair in the old world. He also wrote of the high importance he attached to "the New Sweden in the West." He saw that place as the location where the Lord's blessing "would come in a special and extraordinary way" whereas "in the old fatherland, unbelief and ruin spread with extraordinary, yes horrible waste."[58]

4. Fjellstedt's Impact on Individual Leaders

Of the first six Lutheran pastors ordained in Sweden who came to the United States between 1849 and 1856 before the organization of the Augustana Lutheran Church in 1860, Fjellstedt had contact with five: Esbjörn, Hasselquist, Carlsson, Andrén and Cervin. (He apparently had no contact with Eric Norelius who, however, was not ordained in Sweden but in America). A sixth pastor, Olof Olsson, who emigrated to America in 1869 also came under Fjellstedt's influence. The influence Fjellstedt had on these men was both direct and indirect. The indirect aspect was the nineteenth century religious revival by which all of them were strongly influenced. To the strength of that movement, Fjellstedt through his preaching and journalism contributed significantly.

The second kind of impact, the direct, was in each instance understandably different. With some, as with Esbjörn and Carlsson, it was more intense than with others. The more subtle effects of Fjellstedt's influence upon these men cannot be evaluated fully. Moreover, Fjellstedt had made important contributions to the lives of the hundreds of Swedish immigrants with whom these pastors came in contact.

i. Lars Paul Esbjörn

Lars Paul Esbjörn, the first president of Augustana College, came to America in 1849. He was the first Swedish Lutheran pastor to come to the

[57]Westin, p. 318.

[58]Westin, p. 341.

new world in the nineteenth century. His spiritual kinship with Fjellstedt
was evident in the experience the two had on September 22, 1843. Fjellstedt
had come to Esbjörn's parish in Hille at the latter's invitation. He heard
Esbjörn preach in a school and conduct a service typical of the conventicle
style found in Sweden around the city of Gävle. Fjellstedt gave a talk on
missions. He was highly complimentary of the zeal and enthusiasm of the
congregation and attributed much of this to the relation Pastor Esbjörn had
with his parish. Their mutual interest in missions drew the two men
together.

On the occasion of his visit to Esbjörn's parish, Fjellstedt referred to
Esbjörn as "a friend from Uppsala." It is tempting to assume the friendship
had been of long standing. Two facts, however, contradict such an
assumption. First, at that time Fjellstedt had been to Uppsala only once and
that just a few days earlier. He had spent from September 10 to 16 in
Uppsala where he had preached and given lectures for the cause of missions.

Secondly, an acquaintanceship of long duration between Esbjörn and
Fjellstedt is unlikely because it was on this first visit to Uppsala that Fjellstedt promised "some friends from the Uppsala meeting" to come to
Esbjörn's parish. Almost certainly Esbjörn had been among those "friends
from the Uppsala meeting." It is likely, therefore, that it was from that date
that their friendship had developed.[59]

That contact with Fjellstedt was not the beginning of Esbjörn's interest in
missions. As early as 1840, his congregation under his leadership had been
informed about the work of the Swedish Missionary Society. Esbjörn had
begun at that time to hold prayer services on behalf of missions on the first
Monday evening of each month. Annually on Janaury sixth, he held special
services in support of missions. In 1843 the Hille *Biträdes Missionssällskap*
(Supporting Missionary Society) was organized.

The second contact between the two men was less direct and, from
Esbjörn's point of view, less congenial. The Hille parish pastor's discontent
was not, however, so much against Fjellstedt as against the Lund Institute of
which Fjellstedt was the director. Esbjörn was a strong supporter of the
Swedish Missionary Society. As a pietist, he was drawn to its
interconfessional position. From the beginning of its establishment in his
congregation, the Hille missionary society had sent the money it gathered to
the Swedish Society. In 1847, a bitter conflict arose between Esbjörn and
Jonas Gavell, co-minister at Hille. Gavell proposed that the money gathered
that year by the Hille Society be divided between Lund and the work of the
Swedish Missionary Society in Lapland. Esbjorn bitterly opposed that
suggestion. He employed several arguments. Academically, he saw no
reason why candidates for missionary service needed education beyond
what the schools in Sweden gave apart from the theological institutions.
And, if education in theology were required, institutes such as those at Basel
were available.

Theologically, Esbjörn was opposed to Lund with its high church
orientation. "I and the other religious people cannot find it within us to send

---

[59]Anshelm, 2:58-61 *passim*.

contributions to Lund where there is so little that is spiritual as shown in the instruction at the Mission Institute." In opposition to the constitutional requirement of the Lund Society that the students of the Institute be enrolled with the Lund Theological Faculties, Esbjörn wrote:

> It appears that the intention of the Lund Missionary Council and the unspiritual works of the pastors is to paralyze the cause of missions and make of them a dead form and to that end have begun to undermine the Swedish Missionary Society because the latter Society was considered to be too much under the influence of the läsare, Methodists, Herrnhuters and other manifestations of vitality.[60]

Finally, his practical reason for opposition was his belief that the Lund Institute would invite insufficient financial support for its survival. Moreover, he feared contributions to Lund would weaken the work of the Swedish Missionary Society.

In the controversy, however, Esbjörn did not fault Fjellstedt. "It appears to me that Fjellstedt is bound there in Lund so that he cannot give to the enterprise its true Christian spirit and direction." In that thought, Esbjörn was not entirely in error. Although Fjellstedt was much in support of a thorough education, he too, at that time, was scarcely friendly to the strict confessional position of some of the directors of the Lund Society. But unlike Esbjörn, Fjellstedt desired that a good relationship should exist between the two societies so that "the older society and the newer could extend to each other brotherly hands."[61]

How great a factor Esbjörn's disagreement over policy with the educational requirements of the Lund Missionary Society was as a reason for his emigration is open to question. One historian wrote: "To what extent this controversy influenced Esbjörn to emigrate is difficult to say, but it undoubtedly made his position in Sweden quite uncomfortable."[62] That situation in itself would scarcely have moved him to leave Sweden; other reasons were stronger. As to his position, he was already uncomfortable. His activity with George Scott and Peter Wieselgren identified him with pietism and the temperance movement both of which placed him in disfavor with the church authorities and blocked his chances for promotion. His theological education may also have placed him at a disadvantage since an examination of "the documents relating to Esbjörn's education at Uppsala . . . revealed that [his] theological training

[60]Sundkler, p. 195 and fn. 9.

[61]Sundkler, p. 187. In the constitution of the Society, there was no doubt about the theological stance of the Society and its Institute. In the initial issue of the *Lunds Missions-Tidning* in its feature article, the constitution for the Institute was printed. The fourteenth article declared: "Missionaries shall be faithful to the pure evangelical doctrine according to the unaltered Augsburg Confession; at the same time, the missionary should avoid strife in matters of faith. He shall in the congregations [he organizes] as much as possible establish and administer the order of the Swedish Church." (July 1846), n.p.

[62]Oscar N. Olson, *The Augustana Lutheran Church in America: Pioneer Period 1846 to 1860* (Rock Island, Ill.: Augustana Book Concern, 1950), p. 115.

was designed to meet the minimum requirements for ordination of that day. His highest achievements were in the scientific rather than the theological fields."[63] His own belief that he could exercise a freer ministry, together with letters from friends in America urging him to become their spiritual leader, strengthened his resolve to leave his fatherland in the summer of 1849.[64]

It did not take too many years of residence in America for Esbjörn to change his mind. The conflict both with Americanized Lutherans and non-Lutherans and the formless, traditionless frontier situation in America caused him to look upon the Institute at Lund from a different perspective. In the February issue of the *Lunds Missions-Tidning*, 1852, his letter of November 1851 was published:

> I have since I have come here become more and more convinced of the truth of our pure Lutheran faith and of the necessity to build our Lutheran Church on the true foundation. I thought, for example, when I was at home that the Mission Institute of Lund was little needed, that the institutes at Basel, Barmen, etc. were sufficient. Now I see that the Institute was and is necessary and I hope that it will flourish and send out many pious and properly ordained Lutheran workers who will build not out of wood, hay, or straw but out of gold, silver, and precious stones on the right foundation, Jesus Christ crucified.[65]

After 1852 there appears to have been little direct contact between Esbjörn and Fjellstedt. This does not mean that conflict had arisen between the two friends. Rather, there had appeared on the American scene another Swedish ordained pastor, Tuve Nilsson Hasselquist. To him the leadership of the Augustana Church passed more and more after his arrival in America in 1852. Esbjörn and Hasselquist were not entirely compatible in personality. Differences between the two have been observed. Stephenson wrote: "The free religious atmosphere of America worked like an elixir on Hasselquist; he became more free, whereas Esbjorn was sharply critical and adapted himself to American conditions more from necessity than from choice."[66] Ander wrote:

> There was a great deal of tension between Hasselquist and Esbjörn. Perhaps this was unavoidable. Their personal characteristics were so different that misunderstandings easily arose. They both labored for the same cause; both were earnest in their desire to gather the Swedish people into an American Lutheran Church; both had left a comfortable home in Sweden for the laborious and uncomfortable pioneer life in America. Hasselquist had the qualities of a leader, and in his

[63]Arden, p. 27, fn. 12.

[64]Stephenson, pp. 150-51.

[65]"Brev från en Svensk prest i Nord-America till en vän i Sverige" ["A Letter from a Swedish Pastor in North America to a Friend in Sweden"], p. 28. Perhaps Esbjörn felt the Institute could become an important source of supply for pastors to the United States which in fact it did in its successor institution, the Fjellstedt School.

[66]P. 169.

enthusiasm he took orders from no one. His domineering nature often offended his colleagues, and Esbjörn, especially, who was Hasselquists's senior, believed that he understood the needs in their work as well, if not better than Hasselquist. He was, therefore, often offended when he was not consulted in regard to plans or actions. Some of these differences may have been due to the diverse influences under which they had labored in Sweden. Hasselquist believed in a separation of State and Church, a toleration toward other denominations and in the preaching of law rather than of grace. Such views were considered radical by Esbjörn, who stated definitely that he did not believe in the separation of State and Church.[67]

Ander may have drawn the picture of Hasselquist a little too unconditionally, e.g., his acceptance of separation of Church and State and his toleration of other denominations, both of which were qualified. Still, the contrast drawn by Stephenson and Ander seems on the whole to be accurate. From Hasselquist—who became the first president of the Church beginning in 1860 and held that office until 1870—went the appeals to Fjellstedt.

In summary, two observations may be made of Fjellstedt's impact upon Esbjörn and, in the second instance, perhaps through Esbjörn upon the Augustana Lutheran Church. First, there was confidence shown in Fjellstedt by Esbjörn as well as by the other Augustana leaders in the way they shared their experiences with the Swedish churchman. More than once, Esbjörn sent letters to Fjellstedt who in turn published them in his papers.[68] Thus Fjellstedt kept the needs of the Swedish emigrants before the eyes of his countrymen through his widely read publications.

Secondly, there is reason to believe that Fjellstedt through Esbjörn stimulated in the Augustana Church an early interest in missions outside the United States. In his book, *Foundation for Tomorrow*, the late S. Hjalmar Swanson, who was the first full-time Executive Director of Foreign Missions (1939-1955), stated: "During 1856 *Rätta Hemlandet* [the publication edited by Hasselquist] devoted ten percent of its space to foreign missions, and beginning in 1857, twenty-five percent of the space in the paper was henceforth given to various aspects of foreign missions."[69]

By 1863, the name of *Rätta Hemlandet* (*The True Homeland*) had been changed to *Det Rätta Hemlandet och Missionsbladet* (*The True Homeland and the Mission Paper*). Interest in missions was strong enough to encourage the publication of a separate journal, *Missionaren* (*The Missionary*) between 1870 and 1873 and again between 1875 and 1877. In 1879 that publication was merged with *Augustana*.[70] Even after that change, considerable space was devoted to the cause of missions.

[67]P. 44.

[68]E.g., *Lunds Missions-Tidning*, 3 (January 1848) and 7 (February 1952); *Bibelvännen*, 5 (September 1852).

[69]S. Hjalmar Swanson, *Foundation for Tomorrow* (Rock Island, Ill.: Augustana Book Concern, 1960), p. 7.

[70]*Augustana* was begun as a monthly paper in October 1868, also edited by Hasselquist; in 1879, *Rätta Hemlandet* was combined with *Augustana* and named *Rätta*

When the Augustana Church was organized in 1860, it set forth a four-fold purpose: to educate and ordain pastors, to maintain Lutheran orthodoxy, to give guidance to conferences and local congregations, and *to sponsor missionary efforts in America and foreign lands.*[71] At its second convention as a Church, in 1861 at Galesburg, Illinois, it was decided that a synodical foreign mission board should be created.[72]

One year later, in 1862, an appeal was sent out in the March issue of *Hemlandet.* A majority of the congregations conducted missionary services. A report carried the following information:

> Receipts for the year total $223.61 of which $201.61 has come from Swedish and $22.00 from Norwegian congregations. In accordance with the stipulation of the Synod and the donors, $100 has been sent to the Swedish Missionary Society in Stockholm to be used for the mission in India, $100 to the Hermansberg Mission, [sponsored by Pastor Claus Harms of Hermansburg, Germany. It occupied a field in Natal, India]. Also $3.25 has been expended for postage. The balance in the treasury totals $20.36. . . . The Committee recommends that a sermon on foreign missions be delivered at every synodical convention. May the Lord awaken a time of missionary spirit in order that we and our congregations will be quickened unto a burning love and zeal for the advancement of God's Kingdom.[73]

Two years later in 1864 a letter was sent by Erland Carlsson and Carl Strömsberg entitled: "Ett brev från de Svenska forsamlingarna i Amerika till *Gustaf-Adolphs Stiftelsen* in Göteborg." Among the achievements cited was that a total of $24,097.21 had been raised for purposes outside the local needs of sixty-four congregations. Of that amount, $476.26 had been sent "to heathen missions." The chief recipient of those offerings was the Swedish Missionary Society until 1867. That Society was charged to send the Augustana funds to the mission in India. After that date, for several years, the monies were sent directly to the Indian field.[74]

Money was also to be used for other causes. And. Hökerberg, secretary of *Evangeliska Fosterlandsstiftelsen,* on April 2, 1869, sent a letter from Stockholm to Hasselquist in Paxton, Illinois, thanking him for two gifts: one of thirty *riksdaler* to be used in African missions and another gift of forty-five *riksdaler* which had been sent by Erland Carlsson to Lund (almost certainly Lund Missionary Society). In response, Hökerberg wrote: "That

Hemlandet och Augustana. After 1889, the official Church paper simply carried the name *Augustana.*

[71]James Iverne Dowie, *Prairie Grass Dividing* (Rock Island, Ill.: Augustana Historical Society, 1959), pp. 43-44.

[72]Arden, *Augustana Heritage,* p. 120.

[73]*Protokoll, Augustana Synod, 1862,* p. 10, quoted in Arden, *Augustana Heritage,* p. 121. Between the year of its organization in 1860 until 1870, Norwegian and Swedish congregations constituted the Augustana Church. In 1870, for practical purposes and in a peaceful manner the Norwegians separated to form their own church organization.

[74]*Bibelvännen,* 17 (February 1865), pp. 23, 26.

the brothers in America have not forgotten the Society gives us much joy."[75] Three years earlier, in 1866 when *Fosterlandsstiftelsen* initiated its work in East Africa, Augustana transferred its contributions from the Swedish Missionary Society not only directly to the field in India but also directed a portion of its mission monies to the work of *Fosterlandsstiftelsen*. For more than a quarter of a century thereafter, Augustana continued to support its work.[76]

There were those, however, who were not satisfied with this approach to the support of missions in other countries. Many felt Augustana Church should send its own missionaries. This desire was in part—but only in part—fulfilled when as a member of the General Council, the Church cooperated with several Lutheran bodies in the Council's missionary work in India. From the Council, Augustana's first missionaries, Pastor and Mrs. A. B. Carlson, in 1878 went to work among the Telegu people in Rajahmundry, India. "The Telegu Mission had already been in existence for thirty-six years, but Carlson was a pioneer as far as the Augustana Synod was concerned."[77]

Several years were to pass before Augustana sent out missionaries solely on its own. In 1888, it initiated its first overseas enterprise in Iran. Because of difficulties in that country and declining interest at home, that work was discontinued in 1912. A later effort was more successful. In 1901, a local missionary organization, the China Mission Society, was formed by Augustana members in Minneapolis, Minnesota. This zealous group in 1906 sent to the Honan province Pastor and Mrs. A. W. Edwins. In 1908, the Church took over the work of the China Mission Society. Actually, then, the first mission work which Augustana could claim as its own solely (notwithstanding the unsuccessful work in Iran) was its field in China.[78]

To attribute this early concern for missions by Augustana to the influence of Fjellstedt upon Esbjörn may be difficult to prove. After all, this interest was shown throughout the Church and much of this concern was expressed through *Rätta Hemlandet* of which Hasselquist was the editor. Arden was probably correct when he wrote:

> The religious revivals which were sweeping across Scandinavia during this period awakened a wide-spread interest in the world mission of the Church, and in most parishes of Sweden and Norway where the new evangelical movement took root missionary societies were organized which endeavored to inform and inspire the people, as well as gather

[75]Money was sent, however, to be used for other causes than India. Hökerberg, secretary of the *Evangelisk Fosterlandsstiftelsen* on April 2, 1869 sent a letter from Stockholm to Hasselquist in Paxton thanking him for two gifts: one, of thirty *riksdaler* to be used in African missions and another, of forty-five *riksdaler* which had been sent by Erland Carlsson to Lund (almost certainly to the Lund Missionary Society).

[76]Arden, *Augustana Heritage*, p. 121.

[77]S. Hjalmar Swanson, *Three Missionary Pioneers* (Rock Island, Ill.: Augustana Book Concern, 1945), p. 6.

[78]*Ibid.*, pp. 57-72 *passim*.

funds for carrying on the work. Most of the leading churchmen and evangelists in Sweden were strong supporters of foreign missions.

Arden concluded: "It is not surprising, therefore, to find the Scandinavian immigrants in America giving a good deal of attention to foreign missions even before they had organized themselves into an independent synod."[79]

One fact is certain; none contributed more to the rising interest in foreign missions in Sweden than Peter Fjellstedt. And, among the leaders of the Augustana Church upon whom Fjellstedt left his influence, with none was the interest in missions more explicit than with Lars Paul Esbjörn. It is at least safe to suggest that although interest in missions in foreign lands was general among both clergy and lay people, a special impact came from Fjellstedt through Esbjörn. O. N. Olson wrote of Fjellstedt: "It is largely due to his influence that interest in missions had existed in the Augustana Church from its very beginning."[80]

ii. Tuve Nilsson Hasselquist

Any direct contact between Fjellstedt and Hasselquist while the latter was still in Sweden has not yet been uncovered. Still, the deep confidence and affection which each showed to the other in their correspondence after Hasselquist came to the United States lead one to believe that there had been a relationship between the two before Hasselquist emigrated. That Hasselquist did not know of Fjellstedt is impossible to believe. From 1848 with the launching of Fjellstedt's *Lunds Missions-Tidning* and *Bibelvännen* until 1852 when Hasselquist left Sweden, the latter certainly must have read those publications. That Fjellstedt wrote to Hasselquist about going to America also indicates that the two must have known each other personally.

Certainly, Peter Fjellstedt was one of the influences that brought Hasselquist to America. He had been recommended to Esbjörn by the pious family of Ola Nelson. Esbjörn wrote to Fjellstedt asking him to contact Hasselquist. Evidently, Fjellstedt sent the letter to Wieselgren for him to give to Hasselquist. Stephenson wrote: "On January 24, 1852, Hasselquist wrote to Wieselgren in reply to an important letter he had received from him through Fjellstedt."[81] When Hasselquist replied to Esbjorn's letter, he wrote: "That was an important letter I received from you through Brother Fjellstedt two days ago."[82]

On July 24, 1852, Fjellstedt wrote to Hasselquist. Almost certainly this letter was in response to an earlier one from Hasselquist in which he had asked Fjellstedt for advice as to which would be the best point from which emigrants might leave for America. Fjellstedt replied that it was advisable to leave from Hamburg. For those who did not have sufficient money to go the whole way from Hamburg to New York by steamship, there were sailing

---

[79]Arden, *American Heritage*, p. 119.

[80]O. N. Olson, *The Augustana Lutheran Church* . . . , p. 25.

[81]P. 167.

[82]Westin, p. 48.

vessels which left Hamburg the first and fifteenth of each month. Fjellstedt included other information such as requirements for foods, costs and sources for further information. He closed his letter: "Hearty greetings to your good little wife."[83] In that statement is another clue to the early relationship which seems to have existed between Fjellstedt and Hasselquist before the latter's departure from Sweden.

At the age of eight, Eva Helena Cervin, the future Mrs. Hasselquist, was bereaved by the loss of her merchant father. The family lived in Kristianstad [Skåne] Sweden apparently in financially comfortable circumstances. The eldest of four children, she was nurtured by a remarkable mother, Lorentia Åkerman Cervin, who even that early in nineteenth century Sweden had developed a deep interest in missions. Mrs. Cervin could understand and use the German language. This facility enabled her to communicate easily with the Basel Mission Society. To its Institute she sent financial contributions. In her home she held monthly prayer meetings assisted by Christian teachers.

Upon Peter Fjellstedt's return to Sweden, the future Mrs. Hasselquist's mother became a warm friend of his and of his work for foreign missions. "When Dr. Fjellstedt travelled through Kristianstad, he was always a welcome guest in her house and could with joy rest in that serene and blessed home." The young Eva was not left unaffected by this contact. In the early forties, she experienced a religious crisis. She became concerned about her salvation.

> That feeling was deepened, through her acquaintanceship with Dr. Fjellstedt who during that time, in 1843, made a visit to Sweden as representative of the Basel Mission Institute. Several years later, the Augustana Lutheran periodical [*Augustana*] published notes she had taken on Dr. Fjellstedt's discourse thus demonstrating that she had taken account of what she had heard.[84]

With the strong influence of Fjellstedt on Hasselquist's wife, one can be certain that her husband too knew Fjellstedt.

Tuve Nilsson Hasselquist, destined to become the foremost leader of the Augustana Lutheran Church in its formative years, landed in New York, September 28, 1852. Already in January 1853, he addressed a letter to Fjellstedt in which he appealed to the latter to "send a pastor by the name of Dahlstedt or some other suitable man."[85] Thus, early in his life in America Hasselquist tended to depend upon Fjellstedt as a chief agent through whom pastoral help could be obtained for the struggling Swedish Lutheran Church in America. The unqualified confidence Hasselquist had in Fjellstedt is shown by the fact that he had no hesitation to authorize Fjellstedt to select another person should Dahlstedt decline the offer. This occurred,

---

[83]*Ibid.*, p. 59.

[84]P. A. Cedarstam, "Lefnadsteckning af Fru Eva Helena Hasselquist" ["Biography of Mrs. Eva Helena Hasselquist"], *Korsbaneret*, 1895, p. 81.

[85]Eric Norelius, *T. N. Hasselquist: Lefnadsteckning* [*Biography*] (Rock Island, Ill.: Lutheran Augustana Book Concern, 1900), p. 40.

whereupon the name of Erland Carlsson was inserted. In that choice by Fjellstedt, the Augustana Lutheran Church received one of its most capable and respected leaders. Thereafter, Fjellstedt was the recognized medium through whom calls were extended.

Hasselquist expressed his confidence in another way. A short time later, it was decided that a professorship for Scandinavian students should be established at the State University of Illinois [Springfield]. At the united meeting of the Chicago and Mississippi Conferences [the Scandinavian contingent of the Synod of Northern Illinois] at Rockford, Illinois, September 23-29, 1857, Esbjorn was nominated as the candidate for the professorship. This was confirmed by the Synod.[86]

Hasselquist was not happy with that action. His choice for that position had been Peter Fjellstedt. He had written to Fjellstedt prior to the conference and synodical action. Fjellstedt was sufficiently interested to address a letter to Hasselquist on the matter. He wrote on June 9, 1857: "In response to your question whether I would come if I received the call you mention, it is impossible to give an answer." He then requested Hasselquist to write to him about "Springfield, its situation, its character, and, more important its people, its views of the Church and the middle class, climate, air, water, and living costs."[87] He assured Hasselquist that the salary of $500 would be sufficient and that he would do all in his power to raise that amount himself. Yet, he concluded that if he received the call, he must wait upon the Lord's will to decide. Of course, he did not have the opportunity to reply negatively or positively but Stephenson mused:

> One cannot resist the temptation to speculate upon what might have been the destiny of the Augustana Synod if a man of the broad vision and attainments of Fjellstedt had put its educational activity under way and had projected his compelling personality into Swedish-American Lutheranism.[88]

Not all the letters were of a private nature. Both men were journalists. They used their judgment as to which items of their correspondence should be printed for the public to read. When they felt that the interests of the Church in the new land could be promoted, such action was taken.

Hasselquist's confidence in the printed word to shape the thoughts of the Swedish Lutheran immigrants both to equip them in the struggle against non-Lutherans and to enlighten them in Lutheran teachings led him to his journalistic endeavors. In his frontier surroundings, the necessity to purchase his own printing equipment was imposed upon him. He purchased the necessary machinery in New York. When the equipment arrived in Galesburg, Illinois, one of the first items to come off the press in the summer of 1855 "was a reprint of Fjellstedt's version of *Luther's Small Catechism*. This book was used by the earliest Swedish pastors and congregations to

---

[86]*Ibid.*, p. 64. Although the school had this prestigious name, the institution was not related to the state of Illinois.

[87]Westin, p. 91.

[88]P. 37.

instruct the young in the fundamentals of the faith."[89] In this publication, as in many other ways, Fjellstedt through Hasselquist's work exercised a significant influence on Augustana.

iii. Erland Carlsson

Oscar F. Ander wrote of Hasselquist: "His first appeal to Dr. P. Fjellstedt resulted in the arrival of the able Rev. Erland Carlsson in 1853."[90] This was one of the few successful appeals made by Hasselquist to Sweden for ordained pastors to come to America. This request was not only successful; it was momentous for the history of the Swedish Lutherans in America.

Erland Carlsson was born in Älghult, Småland, Sweden in 1822. Following his ordination in Växjö Cathedral June 19, 1849, upon completion of his studies at Lund, he served as the pastor of the Lessebo parish about thirty miles southeast of Växjö. He served that parish until 1853 when because of his Bible studies and strong temperance stands, he came into difficulty with his bishop. The latter regarded the Bible studies as possible violations of the Conventicle Act. Furthermore, some of his fellow pastors along with the bishop didn't like "this temperance business."[91]

Beginning in January 1853, he served as co-pastor at Härlöv and Öjaby about one-half Swedish mile from Växjö. There he stayed only about six months. On August 13 of that year, he landed as a Swedish immigrant in New York and arrived in Chicago nine days later. There he began twenty-two years of faithful and valuable service at the newly organized Immanuel Lutheran Church. Thousands of immigrants came to Chicago those years either to stay or to go further west to promising agricultural land. Carlsson gave counsel and valuable help to hundreds of these people and because of his awareness of the difficulties Swedish immigrants would face, he wrote a helpful immigrant guide.

Following his ministry in Chicago, he became pastor of the large congregation in Andover, Illinois, where he served from 1875 to 1887. He was also president of the Augustana Church from 1881 to 1888. He served with distinction as president of the Board of Directors of Augustana College during three different periods (1860-70, 1878-82, and 1884-87) as well as treasurer of the institution from 1860 to 1868 and again from 1887 to 1889.

Hasselquist had initiated the action which gave Carlsson the opportunity to come to America. In January 1853, Hasselquist had organized the Immanuel congregation in Chicago and had followed that action, as indicated previously, by writing to Peter Fjellstedt to obtain the services of a pastor.

Fjellstedt was aware of the grave responsibility he owed to the infant Swedish Lutheran Church body in America. After holding the letter of call for some days, he one morning knelt in his home at Lund seeking divine

---

[89]Arden, *Augustana Heritage*, p. 202.

[90]P. 212.

[91]Emory Lindquist, *Shepherd of an Immigrant People: The Story of Erland Carlsson* (Rock Island, Ill.: Augustana Historical Society, 1978), p. 19.

guidance as to whose name he should insert in the call to Immanuel Church in Chicago. While thus engaged, he heard a knock on the door. It was that of a student who handed him a letter as he said: "I do not have time to come in but I wish to leave a letter from Pastor Erl. Carlsson." Fjellstedt took that happening to be an answer to his prayer and inserted the name of Carlsson. He sent the call to the young Swedish pastor along with a letter urging him to accept the call to Chicago.[92]

When Carlsson was a student in Lund, he had lived for awhile in the Fjellstedt home. Historical research at this time has uncovered no record of his impressions from those days. Nevertheless, it is interesting to speculate on the importance of that period in the formation of the character and thought of the young theologue.

One clue may be Emory Lindquist's statement about the moment Carlsson received the call via Fjellstedt and the letter from him: "There is no evidence to indicate that Erland had considered emigration to America."[93] To Fjellstedt and others, America was a mission field. Certainly Fjellstedt's interest in missions would have been obvious and impressive to Carlsson. Coupled with his admiration for Fjellstedt, his close contact with the missionary-minded enthusiast must have influenced the young Carlsson to emigrate.

Fjellstedt aided Carlsson's release from the Church in Sweden with wise counsel. Lindquist described Fjellstedt's helpful advice to his friend about the procedure for gaining permission to emigrate. ". . . .he should write to *Högvälborne Herr Friherr* (his lordship, Baron) Joh. A. Posse of the *Kungliga Riksarkivet* (amanuensis at the Royal Archives) Stockholm"[94] The letter from Fjellstedt to Carlsson in which that advice was given also included the revealing sentence: "He [Posse] is a Christian friend and you do not need to be afraid that he will misinterpret [your request]." Perhaps Carlsson had heard of Esbjörn's somewhat unpleasant experience and may have had reason to feel some anxiety about the response to his request. Fjellstedt promised that he would write also. Posse responded with an encouraging and kind letter in which he counselled Carlsson to contact *Fil dr.* Melander in Växjö to speed up the process.[95] Posse would also "personally talk with Ecclesiastical Minister Reuterdahl in his behalf."[96]

Of Carlsson's affection for his older friend, there can be no doubt. Although the two did not seem to have corresponded frequently after Carlsson's emigration to America—Carlsson wrote rather to Peter

---

[92]Eric Norelius, *De Svenska Lutherska församlingarnas och Svenskarnas historia i Amerika* (Rock Island, Ill.: Augustana Book Concern, 1890), 1:418: Lindquist, . . . , *The Story of Erland Carlsson*, p. 19. An intriguing fact is that nowhere does there seem to be any knowledge about the contents of the letter from Pastor Carlsson that was delivered to Fjellstedt that morning.

[93]Lindquist, . . . , *The Story of Erland Carlsson*, p. 19.

[94]*Ibid.*, p. 20.

[95]Westin, p. 65.

[96]Lindquist, . . . , *The Story of Erland Carlsson*, p. 20.

Wieselgren—he did not fail to include greetings to Fjellstedt. On one occasion he wrote: "A thousand loving greetings . . . to dear Brother Fjellstedt . . . and "Humble and hearty greetings . . . to Dr. Fjellstedt."[97] In one of his letters, he wrote more fully of the dependence Augustana had on their friends in Sweden. "Although we rejoice over our friends here, we can do no other than thank God so long as he allows us some of our old, faithful friends among whom we especially count beloved Farbror [Wieselgren] and Dr. Fjellstedt who yet stay with us on the field of strife and fight with us the Lord's battle."[98]

In one important area, that of the many immigrants who came to and through Chicago, there was reason to be thankful for the influence of Peter Fjellstedt who had been a major factor in bringing Erland Carlsson to Chicago. In the year 1868 during the famine in Sweden, according to the Chicago pastor, "over 30,000 Swedes have . . . passed through or settled in Chicago."[99] Carlssons's *Immigrant Guide*, his counsel, and his material and spiritual aid helped many confused Swedes as they came to a strange and new land.

Nor can his contributions to the Augustana Lutheran Church be forgotten. Pastor, president and occupant of important posts of leadership place the descendants of that Church in deep debt to Erland Carlsson—and Peter Fjellstedt.

iv. Olof Christian Telemak Andrén

O. C. T. Andrén was born in Malmö, Sweden, September 21, 1824. He was born O. C. T. Anderson. As many did, he changed his name at ordination (December 9, 1847). After completion of his studies at Lund and ordination following long years of struggle with poverty [He was left an orphan at the age of five.], he served successively for short periods four parishes. One of these, Osby, was the birthplace of T. N. Hasselquist. Andrén, through his friendship with Hasselquist's relatives, established a close relationship with him under whose leadership in America he later served for four years.

Andrén's life demonstrates the influence Fjellstedt exerted on one person. In the 1840's and 1850's Andrén was stirred by the Swedish evangelical revival which was taking place in Skåne. In the early 1850's during a period of illness, he had a spiritual crisis. A series of presentations by Fjellstedt in 1852 and 1853 "made a profound impression on him. His own preaching became more evangelical with a touch of pietistic legalism."[100]

In his unfinished autobiography prepared as a legacy for his children, Andrén gave two glimpses of Fjellstedt's ministry to him. He related that at Christmas in 1852, he heard a presentation on the Bible by Fjellstedt in

[97]Letters from Chicago to Wieselgren in Göteborg, October 10, 1865 and October 31, 1870, Westin, pp. 123, 285.

[98]Letter of October 31, 1870. Westin, p. 285.

[99]Letter to Peter Wieselgren (Göteborg), March 1, 1869, Westin, p. 223.

[100]Oscar N. Olson, *Olof Christian Telemak Andrén: . . .* , p. 10.

Karlshamn, the location of Andrén's last parish before he left for America. He wrote: "Fjellstedt had already during the course of the year given me good advice which gripped me. It was not so much the word which he spoke but the inner power which goes forth from his natural character and later this power turned my heart away from despair." The second glimpse was five months later on May 28 and 29 when Fjellstedt preached on the subject. "Two Glances Into Eternity." He also gave a Bible study on the epistle lesson for the second Sunday after Pentecost. "A joyful and quickening time it was for my dry soul," wrote Andrén.[101]

Fjellstedt's influence upon Andrén and the call which he received in the autumn of 1855 are in all likelihood related. On December 1, 1850, Esbjörn organized the First Lutheran Church in Moline, Illinois. Under spasmodic and uncertain pastoral leadership at the beginning of its history, the congregation appealed to the Mississippi Conference to call a pastor from Sweden. Out of that action, a call was extended which read in part:

> The Reverend Doctor P. Fjellstedt in Sweden is hereby authorized to call as pastor of the above named congregation Pastor O. C. T. Andrén in Carlsham [sic], or if he should not be able to accept the call then to extend the call to Pastor W. E. Berggren in Philipstad [sic], or if he is not available then to call G. G. Bark in Mistelås, or if also he should be unable or unwilling to accept the call to this mission field, then to issue the call to any pastor who you consider possesses piety, fitness, willingness and ability for the position. The congregation is not only satisfied in all respects with your actions, but pleads earnestly that you, Dr. Fjellstedt, would take to heart the spiritual needs of these people and do all in your power to secure any of the above named pastors or some other faithful worker known for his piety, Lutheran orthodoxy and experience, who could come here this fall and take up the pastoral work among the many countrymen who are as sheep having no shepherd.[102]

The call, dated June 6, 1855, was signed by L. P. Esbjörn as president and Paul Anderson as secretary. The confidence in Fjellstedt was clear.

The relation between Andrén's spiritual experience under Fjellstedt's preaching and teaching and Fjellstedt's forwarding of the call and his accompanying letter unfolded. On September 28, 1855, Fjellstedt wrote to Andrén that he was sending the call from America to him. He did not exert pressure on Andrén but did ask him "to consider seriously and lay before the Lord [the call] in prayer and afterwards as soon as possible, let me know

---

[101]"Olof Chr. Telemak Andrén," *Rätta Hemlandet och Augustana* (July 18, 1872), 17:154-55. Taken from *Församlingsvännen* (1871), No. 4.

[102]O. N. Olson, *Olof Christian Telemak Andrén:* . . . , pp. 12-13. Two interesting aspects of this statement are: first, the writer of this letter thought of the Swedish Lutheran Church as a mission field—a view held by Fjellstedt also. Secondly, and somewhat ironically, although Augustana was opposed to bishops, in a practical sense, Fjellstedt acted in that capacity. Pragmatically, of course, both by virtue of their confidence in Fjellstedt and his knowledge of Swedish pastors, this approach was understandable.

your decision. . . . I do not venture to offer any advice in this important matter; I only send you the call as it is my duty to do, and pray the Lord to make known to your heart and mind what you ought to do."[103]

On October 11, 1855, Andren wrote to Fjellstedt and informed him that he would accept the call. He did not express unqualified confidence in his knowledge of God's purpose.

> I have asked the Lord to show me his way that I may walk in his truth. . . . What is his will? Does he want to bring me to the congregation, through and to which he has called me, in order to bless the work which he committed to me, or does he want to take me home, but first try me in the furnace of affliction on the dangerous journey in order that the dross be burned away and the silver cleansed and purified? I do not know.

Nevertheless, having neither prayed for nor sought the call and probably because it came from Fjellstedt, he concluded: "And now I inform you that I have received and will heed the call. I will commit my way unto the Lord and trust in Him; He will bring it to pass. The Lord grant me grace to receive of his fullness, grace for grace."[104]

Although the letter of acceptance was written in October 1855, Andrén did not arrive in Moline until the following June 30. His ministry in America was not long—only four years. During that time, he won the respect of his congregation and colleagues.

At the meeting of the Norwegians and Swedes in June, 1860 at which the Augustana Lutheran Church was formed, it was decided to appeal once again to Sweden for financial aid. A like request had been rejected by the fatherland in 1859. This time money was needed not for the support of a professorship, but for the much more expensive project of a seminary to educate pastors for service among the Scandinavian immigrants. The newly formed Augustana Lutheran Church at its organizational synod decided to send a personal representative to present the Synod's appeal. Because of the confidence and love his brethren in the ministry had for him, Andrén was chosen for the mission.

There was no indication when Andrén went on that commission from Augustana that he intended to stay in Sweden. His plans to return, however, were changed because of poor health. Unlike Esbjörn who grew to dislike America, Andrén expressed a deep love for the Augustana fellowship. On March 10, 1863, he wrote to Hasselquist:

> I have a special love for you out there; I feel more of a stranger here at home than out there, due to the difference in church conditions. When I was in America the Spirit wanted to be there, but the flesh longed to be here, but now the flesh wants to remain here, but the Spirit longs to be out there."[105]

Andrén's use of the term "flesh" apparently had no theological implica-

[103]*Ibid.*, p. 13.

[104]*Ibid.*

[105]*Ibid.*, p. 53.

tions but was a reference to his limited health. Twice his former congregation in Moline sent him calls to return (May 17, 1861 and November 16, 1863). To one of these he responded: "My heart says YES, but the body says NO."[106]

v. Jonas Swensson

Jonas Swensson was born in Snollebo in the county of Jönköping and the Province of Småland, Sweden, August 16, 1828. After completion of his studies at Uppsala University, he was ordained in the cathedral at Växjö on October 8, 1851. Until 1856, he served the parishes of Unnaryd and Jälluntofta.

During his student years in Jönköping, Norelius, in his classic history of the Swedish Lutherans in America noted that Swensson came into contact with the revival which occurred in that region. Swensson "did not appear to have much faith in this movement."[107] He was influenced rather by Anders Nohrborg who placed an emphasis upon personal improvement which precedes conversion. In this sense, Swensson placed less emphasis upon feeling than the revivalists with whom he came in contact.

Swensson struggled during all his life between joy and doubt. Norelius wrote of him: "Such a blending of light and darkness marked his whole spiritual life." And so that struggle occurred one day in May 1855 when he read in the paper, *Väktaren*, that he had been called to a congregation in America. He wrote: "This became for me an occasion for new strife."[108]

On June 24, he received the letter from Fjellstedt in which was included the call. It was dated April 17 and was signed by Esbjörn, Hasselquist and Carlsson. The important role Fjellstedt played as an intermediary for the Augustana Lutheran Church in procuring pastors for its congregations is shown in that this document [the call to Swensson] included the names of several other pastors whom Augustana leaders had designated in the hope they would be willing to come to America.

In August, Swensson met with Fjellstedt who encouraged him to accept the call. Swensson was concerned about the expense involved for which Fjellstedt promised to obtain a loan for the young clergyman. Such action became unnecessary because friends including many of Swensson's own congregational members provided the money. Fjellstedt was among those friends; he gave Swensson fifty *riksdaler* for his travel expenses. Swensson attributed these gifts to the providence of God. "Now I see how the Lord keeps his promises, and how he has provided the means, without my concern; for without seeking a loan I now have over 800 Rd."[109]

In late April 1856 on their way to America, the Swenssons stayed several weeks in Göteborg. There Swensson met a number of church leaders among

---

[106]*Ibid.*

[107]*De Svenska Lutherska . . . historia i Amerika,* 1:191.

[108]*Ibid.,* p. 204.

[109]Evald B. Lawson, *Two Primary Sources For a Study of the Life of Jonas Swensson* (Rock Island, Ill.: Augustana Historical Society, 1957), p. 29.

whom was Fjellstedt with whom "he seemed to have the most in common." In his diary, Swensson wrote of his meeting with Fjellstedt: "We conversed about a number of things: concerning the call I had received, conditions in our fatherland, and especially concerning the recent spiritual movement. We were in perfect agreement. The leave-taking with this beloved man was tender."[110]

Swensson became the pastor of the dual parish of Sugar Grove, Pennsylvania and Jamestown, New York. In 1858, he succeeded Esbjörn as pastor of the Lutheran Church in Andover where he remained until 1873 when he died on December 20 at the age of forty-five. He had been elected to succeed Hasselquist, the first president of the Augustana Lutheran Church, in 1870 and was serving the Church in that capacity at the time of his death.

There is no evidence that Fjellstedt and Swensson kept contact with each other after the latter emigrated to America. This is not surprising. The involvement of both men with heavy responsibilities left little time for friendly correspondence. Still, through Swensson as through the other Augustana leaders, Fjellstedt made a significant contribution to the Church.

Fjellstedt was acquainted also with two later leaders who emigrated to America after the organization of the Augustana Lutheran Church. They were Anders Richard Cervin and Olof Olsson.

vi. Anders Richard Cervin

A. R. Cervin was born in Kristianstad, Skåne April 20, 1823, the younger brother of Eva Helena who became Mrs. Hasselquist. Following his early education under the tutelage of his capable mother and the school in his home city, he began studies at Lund. Ten years later he received the doctor of philosophy degree and subsequently began teaching in elementary education in Helsingborg where he remained for five years. In 1856 he went to America when he was responsible for Fjellstedt's two sons who travelled with him. For fifteen months he stayed in Galesburg with his sister and brother-in-law, Eva and T. N. Hasselquist, and helped the latter in editing the two papers: *Rätta Hemlandet*, a religious oriented publication, and *Gamla och Nya Hemlandet* which was more political in character.

In the fall of 1857, Cervin returned to Sweden to assume a new teaching position at Kristianstad. After three years in this work, he began studying for the ministry at Lund and was ordained there in 1864. Between 1860 and 1864, he also spent some time in study at Uppsala. Following his ordination, he, with his wife, Emma Thulin, emigrated to America to assume the editorship of *Hemlandet* which was published in Chicago. In 1868, he was called to be professor at Augustana College and Seminary in Paxton, Illinois. He also assisted Hasselquist in preaching and editing the monthly paper, *Augustana*. Never of strong health, he suffered increasingly during the last twenty-five years of his life. In that last quarter century, he taught some at Augustana in Rock Island and did some editing but for the greater

---

[110]*Ibid.*

part of the time, especially after 1880, he was largely confined to his home. He died January 5, 1900.

In the material available on Cervin, no mention is made of any influence of Fjellstedt upon him. His emigration to America was through his relationship with his sister and brother-in-law. Yet, in view of the high esteem with which Fjellstedt was held in the home of the widowed Mrs. Cervin and his importance in the life of his sister, it would appear that Fjellstedt also left his mark on Cervin. That Fjellstedt and Cervin were close friends is strongly suggested in that the former placed his two sons in the latter's care on their journey to America.

vii. Olof Olsson

Olof Olsson, the third president of Augustana College (1891-1900), was born in Karlskoga, Värmland March 31, 1841. His early education was in a folk school near Karlskoga and a year of private study with Sven Hedström, a parish clerk and organist. A religious revival during the time of Olsson's youth was accompanied by a growth of interest in the missionary responsibilities of the Church. On one of his many preaching tours, Fjellstedt, during the second half of the 1850's, came into that area as a "mighty rousing mission call."[111] Olsson was moved to give his life for missions. He had a personal interview with Fjellstedt. Since a basic objective of the Mission Institute was to provide opportunity for promising students who lacked funds to be educated for pastoral work at home or in missionary activity, the Institute, then located in Stockholm, was ideal for Olsson.

The seventeen year old Värmland youth entered the Institute in the autumn of 1858. He felt at home immediately in the warmth of the evangelical atmosphere. Both spiritually and academically, he made remarkable progress—so much so that after one year of study, it was decided by Fjellstedt and the administration that Olsson along with four other students should go to the mission school at Leipzig.

That decision turned out to be an error at least for the immediate future. The authorities of the Institute had been correct in assessing the superior quality of Olsson's intellectual and spiritual gifts. What unfortunately was overlooked was the inexperience of the young Olsson. Some years later, a successor (not immediate) to Dr. Olsson at Bethany Church, Lindsborg, Kansas wrote:

> Alas! The rigid orthodoxy and high churchly style at Leipzig, for the time being, squelched Olsson's desire to become a missionary. Of this situation, it is written: 'Too late the administration of the Mission Institute at Stockholm saw its mistake and Dr. Fjellstedt had difficulty in reconciling himself to the circumstances which lost to the cause of missions to the heathen one of the doctor's most promising students.[112]

[111]Johannes A. Nyvall, "Dr. O. Olsson," *Korsbaneret*, 1901, p. 154.

[112]Alfred Bergin, *Lindsborg: En Svensk-Amerikansk Kulturbild Från Mellersta Kansas* [*Lindsborg: A Picture of Swedish American Culture From Central Kansas*] (Rock Island, Ill.: Augustana Book Concerns Tryckeri och Bokbinderi [Printer and Book Bindery], 1909), p. 89.

Olsson returned to the Institute for a brief period and then to his home much discouraged and with a sense of defeat. So intense was the experience that twenty years later when Olsson as professor of theology took a journey to Europe for reasons of his health, he recalled his difficult days as he revisited Leipzig. He wrote:

> Before leaving Leipsic [sic] I desired to see once more the mission house where I had spent a year and where I had to fight such bitter spiritual battles, within and without, that I expected nothing but disaster to body and soul. Those struggles and the studies and cares of that year broke my health and strength for the remainder of my earthly life.[113]

Healing, however, came quickly. He met the young lady, Anna Lisa Jonsson, who later became his wife; she was of great help to him. By the autumn of 1860, he was able to assume studies at Uppsala which culminated in his ordination into the ministry in December 1863. He began his work as pastor in Brunskoga congregation, Karlstadt diocese. There he remained only a short time. After an interim period of service there, he moved to Sunnemo where he remained until the spring of 1869. All of these congregations were in the province of Värmland.

Dissatisfaction with the state church in Sweden and his own zeal born from the religious revival combined to turn Olsson toward America. He had hopes of creating a free church there—hopes which were soon frustrated. In the spring of 1869, with his wife, he emigrated to America. His influence in the last two parishes he served was shown by the large number of persons from those places who accompanied him. "He [Olsson] and a group from Sunnemo, who started first, were followed by another group from Persberg and the surrounding mining region. . . . Eighty families are said to have made up the two groups, the emigrants numbering about two hundred and fifty in all."[114]

He began his work in Lindsborg, Kansas, where he organized the Bethany Lutheran Church. He served there from 1869 until 1876 when, first on a temporary basis and then on a permanent call, he became professor at the Augustana Seminary. He served the Church in that capacity until 1891. Upon the death of its second president in that year, T. N. Hasselquist, Augustana College received as successor Dr. Olsson. He served in that office until his death in 1900. During his thirty year ministry in America, Olsson did considerable work as editor and assistant editor on various papers of the Church.

There is no record that Olsson had close contact with Fjellstedt following the conclusion of his studies. During the sixties, both were very busy in their respective work in Sweden. After Olsson's departure from there in 1869, only a few years remained before Fjellstedt retired. Still, the feeling of friendship continued. Even the Leipzig experience did not chill Olsson's gratitude for what Fjellstedt had made possible for him. On his visit to Leipzig in 1879, he remembered the difficult experience when he left the Mission Institute during its 1859-1860 academic year. Of that trying time,

[113]Ernst W. Olson, *Olof Olsson . . .* , p. 175.

[114]*Ibid.*, p. 62.

he wrote that he was permitted to leave Leipzig by "min oförgätliga andliga fader, d:r P. Fjellstedt" ("my unforgettable spiritual father, Dr. P. Fjellstedt")[115]

Certain interesting similarities can be noted between Fjellstedt and Olsson. Both came out of homes of poverty from the same province, Värmland. Both early had the desire to become preachers. Later in life, both engaged in preaching tours, Fjellstedt more extensively than Olsson but Olsson did go out and preach and on those tours preached every day "in some country cottage, in a large barn, in a forest clearing or in churches and always to a large crowd of people."[116]

No cause and effect relationship can be ascribed to these similarities. There is another factor, however, in which Fjellstedt might have influenced Olsson. Both were interested in missionary work among Blacks and Native Americans.[117] Fjellstedt wrote several articles in his condemnation of slavery and the need to bring the Gospel to those people. Most of his writing on the subject occurred before the freeing of the slaves. His solution was set forth in an early edition of the *Lunds Missions-Tidning*:

> The only certain way to abolish this business and to protect our equals against such violence is to make our brothers in Africa Christian. That we could do in the name of the Lord, for he has given us the light which enlightens the world and which teaches us to love one another as brothers. If Africa's children become Christian, then they will cease to sell each other and will in their own land find right ways to earn all that is needed for this temporal life. By diligent work and praiseworthy manners, they will among themselves be at the same time holy in their duty and have the greatest gains as they protect one another from violence.[118]

Fjellstedt also wrote extensively on the condition of Native Americans. He condemned the way other Americans treated them. In an article written in 1867, he wrote that America had just come through one tragedy—the Civil War—but was now committing another one. It was fighting and killing Native Americans as immigrants robbed those people of their land. Money was actually offered, according to Fjellstedt, for Native American scalps: one hundred dollars was paid for the scalp of a male adult, fifty dollars for a female adult, and twenty-five dollars for a child under ten years of age. He blamed this cruelty on state governments rather than the federal. He concluded: "Nothing other than Christianity can affect love between people and peach upon earth for which we all long and for which we daily pray."[119]

[115]*Helsningar från Fjerran: Minnen från en resa genom England och Tyskland* [*Greetings from Afar: Memories from a Trip Through England and Germany*] (Moline, Ill., 1880), p. 182.

[116]*Korsbaneret*, 1901, pp. 158-59.

[117]I use the term "Native American" because of the negative connotation the former term has assumed.

[118]"Slafhandeln" ["Slave-handlers"], 2 (May, 1847), pp. 6-7.

[119]"Indianera i Nord-Amerikas forenta states" ["The Indians in the United States of North America"], *Lunds Missions-Tidning*, 22 (December 1867), p. 182. Other articles on

Olof Olsson showed a similar interest in both groups of these oppressed people. Among the first of the Swedish immigrants to propose mission work among the recently emancipated slaves, he wrote in response to Hasselquist who had invited him to come to America in April 1867: "One of the main reasons why I should like to come to America is that I might spend part of the year to work among the Negroes. Will you now be so good to inform me as to whether such a proposal could be implemented? I desire to be stationed in some Swedish Lutheran congregation in the West on the condition that part of the year I could go out to these people."[120]

Nothing came of this work, partly because of the lack of human resources to carry on such a mission. Too, it is probably true that there may have been a language barrier. Also, the expression of the Christian faith in which the black Americans had been nurtured, largely by the freer Baptist and Methodist modes of worship, would have made the Swedish Lutheran form of worship and church life quite foreign.

Augustana Lutheran Church went a bit farther in its proposal to minister to the Native Americans. In this possibility, too, Olsson showed his interest. Apparently as a result of Olsson's initiative, the Augustana Church at its Synod in 1874 instructed its mission board to make inquiry into the possibility of beginning missionary work in the Delaware tribe and others. In 1875 Olsson was selected to make this study but due to his heavy schedule, he was not able to fulfill this commission until 1876. In May of that year, he went by way of Topeka, Kansas and visited the Delaware tribe. He met the chief, Charles Journeycake who was a Baptist preacher. Journeycake favored the establishment of a Lutheran mission among the Delawares. Olsson, however, felt work should be initiated among people who had not yet been approached by the Gospel. The chief suggested the Pawnee tribe and his willingness to go along with the Swedish pastor to introduce him.

Olsson reported to the Church with the strong recommendation that work among Native Americans be started. He believed the endeaver should begin with the establishment of a children's home or a boarding school. The Church decided to begin work in the Pawnee tribe and sent one of its pastors, John Telleen, to make a further survey. No work was begun. Later, in 1879, Matthias Wahlström was sent to work among the Comanches but was forced to leave because of war between the Comanches and neighboring tribes. Year after year, the mission board reported no progress. By 1885, the issue was all but dead.

The question arises: Was there a cause and effect relationship between these similar interests of Fjellstedt and Olsson? It is highly likely that the younger of the two friends was acquainted with some of the articles in Fjellstedt's widely read papers. His high regard for his older friend and his early desire to be a missionary to foreign people may well have combined to stimulate his interest in the American Blacks and Native Americans. If true,

Native Americans appeared in this journal in June 1854; November 1860; September 1865 and others. In *Bibelvännen* on the same subject, January 1855 and June 1857.

[120]From Karlstad and Noretorp, February 18, 1868 in Westin, p. 163.

the impact of Fjellstedt upon one of Augustana Lutheran Church's leaders is further extended. Beyond these possibilities, one cannot with certainty ascribe Olsson's missionary interest among these Americans to Peter Fjellstedt.

Thus far, the influence of Fjellstedt has been confined to seven leaders of the Church: Esbjörn, Hasselquist, Carlsson, Andrén, Swensson, Cervin and Olsson. Much more difficult to identify is the influence he had upon laypersons who came to America and became members of Augustana. The seven leaders had all come from southern and central Sweden, none from the northern part. Fjellstedt's work had been concentrated in those areas; Rosenius too had been active in that same region. Most of the mid-nineteenth century Swedish immigrants had come from southern and central Sweden. Sten Carlsson has shown that in the period from 1845 to 1854, just when the first of Swedish American Lutherans were coming to America, the areas from which most of the emigrants came were in central and southern Sweden: Östergötland, northern Småland, Hälsingland, eastern Dalarna, northwestern Uppland, the Karlskoga mining districts, the southern sector of Kronobergs län (comparable to a county) in Småland, and the Jämshög area in Blekinge. Most of these immigrants settled in the Middle West. During the two later periods under study by Carlsson (1868-1873 and 1879-1893) when thousands who became members of the Augustana Church came, the situation was much the same. In the first of these periods, the highest emigration rates were registered for northern Småland, southwestern Östergötland, the Karkskoga mining district, and sections of Hälsingland. High rates were also recorded for large areas of southeastern Småland, western Blekinge, northern Dalarna and Jämtland. In the latter period (1879-1893), Carlsson again showed that from the same areas the largest number of emigrants went to America.[121]

Nor did the fact that most of them went to the Middle West change much. Augustana had its greatest strength in that area of the country. Hans Norman has shown that in 1880, 76.54 percent of people born in Sweden then living in the United States lived in the midwest. In the states of Minnesota and Illinois, where Augustana members were most numerous, 20.16 and 21.83 percent respectively lived. Add to that the 9.04 percent of Swedish-born persons in Iowa, 5.77 in Kansas, and 5.23 in Nebraska, states where there were heavy concentrations of Augustana members, and a total of 62.03 percent of all Swedish-born immigrants in 1880 were in prominent Augustana territory. In 1900, one out of every ten Swedish-Americans lived in Chicago thus ranking that city next to Stockholm with the largest Swedish population.[122]

Although it is difficult to evaluate precisely the degree to which Fjellstedt had shaped the religious outlook of the Swedish-American laity, the fact that such a large number came from the area in Sweden where Fjellstedt had been so active indicates his influence must have been considerable.

---

[121]"Chronology and Composition of Swedish Emigration to America," Runblom and Norman, pp. 119-120.

[122]"Swedes in North America," Runblom and Norman, pp. 242, 252.

Moreover, several of the leaders had been accompanied by large numbers of laypersons. With Esbjörn, came 146 persons; with Hasselquist, came about 100; Carlsson led a group of seventeen families numbering about 150 people.[123] From two of his congregations, Persberg and Sunnemo, Olsson was accompanied by 250 people. So the pastors came with an important nucleus of lay co-workers which no doubt greatly aided their work here. How many of those persons had been influenced by Fjellstedt? The question is probably unanswerable but of these people, Norelius wrote:

> They were not unacquainted with the spiritual revival; on the contrary they had been to a greater or lesser degree stirred and wished to hear the living Word of God declared in common language as they had heard in their fatherland from Pastor Fjellstedt, J. M. Lindahl, J. Colliander, Oskar Ahnfelt, C. J. Lindberg and others.[124]

The establishment of connections between Fjellstedt and individual laypersons is beyond the scope of this research and perhaps would be impossible to ascertain. Still, one fact seems certain; Fjellstedt was a vital force in the creation and nurture of a climate which was an important factor in the emigration of Swedes to America. Here they built their homes and organized their congregations according to their convictions—something they believed impossible to accomplish in Sweden.

5. The Channels of Fjellstedt's Influence

Important as was Fjellstedt's influence upon the individual leaders of the Augustana Lutheran Church, equally important was the help he gave this community in America to which he never came but which continued to be for him an important concern. And from America, the members of the Church recognized that they had a capable champion in Sweden upon whom they could depend. There were three ways in which Fjellstedt was helpful to Augustana during its formative years: his work as advocate, counsellor and recruiter; his theological influence; and through the Fjellstedt School.

i. Fjellstedt as Advocate, Counsellor and Recruiter

Fjellstedt employed three channels as advocate, counsellor and recruiter: correspondence, journalism and financial aid. He defended the young church in America against its critics in Sweden, gave advice particularly to Hasselquist for the benefit of the Swedish-American Lutherans, and helped recruit men for its ministry.

(1) *Correspondence*

In terms of Fjellstedt's relation with Augustana, no correspondence between the Augustana leaders and Fjellstedt appears to be in existence until the late 1860's. There may be three reasons for the situation. First, the

---

[123]Lindquist, . . . , *The Story of Erland Carlsson*, p. 21.

[124]*De Svenska Lutherska . . . historia i Amerika*, 1:492.

correspondence has been lost if there had been any. Secondly, the early arrangement with Fjellstedt to have authority to call pastors for Augustana churches may have shaped what correspondence there was into formal documents which have become buried in congregational or other records. Finally, Fjellstedt worked with the *Evangeliska Fosterlandsstiftelsen* to whom the Augustana leadership also made appeals. With Fjellstedt, this organization worked closely to procure men and money for the Swedish Lutherans in America. From this organization, letters were sent to President Hasselquist early in the 1860's. On January 10, 1863, for example, a letter was sent to Hasselquist in response to one he had sent the previous October 16. A promise was given for financial support for work in Swedish Lutheran congregations in America. Again, on July 11 of the same year, *Fosterlands-stiftelsen* regretfully reported unsuccessful attempts to procure a pastor for work in New York. Information was also given about copies of *Gezelli's bibelverk* (*Gazell's Work on the Bible*) which would be sent to Hasselquist in the near future.

While the absence of letters from Fjellstedt to the Augustana leaders between 1860 (the organization of the Church) and 1867 poses a problem, it does not detract from the important role he played. The frequency with which his name was mentioned in historical works dealing with Augustana history bears eloquent testimony to his importance. The fact that fifty years after his death, Fjellstedt was eulogized in a publication of the Augustana Church gave witness to his rich contribution. Emil Lund wrote: "The fiftieth anniversary of the passing from the field of battle on earth to peace in heaven of this remarkable man of God was celebrated in the beginning of last year both in his home land and other places in the world including here in America especially through memorial sketches in journals and brochures."[125] The vivid memory of what Fjellstedt had done so significantly for Augustana prompted the acts of remembrance.

The exchange of letters particularly between Fjellstedt and Hasselquist occurred between April 1867 and September 1872. The topics which were considered were three.

First, there was the need for encouragement. As Hasselquist complained about the unwillingness of pastors from Sweden to come to America or expressed his feelings over hard conditions borne by the Swedish immigrants, Fjellstedt became a source of encouragement simply in the opportunity Hasselquist took to write to his friend in Sweden. On February 28, 1868, he wrote: "Some of the new evangelism from the Swedish Church we have learned to know in its very worst characteristic and we are afraid of it." Hasselquist was referring apparently to the tendencies which later erupted in the Waldenströmian controversy. He complained because he felt the "new evangelism" was opposed to the confessions of the Lutheran Church. He continued:

> In truth we need capable men from the fatherland. Many of our congregations are without care and plead bitterly their need and cry for help and we have yet no help to send. . . . We have here people who

[125]"Peter Fjellstedt," *Korsbaneret*, 1932, p. 20.

deny the Christian faith. They show their contempt through a new paper, *The Swedish-American,* through which even the Episcopalian Church seeks to win a foothold among us."

He was relieved in writing of his burden apparently for he ended the letter with a postscript: "It may appear from the foregoing that we have among our pastors those of the new evangelism but that is not so. Although we have different endowments, natural and spiritual, yet we stand faithfully by each other's side and work together in brotherly love."[126]

Need for encouragement was not only implicit. At least on one occasion, Fjellstedt was asked to come and visit The Augustana Church. In the spring of 1867, Hasselquist wrote: "Two of our largest conferences which have held their conventions recently decided through me to send to you a humble and hearty invitation to come and see us in our district land." He apologized for what he thought might be an imposition on his older friend. "I thought enough of my old revered Brother Fjellstedt and believed your sixty-six years should protect you from an invitation of this kind." The determination and deep desire of the delegates, however, overruled Hasselquist's hesitation. No doubt he also wanted his friend to come. "Your visit among us and our congregations would, we are convinced, through God's grace be a rich encouragement, would strengthen the wavering, and restore the misguided." As he continued, Hasselquist spoke of troubles the Church was experiencing. "It seems as if we just this year have come to need support in view of several troublesome issues that already confront us." Among the troubles he listed was the case of a young pastor who had been defrocked "having fallen," the presence of a new Swedish newspaper which promoted unbelief, and the power of the sects.[127]

Not only encouragement but counsel was also sought from Fjellstedt as well as Wieselgren. Hasselquist was disturbed because he had not heard from Fjellstedt for some time. He said: "We need so much the judgment of one upon whom we can depend, the judgment of one who has time to involve himself with our concern and besides is widely travelled. . . . We need help because I dare not without advice take the offers of which I receive not a few from unknown men."[128]

Hasselquist then came to the specific matter on which he was seeking counsel. The question had arisen whether the Augustana Church should cooperate with the newly organized General Council (1867) which had arisen as a more confessional Lutheran group in reaction to the Americanized General Synod. The area of work where Augustana and the General Council might work together was in theological education. There was a proposal from the General Council that a seminary be organized under its auspices in Chicago. The president of Augustana felt that the Church which he represented should have greater control over theological education. In his uncertainty, he wrote in the same letter: "I wish I could hear your and Dr. Fjellstedt's thoughts on this issue. I can then take your

---

[126]Westin, pp. 169-70.

[127]April 6, 1867, Westin, pp. 143-44.

[128]Westin, p. 254.

expressions to Augustana and enlighten them all. This will bring about what we perceive to be the right understanding of the question."

Secondly, correspondence between Fjellstedt and Hasselquist was carried on out of Augustana's need for pastors. No topic was written about more often than this one. On February 28, 1868, Hasselquist wrote to Fjellstedt urging him to encourage more men to come to America because the need for pastors was great and "many of us who are working here will soon be worn out." Specifically he wrote about a pastor, C. Torin. An exception had been made in that instance. Augustana's leaders had called Torin directly rather than through Fjellstedt "because the information we had on him entitled us to do so." But Hasselquist wrote they had been upbraided harshly for that act. "We fear to call directly because we have received chastisement from Com. Karlén which we shall not easily forget."[129]

In his reply dated January 14, 1871, Fjellstedt wrote from Göteborg that he had discussed with Wieselgren the situation of Pastor Torin. It was not yet certain, Fjellstedt said, that Torin would come. Further information was requested. Under what conditions would a pastor be required to work in America "for it is not easy for a pastor with a family to work in unfamiliar surroundings?"[130] The attempt to procure the services of Torin for Augustana apparently ended in failure. There is no record that he ever held membership in the Augustana ministerium. The long period of elapsed time between Hasselquist's letter to Fjellstedt (February 28, 1868) and the latter's reply (January 14, 1871) does not suggest a high level of enthusiasm on the part of Torin.

Another letter to Fjellstedt from Hasselquist (July 27, 1869) further emphasized the need for pastors. At its recent annual meeting, the president of the Augustana Church reported that eleven men had been ordained. He added: "But what does this suffice among so many in a place where so much unbelief exists and where so much bad seed is being sown."[131]

By 1870, Hasselquist had come to the conclusion that the Lutheran Church in Sweden was an unreliable source for pastors who would come to America. Following his visit to Sweden in the summer of that year, he recalled his report to the pastors of the Swedish Church. He told them "the Augustana Synod comprised a community of about 16,000 communicants with a total number of about 30,000 souls." He deplored the fact that that was a small percentage of "the 150,000 Swedes who had immigrated into the United States of whom the majority had disappeared as raindrops in the sand." He noted: "I asked the mother Church how much she had sacrificed to prevent this condition. Yes, six pastors had been sent of whom two had returned." Obviously this was a miserably small contribution between the years 1849 and 1870. Hasselquist stressed the fact that the need for pastors remained urgent. "Who is responsible for taking up the work to which the Lord calls if not the Church in the fatherland from whom these scattered

[129]Westin, p. 169. Karlén was a Swedish official.

[130]*Ibid.*, p. 293.

[131]*Ibid.*, p. 239.

people have come?"[132] It was to another source that Fjellstedt turned to help Augustana.

Thirdly, Fjellstedt appealed to Swedish students to come to America. Benson and Hedin wrote:

> The State Church authorities did very little to supply the need. Rather was it individuals, far-sighted and liberally inclined clergymen like Wieselgren and Fjellstedt who advised their young friends in the Church to emigrate, especially those who had made themselves objectionable as pietistic or *läsare* preachers or as temperance leaders.[133]

These "young friends" of whom mention was made referred to the students whom Wieselgren and Fjellstedt encouraged to come to America, complete their education under the auspices of Augustana and become pastors in its congregations. It was from these young students that Augustana would receive its greatest number of pastors from Sweden with the splendid help of Fjellstedt and Wieselgren.

"Through Wieselgren and Fjellstedt several recruits from the ministry were obtained in the years from 1866 to 1869."[134] Not all of these men proved to be an unmixed blessing to Augustana. One example was the case of Peter Sjöblom. On Wieselgren's recommendation, Sjöblom came to America. He was ordained after a short apprenticeship under Erland Carlsson in Chicago. Shortly thereafter, he began to write letters to Sweden warning Swedes against coming to America. His penchant for making trouble continued into the eighties when he was a leader in an attempt to create a schism in the Augustana Church.[135]

Accordingly, the Augustana leaders depended upon Fjellstedt not only to recruit students but also to judge the fitness of those who were to be sent. On July 27, 1869, Hasselquist wrote about two students at the Fjellstedt School, one named Joh. Sandén and the other simply identified by his last name, Wikstrand. Hasselquist wrote that students from Sweden could not be accepted except on the recommendation of "Br. Fjellstedt or someone else upon whose judgment we lean." If Fjellstedt could give a positive judgment upon these two men, "they could come this fall so as to continue and complete their studies here."[136]

Nearly a year and half later on January 1, 1870, Fjellstedt responded to Hasselquist's letter. This long delay was not entirely the fault of Fjellstedt. The letter had been sent on the postal ship *Germania* which sank. Amazingly, the letter was recovered and was legible in spite of its exposure to water.[137] In regard to Sandén, Fjellstedt wrote that he could "without

---

[132]Norelius, *T. N. Hasselquist*, pp. 162-63.

[133]Adolph B. Benson and Naboth Hedin, *Americans From Sweden*, The People of America Series (Philadelphia: J. B. Lippincott Co., 1950), p. 202.

[134]Stephenson, p. 228.

[135]Arden, *American Heritage*, pp. 194-95.

[136]Westin, p. 239.

[137]Other reasons why it had taken Fjellstedt so long to answer Hasselquist's letter were:

hesitation recommend him for a call." He was also positive, though less so, toward Wikstrand. On the basis of information from another student, Fjellstedt had discovered that Wikstrand was economically poor but sufficiently gifted so that Bishop Sundberg had given him a license to preach in the Tveta Church in Åmål. Fjellstedt concluded: "Should one consider him? He is strongly awakened spiritually, has good gifts. More I dare not now say."[138]

Another example of Fjellstedt's willingness to put forth considerable effort in the selective process to obtain satisfactory recruits for Augustana was illustrated in a letter from Göteborg, February 5, 1872. He accompanied his letter with biographies and recommendations for two students who were not named. On the information he had, he felt he could recommend them to Hasselquist. They had been preaching in the diocese of Halland under the supervision of a bishop who was well known for allowing licenses only to those who were of "irreproachable conduct, have essential knowledge, pure learning, and in whom is beginning the work of God's Spirit."[139] Fjellstedt did not force his judgments upon Hasselquist but left the final decision to him. At the same time, he made it clear he believed the young men were worthy of investigation on their merits.

An examination of the correspondence between Fjellstedt and Hasselquist shows the undoubted interest Fjellstedt took in his fellow Swedes in America. The neglect of which he believed the Church in Sweden was guilty created in him both a critical view of that Church and all the stronger determination to promote and support the work among the Swedish immigrants in America.

(2) *Journalism*

In a sense, journalism was even more important than correspondence because it came to the attention of more than one recipient. During the course of his twenty years as editor of two widely read papers, the *Lunds Missions-Tidning* and *Bibelvännen*, Fjellstedt published articles both from his own authorship and from the leaders of the Augustana Church. From the abundance of material, only representative examples can be given.

In the October issue of *Lunds Missions-Tidning* 1849, Fjellstedt reported the departure from Sweden of two emigrant groups: Esbjörn and his group and the Jansonites. The thrust of this article was threefold. First, the author set forth the unfortunate condition of the Jansonites who were deluded by Eric Janson who, they thought, was giving them bread for their souls. Instead, they were being taught wrong interpretations of the Bible.

Secondly, he indicted the Swedish Church and State. He asked the question what the Church and State were doing to win such people away from their errors. Here was the implication that Church and State were themselves guilty of providing inadequate spiritual food for Swedish

Fjellstedt's weakness and age, his lack of personal acquaintance with Sandén and Wikstrand, and the difficulty he had encountered in trying to get the desired information.

[138]Westin, p. 257.

[139]*Ibid.*, p. 324.

citizens. Else, why should Lutherans like Esbjörn and his company be leaving Sweden?

Finally, Fjellstedt asked his readers to pray for Esbjörn and those who accompanied him. He may have been moved by his own doubts about the wisdom of Swedes moving to the frontier of America. Of greater importance, no doubt, was his concern that the ministry of the Church be available to those people.

Another example of help for Augustana from Fjellstedt's journalistic work was the publication of the long letter from Esbjörn already referred to, published in the September issue of *Bibelvännen*, 1852.[140] This was a particularly valuable article because it brought into view for Fjellstedt's Swedish readers the unusual religious situation in America. The need to inform the Swedish people of conditions in America was great, but of even greater significance was the appeal Esbjörn made for help. His Macedonian call, "Come over and help us" could scarcely fail to stir at least some of the most sensitive readers of *Bibelvännen*.

A final example is an article from Fjellstedt which was a response to the continuous call from America for support. In his article, "Skall jag taga wara på min bröder?" ("Shall I Take Heed of My Brothers?"), he took up the cause of the Augustana Church. Fjellstedt had a fourfold concern. First, there was the frontier condition in America with all its dangers and rigorous demands upon the pioneers. Secondly, the needs of the Swedish immigrants for the ministry of the Lutheran Church were continually addressed. Thirdly, he faulted the Church in Sweden for its neglect of the spiritual ministry to the Swedes in America. This was a responsibility which could not be neglected without serious consequences for the Swedish Church. Finally—and this was the most important—Fjellstedt kept before his readers that in America, they had brothers and sisters who had needs to be fulfilled.

In addition to the value of his journalism on the corporate life of Augustana, one can only speculate on the breadth of Fjellstedt's influence upon individual persons who later came to America and contributed to the life of the Church. Johan A. Enander, who from 1869 was for several years editor and part owner of the journal, *Hemlandet*, wrote in his *Autobiography*: "The first periodical I studied was Dr. Fjellstedt's *Bibel vän* [sic] which was widely read in the community where my parents lived in Sweden."[141] Both Enander's example and statement give high credence to the probability that through his work as journalist, Fjellstedt affected many people whose lives are difficult to reach through historical research but who contributed much to the life of the Augustana Lutheran Church.

[140]See above, pp. 243-47.

[141]"Autobiography of Johan A. Enander: Student at Venersberg High School," trans. Conrad Bergendoff (Handwritten; Archives, Denkmann Memorial Library, Augustana College, 1869), p. 3. From 1890 to 1893, he was professor of Swedish language and literature at Augustana College. He was also an author of some distinction (Conrad Bergendoff, "A Significant Enander Document," typewritten; Rock Island, Ill.: Archives, Denkmann Memorial Library, Augustana College).

(3) *Financial aid*

In the realm of finances, Fjellstedt's help was also sought. This dependence was shown in a matter that involved a gift from the "Swedish Nightingale," Jenny Lind Goldschmidt. From the earliest years of the Church, Augustana leaders recognized the need to establish facilities for the education of pastors in America. One option was the possibility of working with non-Swedish Lutheran institutions through the establishment of Scandinavian professorships—a procedure which was actually tried and failed between the years 1858 and 1860 at Springfield, Illinois.

Some years earlier in 1852, Mrs. Goldschmidt gave $1500 to the Board of Directors of Capital University, a Lutheran school in Columbus, Ohio. The money was to have been used for the establishment of a Scandinavian professorship at Capital. That intention was never fulfilled.

In 1860, when Augustana established its own seminary in Chicago, Esbjörn attempted to procure the money from Capital authorities for the benefit of the new school. The University authorities at Columbus promised to give the funds to Augustana but never did. Efforts continued for over a decade to get the money. On May 5, 1871, Hasselquist wrote to Mrs. Goldschmidt and asked her to send a letter through either Wieselgren or Fjellstedt to the "Board of Directors of the University of Columbus and instruct them to turn over the $1500 which had been left for the establishment of a Scandinavian professorship."[142]

Fjellstedt responded to this request and made some inquiries. In a letter to Hasselquist dated May 2, 1872, he wrote that so far he had not been successful. But he wrote: "I shall try further but I do not have much hope because the Synod [Augustana] is not considered to have enduring, fixed authority and also they [the authorities at Capital] are not satisfied how the principal would be secured and how the interest would be paid."[143] Although in this instance, Fjellstedt was unable to aid his friends in America, the fact that the Swedish immigrants called upon him in a financial matter testifies to the range of confidence they had in him.

Fjellstedt not only offered financial advice to Augustana; he also helped in concrete financial support. His journalism efforts were related to this aid. This was shown in an article which appeared in the September issue of *Lunds Missions-Tidning*, 1859. From Augustana had come grateful acknowledgment for fifty dollars which had been sent by the Lund Missionary Society. The money had been received by the Society from people who had been moved by articles they had read in Fjellstedt's journal about the work in America. Of the response to the gift on the part of the American immigrants, Fjellstedt wrote: "This little gift has brought great joy to our Church friends there."[144]

[142]Westin, p. 303.

[143]*Ibid.*, p. 325. Apart from the main topic of the financial issue, this statement is interesting in the insight it gives about the relationship between the Swedish Lutherans and some of the non-Swedish Lutherans in America—scarcely a relationship of mutual confidence and love.

[144]*Ibid.*, p. 143.

The Lund Society made other contributions. According to financial reports which were published periodically in an appendix of the *Lunds Missions-Tidning*, a total of 1064.57 *riksdaler* was given to the Augustana Church between the years 1858 and 1861.[145]

Fjellstedt also obtained aid for Augustana from *Gustaf Adolf Stiftelsen* (Society), Fjellstedt played an active role in this Society; he was for awhile its secretary and addressed the Society at its annual meeting in 1864.[146] At its meeting in Göteborg some years later, the decision was made to send 250 *riksdaler* to "a Swedish congregation in North America."[147] Again, in 1871, Fjellstedt informed Hasselquist that the Society had decided at its November 11 meeting to send 300 *riksdaler* to a needy congregation in America. Another 261 *riksdaler* were placed at the disposal of Hasselquist to use as he saw appropriate.[148]

The Society also gave aid to young men who came from Sweden to become pastors in Augustana. "The expenses of their journey were paid by *Gustaf Adolf Stiftelsen* with contributions collected by men like Wieselgren and Fjellstedt."[149] Without the deep interest of these men, it is doubtful whether the need of these students—and of the Augustana Church in America—would ever have been brought to the attention of the Society.

In two dramatic instances, Fjellstedt acted as advocate in behalf of Augustana in its appeal to Sweden for financial support. In 1859, a petition had been addressed to the King of Sweden that he give permission for a collection to be taken in the Swedish Lutheran churches for the support of the Scandinavian professorship at Illinois State University. Archbishop Reuterdahl exerted his authority to deny the request partly because of his dislike for the pietistic, free-church character of the Swedish emigrants. Perhaps he knew that Hasselquist had deplored his appointment to the archbishopric in 1856 and that fact may have colored his decision.

The next year a radical change occurred with the separation of the Scandinavian Lutherans from the Synod of Northern Illinois and the organization of the Augustana Church. This occurrence was important for two reasons. First, the new church body could no longer depend upon support from the American Lutherans. Secondly, Augustana, even by its name, had shown itself to be confessionally Lutheran, a fact which not even so conservative a person as Reuterdahl could deny. After all, critical as the leaders of Augustana were of the Church in Sweden, they yet remained faithful to it. The Lutheran confessions were highly prized. No doubt to this faithfulness toward the "Mother Church" and its confessional basis Fjellstedt contributed.

[145]Lunds Missions-Tidning, 7 (December 1859); 12 (March 1860); 14 (February 1861); 15 (February 1862).

[146]"Gustaf Adolphs Stiftelsen," *Bibelvännen*, 18 (February 1865), 28-32 and (March 1865), 36-38.

[147]"Wedergällningen" ["Retribution"] *Bibelvännen*, 20 (March 1867), 45.

[148]November 20, 1871, Westin, p. 317.

[149]Stephenson, p. 653.

Viewing themselves as significantly related to the Church in Sweden, leaders of Augustana renewed their appeal to the king. O. C. T. Andrén became the emissary to carry this request to Sweden.[150] Reuterdahl lacked sympathy for the proposal but this time the Archbishop was overruled. "Through an audience with the king and the support of Dr. P. Fjellstedt, the petition was granted, and collections were taken up in the churches of Sweden for the benefit of Augustana Seminary."[151]

The second advocacy by Fjellstedt was also performed in 1860 and in relation to Andrén and his mission. Judge T. H. Odencrantz and K. W. Almquist encouraged the Swedish Missionary Society to gather funds for work among the Swedish-American Lutherans. (The proposal was also urged by the Lund Missionary Society)[152] Andrén was present at the meeting and made an eloquent plea for such help. "Fjellstedt powerfully supported Andrén's effort. It was decided that the Swedish Missionary Society would allow 2000 *riksdaler* of the reserve fund of the Lund Missionary Society to be used to that end."[153]

Fjellstedt gave valuable assistance to Augustana not only with cash but with other forms of aid. In his letter from Göteborg of November 20, 1871, Fjellstedt wrote to Hasselquist that he was urging a student, Jörlander by name, whom he was sending to America to bring "a packing case of excellent works such as Starkes and Wilischens *Bibelverk* [a commentary], etc. as a contribution to the library of Augustana College in Paxton. I hope both Jörlander and what he is bringing will arrive safely.[154]

Finally, how many individual pastors who came to America were helped by Fjellstedt is unknown but that he personally contributed to the travelling expenses of some is a matter of record. Mention has been made of the gift Fjellstedt gave Jonas Swensson when he left Sweden for America. A. W. Dahlsten, a student at the Fjellstedt School while it was in Stockholm, wrote that when he came to America, he did so at the expense of Dr. Fjellstedt.[155]

ii. Fjellstedt as Theological Mentor

The second area in which Fjellstedt made significant contributions to the Augustana Lutheran Church was in its theology. This aspect of the Swedish churchman's activity has not been explored extensively. As a consequence, it may be that Augustana itself has been ignorant of an important

[150]See above, p. 281.

[151]Oscar O. Ander, *T. N. Hasselquist: The Career and Influence of a Swedish-American Clergyman, Journalist and Educator* (Rock Island, Ill.: Augustana Historical Society, 1931), p. 215.

[152]It will be recalled that in 1855, it was decided to join together the Swedish Missionary Society and the Lund Missionary Society. The latter organization, however, was not dissolved. It became an associate or supporting society and retained some autonomy. It retained 20,000 *riksdaler* of its treasury as a reserve fund.

[153]Sundkler, p. 558.

[154]Westin, p. 318.

[155]*Korsbaneret*, 1919, p. 142.

dimension of its basic character. Through the years, it has associated itself quite exclusively with the Rosenian tradition. Augustana has regarded itself as essentially shaped by the nineteenth century religious revival in Sweden which prospered under the leadership of Carl Olof Rosenius.[156]

Conrad Bergendoff, president emeritus of Augustana College and the former Augustana Theological Seminary, has made two observations which counteract this popular notion. First, it is his conviction that whereas Rosenius had much influence on the laity, it was Fjellstedt who was more important in shaping the views of the clergy. "More than ever I am convinced that his [Fjellstedt's] influence on Augustana's formative years was of prime importance. Rosenius had left his mark on the laity, but I think Fjellstedt affected the ministry in a more substantive degree."[157] There is good evidence for this view in relation to the doctrine of the ministry and the Church affirmed by Augustana.

Secondly, Bergendoff provocatively noted another difference between Fjellstedt and Rosenius: "Again contrasting Rosenius and Fjellstedt: while the former nourished piety, the latter was willing to tackle hard intellectual problems. The one helped form Bible Schools, the latter, college and seminary."[158]

Certainly this view is suggested both by Fjellstedt's rigorous requirements for the Mission Institute he led in Lund and the active support he gave to Augustana College and Seminary during the early years.

Professor Carl Hallencreutz, Professor of History of Religions at Uppsala University, has further elaborated upon the difference between the influences of these two men upon Augustana. Plainly, the widely read *Pietisten* by the laity as well as pastors was a strong force in the shaping of Augustana. Yet, Hallencreutz observed that the difference in the background of the two men oriented Fjellstedt more toward the clergy. He was himself a clergyman; Rosenius, a layman. Both were zealous in the missionary endeavor but Fjellstedt, as educator and pastor, had spent actual time on mission fields. This uniquely equipped him as a counsellor for the Augustana leadership. Admittedly somewhat weak in the details of administration, he was, nevertheless, an organization man. For a decade and a half, he was head of the Mission Institute which began in Lund. Rosenius, although also international in outlook, was more pastoral in his writings and preaching than Fjellstedt. By contrast, the different nature of Fjellstedt's journalism and his experience with organizations such as the Lund Missionary Society and the Mission Institute gave him a greater entré into the confidence of Augustana's leaders, especially Hasselquist who came to rely on Fjellstedt so much and who more than any other person shaped the theology and organization of Augustana during its formative first three decades of existence. Important in this respect was the relationship of Fjellstedt, as educator, with Augustana College and Seminary, again especially through Hasselquist. There is little wonder that Fjellstedt with his

[156]See above, p. 37.

[157]Letter to the writer, dated April 8, 1979, Rock Island, Illinois.

[158]*Ibid.*

wider and more varied background became more of a guide to the leaders of Augustana than Rosenius.[159]

Before entering into a consideration of specific theological doctrines, two general observations about Fjellstedt's theological influence can be made. First, his theology shaped the thought of individual parish pastors. Particularly significant was his three volume commentary, *Bibeln med Förklaringar*. When this work was published, A. G. Sefström, a pastor from Sweden, wrote to Esbjörn on April 29, 1853, and informed the latter that *Bibeln med Förklaringar* had been published. Of its author, Sefström wrote: "Praise God for this pillar in our Zion."[160] There is no record of Esbjörn's response but it is safe to assume that he reacted positively to the news. Many Augustana pastors owned and used Fjellstedt's commentary.[161]

An example of the use of Fjellstedt's work was demonstrated in the Augustana Annual, *Korsbaneret*, for 1905. The editor, J. G. Dahlberg, chided but also encouraged Augustana congregations to give more generously for the work of the Church. He used two arguments: first, although God gives the promise, the law and the order for worship, the communities described in the Old Testament and the New Testament and the Augustana Church as well must provide the means (e.g., buildings, appropriate instruments). Secondly, in response to the gracious and abundant love of God, the people should respond with their gifts freely and generously. To support his pronouncements, Dahlberg used Fjellstedt's *Bibeln med Förklaringar* with its interpretation of I Chronicles 22:14, Genesis 4:26 and Proverbs 15:8.[162] That an Augustana pastor in an important communications position should make reference to this work nearly twenty-five years after the death of its author is significant.

A second general observation concerned the growing confessionalism which was evident in the thought of both Fjellstedt and the leaders of Augustana in the decade of the 1850's. Like Fjellstedt, as the years went on, the Augustana leaders became more conservative and confessional in their theology.

Admittedly, one cannot prove a cause and effect relationship between the growing confessionalism of Fjellstedt with that of the Augustana leaders. Still, communication between these persons was active. Also, the unqualified confidence the American churchmen had in their friend in Sweden adds credibility that here, too, Fjellstedt influenced them theologically. Bergendoff rightly asks:

[159]Carl Hallencreutz, letter to the writer, dated June-July, 1980, Uppsala, Sweden.

[160]Westin, p. 68.

[161]For example, I had little difficulty in purchasing a set from the widow of a pastor living in California. At the time I was doing research on this manuscript in the autumn of 1978 in the archives of the Denkmann Library of Augustana College, Professor Alan Swanson in the department of Swedish was doing research on a parish pastor who had lived in East Sveadahl, Minnesota. A sermon by that minister dated November 10, 1880, made use of Fjellstedt's Commentary on II Timothy 2:12-21. It is a safe conjecture that many other pastors relied in Fjellstedt's work.

[162]"Kommunikantafgiften och andra gåfvor" ["Offerings and Other Gifts from Communicants"], 26:65-88 *passim*.

147

> Why did these older Lutherans succumb to the environment [Anglo-American revivalism] in Protestantism while the opponents [Swedish Lutheran immigrants] fell back on more churchly, traditional, confessional elements of their heritage? When these Augustana leaders broke with the "Americanizers" were they not in line with Fjellstedt's principles?[163]

in three particular instances the influence of Fjellstedt can be noted: the view of the Church, the ministry and episcopacy.

(1) *The view of the Church*

Hasselquist may serve as a representative of the Church's theology when a single spokeman is sought. He wrote far more extensively than any of the other Augustana leaders. Also, when he died February 4, 1891, he had served as the second president of Augustana College and Theological Seminary for over thirty-seven years. During much of that time, he had also served as professor of theology. It is hard to imagine any other person who exerted such an influence on the formation of Augustana's theology. Both through his instruction as professor of the Church's pastors and his participation in the forging of statements regarding doctrine, the voice of T. N. Hasselquist was strong.

Hasselquist's view of the Church in a figurative sense was essentially that of St. Paul in his use of the head and the body with its several members as representative of the Church. In the one book he published—a commentary on the letter to the Ephesians—he used that figure at least twenty-two times. On one occasion, Hasselquist wrote: "Above all, I want to remind you that the Apostolic order for the congregation is like a body of which the individual Christian is a member. These should be as near to one another as the members in a natural body so that the body is healthy and can accomplish its work" Fjellstedt, too, used that figure but for him, it was not the only one he employed. Hasselquist deplored that this basic understanding of the Church was being neglected even by such a well edited paper as *Budbäraren* (Messenger), the journal of *Fosterlandsstiftelsen*. He added: "As long as *Bibelvännen* was in the hands of Dr. Fjellstedt, the question of the nature of the Church as it concerned doctrine and order was frequently considered."[164]

A more important observation of this issue was the context in which Hasselquist employed his view of the Church. He defended his opposition to what he called "independentismen" [sic] (Actually congregationalism and sectarianism).

> Christ's work concerns the whole. It refers to the individual members as part of the whole and only in connection with the whole body. This should be warning enough against "independentismen" [sic] according to which each and everyone is whole in oneself and each and every congregation independent of others. Jesus said before he actually began to build his body: "I shall myself build my Church," not churches. He is

[163]Letter, April 8, 1979.

[164]Quoted in Norelius, *T. N. Hasselquist*, pp. 167-68.

the head of only one body as is confessed in the Apostles' Creed: "One, holy, catholic Church, the communion of saints.[165]

Fjellstedt was likewise opposed to sectarianism and separatism. To insist that Hasselquist's use of the body and its members as a picture of the Church or that his opposition to congregational polity and separatism was caused by Fjellstedt's influence is impossible to affirm as conclusive. For instance, the context in which each man developed resistance to separatism was different. Fjellstedt expressed his opposition in the highly religiously homogenized culture of Sweden. His battle was based very much upon a reflective consideration of the Lutheran confessions. By contrast, Hasselquist fought the separatists in the religiously pluralistic frontier of a new country. Although he too was guided by the confessions, there was also a strong element of pragmatic necessity. Little time was available for reflection on theological issues. Hasselquist and his colleagues were fighting for their very survival.

Nevertheless, evidence is not lacking that Fjellstedt did influence Augustana's thought in its view of the Church. Hasselquist's reference to Fjellstedt's support of this outlook as editor of *Bibelvännen* is not without significance. Also, although Fjellstedt used many biblical figures to describe the Church, that of the body and its members was important to him. In his doctoral dissertation, the figure was used prominently. He wrote: "In this faith in the crucified and risen high priest, Christ ever lives and prays for them [his followers], Hebrews 7:25, and in this relationship with Him, they are members of the spiritual body, of which He is the Head."[166]

(2) *The doctrine of the ministry*

There is good evidence that Peter Fjellstedt strongly influenced the doctrine of the ministry in the Augustana Lutheran Church. Hugo Söderström wrote: "The Augustana view of the ministry was in fact similar to the concept of some Swedish low-churchmen, with whom the immigrant pastors kept contact. Especially the concept of Fjellstedt, the well known missionary and biblical scholar, seems to have influenced the leaders of the Synod."[167]

In his doctoral dissertation, Fjellstedt's main contention on the basis of his interpretation of scripture (e.g., Ephesians 4:11ff, I Corinthians 12) was that the ministry was an institution ordained by Christ with rootage in the Old Testament priesthood. This order was not, therefore, an invention or product of the Church or the individual congregation but Christ's gift to the Church through which his service was continued. Thus, there was, by virtue of this order, a certain authority and independence which the

[165]T. N. Hasselquist, *Försök Till En Grundlig Och Dock Lättfattlig Förklaring Af Paul's Bref Till Efeserna* [*An Attempt Toward a Comprehensive and Yet Understandable Explanation of Paul's Letter to the Ephesians*] (Rock Island, Ill.: Augustana Book Concern, 1887), p. 248.

[166]*Några Grunddrag Af Nya Testamentets . . .* , p. 3.

[167]P. 87.

ministry exercised apart from, although in relation to, the congregation. Other features of Fjellstedt's view of the ministry included the requirement that one entering into the ministry must possess both an inner and an outer call. Also the investment of a man into the office of the ministry occurred only through the laying on of hands by those who had previously been ordained. In relation to this last characteristic, he wrote: "It is not in accordance with the Scripture for a group of Christians to elect a person whom they want as a pastor or teacher and ordain him."[168]

Hasselquist could not speak from the view of the episcopacy; nevertheless, he also argued that the ministry was ordained by God. In the absence of a bishop, the authority to call a pastor was delegated to the congregation. This was itself an orderly process which prohibited any person from coming into a parish on one's own accord. Hasselquist appealed to the fourteenth article of the Augsburg Confession for his position. "No one should publicly teach in the Church or administer the Sacraments, unless he be regularly called." But not anyone could be called; only those who had been ordained could be installed into a parish. Hasselquist rejected both the Roman Catholic view of ordination as a sacrament and the approach that every Christian was a priest, that is a view which saw nothing significant about ordination.

He reasoned in a fashion strikingly similar to Fjellstedt. Hasselquist based his understanding of the ministry on Ephesians 4:11 ("some to be apostles, some to be prophets, etc.) as did Fjellstedt (along with other similar biblical passages). Hasselquist wrote: "The office is thus not only a necessary human order for the prevention of unedifying confusion but it is also a divine order which the Christ, according to God's order, would have in the Church and would have us follow."[169]

This view which separated the ministry as an order within the Church, the priesthood of believers, was not universally accepted in Augustana. The differences, however, appear to have been more on political than theological grounds. Quite severe controversy continued for three decades as to whether the constitution of the Church should be on the basis of a congregational polity with the authority in the congregation or a presbyterian type in which an independent and separate authority of the ministry was established. The latter view was early expressed in the constitution adopted at the founding of the Church in 1860 when Synod was defined as consisting of ordained pastors and lay delegates who represented the congregations of the Synod.[170] Eighteen years later, in 1878, a revised constitution enunciated the congregational polity in its statement. "The Synod shall consist of all the congregations regularly connected with it, and at the synodical conventions shall be represented by the pastor and one elected delegate from each congregation." G. Everett Arden interpreted the change thus:

[168]*Bibelvännen* (June 1856), quoted in Söderström, p. 88. See p. 320 for an exception in Fjellstedt's view.

[169]*Augustana*, 1889, quoted in Norelius, *T. N. Hasselquist*, p. 258.

[170]For clarity, it is well to make the term "Synod" synonymous with "Church."

With the adoption of this proposal the pendulum had swung to the opposite extreme, relegating the ministerial office to a delegatory status only, while making the congregation, as such, the constitutive element of the Synod. This was tantamount to outright congregationalism wherein the *congregation* and the *Church* became virtually synonomous terms.[171]

In the early 1880's, there was actually a plot to divide the Minnesota Conference from the Augustana Church on the basis that there was no distinction between the office of the ministry and the congregation as the priesthood of believers; the office of the ministry was simply functional. Finally, in 1890, a proposal was made which read: "This Synod shall consist of all ordained pastors and all congregations which are regularly connected with the same, and shall be represented at synodical conventions by elected delegates." With slight revision, this statement became constitutional in 1894. Of that action, Arden wrote:

> The new constitution defined the Synod as consisting of *pastors* and *congregations* in regular connection with the same, *indicating that the ministerial office, like the congregation, is divinely instituted* [emphasis mine]; the office is not a mere *function* created by the congregation; nor is the Church the creation of the ministerial office. Neither the Church nor office have [sic] priority over the other, but together constitute the divine institution ordained by Christ.[172]

Certainly the political aspects of the formulation of a doctrine of the ministry (and of the Church) in Augustana history are clear. Still, the actions of the Augustana Church followed closely the thought of Fjellstedt. Söderström's view that Augustana's understanding of the ministry seems to have been influenced by this Swedish leader appears to be well founded.

(3) *View of episcopacy*

Early in the history of the Swedish Lutheran immigrants, episcopacy confronted them as a threat at least in the minds of Esbjörn, Hasselquist and Carlsson. This danger was in a sense more threatening than that from the Anglo-American revivalism of the Baptists and Methodists. The Episcopalian challenge came from one of their own countrymen, Gustaf Maurius Unonius.

Unonius came to America nearly a decade before Esbjörn. Educated at Uppsala in law, medicine and the humanities, he came to America in 1841. He was instrumental in influencing several fellow Swedes to come and in 1842 began a settlement near Pine Lake, Wisconsin, about thirty miles west of Milwaukee. The colony was called New Uppsala but did not succeed as a community enterprise.

New Uppsala had been visited by an Episcopal clergyman, Rev. J. Lloyd Breck, rector of the school near Nashotah where men were educated for the Episcopal priesthood. Unonius was deeply impressed with what he thought

---

[171]Arden, *Augustana Heritage*, p. 193.

[172]*Ibid.*, p. 196.

151

was the close similarity between the Lutheran Church in Sweden and the Episcopalian Church. "Both were governed by bishops. And had not the Swedish churches on the Delaware been turned over to the Episcopalians?"[173]

In the light of his conviction, Unonius attempted to draw the newly arrived Swedish Lutheran immigrants into the Episcopalian Church but on the basis that they could remain Lutheran. A congregation was founded under the name: "The Scandinavian Parish at Pine Lake." This enterprise also failed. The parish soon divided into the St. John's English Lutheran Church and the Holy Innocent Episcopal Church. Unonius went on to study at the new Episcopal seminary at Nashotah, Wisconsin, and was ordained into the priesthood of the Protestant Episcopal Church. In 1849 he was called to Chicago to take charge of the newly formed Swedish-Norwegian parish, St. Ansgarius.

The nine years Unonius labored in Chicago before he returned to Sweden in 1858 were marked by bitter antagonism between him and the Swedish Lutheran pastors. The relationship was not helped by the statement of the priest of St. Ansgarius that the Swedish pastors were not Lutherans and had abandoned the Lutheran practices in Sweden. The basic ground for this accusation was that Esbjörn and Hasselquist did not wear the customary Swedish ministerial garb. This was a concession which the two pastors had made out of anxiety that the Swedish clerical vestments might offend their more pietistic congregations in Andover and Galesburg, Illinois.[174]

Some years later, the old dream of Unonius for a union between the Swedish Lutherans in America and the Protestant Episcopal Church was revived. The leading figure who worked for a union was Henry J. Whitehorse, Protestant Episcopal Bishop of Illinois. In 1865 and 1866 he was appointed by the Bishop of London, A. C. Tait, to inspect the Anglican congregations in Sweden. A close friendship developed between Bishop Whitehorse and Henrik Reuterdahl, Archbishop of Uppsala. The American bishop invited the Swedish prelate to participate in the consecration of the new Anglican church in Stockholm, the Church of St. Peter and St. Sigfrid on June 13, 1866. This Archbishop Reuterdahl did along with other Swedish ecclesiastical dignitaries. Whitehorse left no doubt as to his acceptance of Swedish apostolic succession as valid and communicated that attitude to his fellow Anglicans.[175]

[173]O. N. Olson, *The Augustana Lutheran . . .* , p. 60. The reference to the "Churches on the Delaware" is in relation to the colonial settlement of Lutherans at Fort Christiana (now Wilmington) Delaware in 1638. At least seven Lutheran parishes (Pennypach, Kristina, Racson, Pennsneck, Vicasou, Kingsessing and Upper Merion) were established. As the years went by, the inability and unwillingness of the Lutheran Church in Sweden to supply pastors plus the acculturation of the Swedish people toward the American language changed these parishes into Episcopal churches. See Carl Henrik Lyttkens, *The Growth of Swedish-Anglican-Intercommunion Between 1833 and 1922*, trans. Neil Tomkinson (Bibliotheca Theologiae Practical Series; Lund: CWK Gleerups Förlag, 1970), pp. 81-82.

[174]Lindquist, . . . , *The Story of Erland Carlsson*, p. 56.

[175]Lyttkens, pp. 55-57.

Whitehorse hoped to use the ministry of the Protestant Episcopal Church
in America to work among the Swedish Lutheran immigrants. To that end,
three years after the departure of Unonius, Whitehorse accepted from
Sweden a Swedish Lutheran minister, Jacob Bredberg, to be priest in the St.
Ansgarius parish in Chicago where Unonius had served.[176] Bredberg
worked there from 1861 to 1877. He was not required to be ordained as an
Anglican—another indication of Whitehorse's acceptance of the
authenticity of Swedish Lutheran orders.[177]

Four years after Whitehorses' visit to Sweden, Dr. J. P. Tustin in 1870
was sent from America to Sweden to further union between the Protestant
Episcopal and the Augustana Churches. One factor in favor of the
Episcopalian's hope was the attitude of Archbishop Reuterdahl. The latter's
view toward the Augustana Lutherans continued to be negative. Because it
did not have an episcopate, he had grave doubts that the Swedish Lutheran
Church in America could avoid disintegration. Therefore, he was favorably
inclined toward an episcopacy for Augustana.

But there were counteracting forces. One was, interestingly enough,
Hasselquist who was also in Sweden during the spring and summer of 1870.
He was fully aware of the gestures being made by the Episcopal Church.
Although his chief purpose for the journey was to recruit ministers for
Augustana, he also went to Sweden to oppose the designs of the Protestant
Episcopal Church.[178] Hasselquist and Tustin met in Fjellstedt's home in
Göteborg. Tustin proposed that a pastor from Sweden should be
consecrated as bishop so that the Augustana and Protestant Episcopal
churches could have eucharistic fellowship.[179] Hasselquist saw this as a
threat not only to the existence of Augustana as a church but as a move to
proselyte Swedish Lutherans in America to become Episcopalians.

One might assume that in view of his friendliness to the Anglican Church
in his earlier days, Fjellstedt would have been sympathetic to such a
proposal. Not so. Fjellstedt argued from the Lutheran confessions that the
congregation had power to install a minister. On the basis of the Smalcald
Articles, he was referring to the statement that if bishops are unwilling to be
responsible for providing faithful and true ministers, then the Church is not
compelled to follow them. The confession states:

---

[176]In his letter from Paxton on April 6, 1867, Hasselquist wrote: "The Episcopalians
have certainly constantly sought after the Swedes but have been unable to accomplish
anything, mostly because of their poor priestly representatives, first Unonius and later
from Sweden the infringement of Bredsberg." Hasselquist appealed to Fjellstedt for his
help "not your theological thought, only your brotherly opinion on the question."
Interestingly, Hasselquist did not indict episcopacy as such. "We do not fight against the
principle of the office of bishop as such but we must as Lutherans make battle against
"Apostolic Succession," a teaching which is against the material principle of the
Reformation." Westin, p. 146-47.

[177]Lyttkens, p. 103.

[178]Stephenson, pp. 233-34.

[179]Anshelm, 3:350-51.

> We have an ancient example in the Church of the fathers that we ourselves should ordain those men who are sent. The Pope could neither forbid nor advance this practice according to his own law. . . . The holy Hieronymus in the Church at Alexandria noted that in the beginning the Church was guided without bishops over the lower clergy.[180]

On that basis, Fjellstedt agreed with Hasselquist. In an irenic statement, he wrote:

> I bow in deep humility to the apostolic order, but papist orders we are bound to reject, and this very house the Protestant Church needs to be on guard against popish elements. The successionist idea marks a return from spirit to flesh, from Christ to the sons of Aaron, and it is in fact contrary to the letter and spirit of the New Testament. As transmitted through a chain of popes the succession becomes still more unreasonable.[181]

A change in Fjellstedt's earlier favorable impression of the Anglican orders is obvious. Two factors have to be taken into account. First, Fjellstedt had a big investment in the Augustana Lutheran Church. Its polity was much more in keeping with his own church orientation than was the episcopal order either of England or Sweden. He had been instrumental in recruiting several men for the Augustana ministry. By 1870 the Augustana Lutheran Church was an independent functioning body which could point to a growth since its founding a decade earlier of more than fourfold (from 3747 to 16,376 communicants).[182] Although this Church could claim only 16.8% of the total Swedish population in America, the figure of one out of six is not unimpressive when the chaotic frontier, conflict with other religious bodies, the difficult adjustment to radically different conditions as an independent church body in contrast to the stable and traditional Swedish situation, and the scattered locations of the Swedish immigrants are taken into consideration. Fjellstedt could not help but be encouraged as he saw the Church as he understood it enjoying success; he had contributed significantly to its development.

Secondly, the confessional view which had developed in Fjellstedt governed his position. Had he spoken earlier in his life from his experience with the Anglicans, he might have come to another stance. Fjellstedt, however, was too confessionally oriented to come to a different conclusion. Asserting his view from that of the Lutheran confessions, he was encountering not Anglicanism but the Roman Catholic position from the sixteenth century. Not untypical of nineteenth century Protestantism, Fjellstedt was definitely convinced of the grave errors of the Church over which the Bishop of Rome presided. His utterances against that Church were numerous. In 1846, he wrote:

---

[180]Article III in *Svenska Kyrkans Bekännelseskrifter*, p. 335.

[181]Ernst W. Olson, *The Swedish Element in Illinois: Survey of the Past Seven Decades* (Chicago: Swedish American Biographical Association, 1917), pp. 89-90.

[182]Arden, *Augustana Heritage*, p. 127.

> The members of the Catholic Church do not have the good fortune to possess the pure, unadulterated teaching such as our churches teach and confess. Their teaching is blended with much dangerous heresy. But they are much more zealous to spread their teaching and widen the influence of their Church than we Lutherans are to spread our pure, unadulterated teaching and to work for the extension of our Church.[183]

It is not surprising, therefore, that Fjellstedt responded as he did to the Protestant Episcopal attempt to form a union with the Augustana Lutheran Church, notwithstanding his earlier positive attitude toward Anglican orders. There is no evidence that he ever lost his appreciation of, and gratitude for, the Anglican Church. Yet, when faced with the principle of apostolic succession within the confessional position which he cherished in the Lutheran Church, together with the pragmatic situation of the Augustana Church to which he had such a close relationship, he could react in no other way.

Fjellstedt was important to Augustana as it forged its view of the Church. The use of the figure of the body and its members gave to Augustana a sense of unity beyond that of an individual congregation. Associated with its commitment to Word and Sacrament as the means of grace, the body/member served as a bulwark against separatism. Its view of the ministry as influenced by Fjellstedt provided a protection against a destructive individualism which was especially strong in nineteenth century America. Too, its rejection of the episcopacy was important not in the sense that a particular form of polity was questioned. Rather, Hasselquist sensed the wrong use of episcopal polity. In this, Fjellstedt, more sympathetic to that form of Church government, nevertheless, supported Hasselquist. Fjellstedt was able to do this, first, because he was not tied to a particular form of polity. Secondly, he was sufficiently incisive to recognize that a system could be corrupt.

The conclusions on the basis from which Fjellstedt—and the leadership of Augustana—worked were sound. Fjellstedt came to an understanding of the Church, first, on biblical grounds. Secondly, he was theological (in the sense of God-oriented) and Christological in his thought. Finally, he knew well the position of the Lutheran confessions. By addressing these issues, he greatly helped Augustana. To know itself as the Church as formulated in its doctrine was to have an answer to the important problem of self-identity. Assuming the soundness of its ecclesiological doctrine, Augustana was able to go forward, face its failures as well as successes and thus make a contribution, not only to America, but to the ministry of the one, holy, catholic, apostolic Church. To that end, Fjellstedt's influence was highly significant.

iii. The Fjellstedt School

Among the channels through which Fjellstedt impact was exercised upon the Augustana Lutheran Church, none was more concrete than the third: the institution which he founded and eventually bore his name, the Fjell-

---

[183]*Lunds Missions-Tidning* (December).

stedt School.[184] In his comprehensive study of Augustana pastors, Conrad Bergendoff has identified twenty-nine men, ordained between the years 1860 and 1910, who came to Augustana as students from this School.[185] The students completed their studies at Augustana College, and, upon a call from a congregation, were ordained into the Augustana ministry. The influence of these men upon the many people they served in the several congregations is impossible to ascertain. Certainly their contributions were considerable.

(1) *Problems of relation of Fjellstedt to the School*

Before a consideration of the character of the Fjellstedt School and its specific contribution to Augustana can be undertaken, it is necessary to face the problem of Fjellstedt's relation to the School. Only three of the men who became pastors of Augustana churches (Olof Olsson, Gustaf Peters and A. W. Dahlsten) attended the School while Fjellstedt was director of it. He left at the end of the academic year in 1861 and did not return to the Institution until 1877 when he took up residence there for the final four years of his life. During that latter period, only four Augustana pastors attended the School (A. Palmstrom, J. Torell, J. E. Nystrom and E. J. Werner). There is little doubt that the respected churchman through his teaching, preaching and simply his presence had much influence upon these men. Still, the fact remains that twenty-two men who later were ordained into the Augustana ministry or nearly three-fourths of all who attended the Fjellstedt School were students there when Fjellstedt was no longer associated, in an official capacity, with the School. During the 1860's, after Fjellstedt left Uppsala, he had little direct connection with the School. With the beginning of Johannes Kjerfstedt's rectorship in 1870, Fjellstedt again became more active. In the last decade of his life until his death in January, 1881, the School came increasingly to occupy Fjellstedt's central interest. Still, one must ask, can this Institution be regarded as an important channel through which he influenced Augustana?

The response to this question must be answered positively. In the first place, education was a central concern of Fjellstedt all his life. Carl Anshelm observed that beginning as a tutor at the age of eleven until his final

---

[184]When the School first bore the name "Fjellstedt" is not clear. One view holds that this occurred in 1862 after it had been in Uppsala since 1860. (C. A. Cornelius, *Handbok I Svenska Kyrkans Historia* [*Handbook of Swedish Church History*] (Uppsala: Edquist and Bergland, 1867, p. 282). Carl Anshelm, however, wrote that with the departure of Fjellstedt from the active leadership of the School, the institution came to be known as "The Former Fjellstedt School," a designation it was to bear for several years. (*Peter Fjellstedt Och Hans Betydelse Förtillkomsten Av Fjellstedtska Skolan* [*Peter Fjellstedt and His Significance to the Origin of the Fjellstedt School*] Uppsala: Almquist och Wiksells Boktrycken, A.B., 1931), p. 19.

[185]Conrad Bergendoff, *The Augustana Ministerium: A Study of the Careers of the 2504 Pastors of the Augustana Lutheran Synod/Church: 1850-1962* (Rock Island, Ill.: Augustana Historical Society, 1980).

residence at the Fjellstedt School in Uppsala, he was almost continuously engaged in education.[186] During his school years both in Karlstad and Lund, he supported himself as a tutor. His decade of work on the mission fields in South India and Asia Minor was basically as an educator. Even before leaving Europe for Asia, he had been at Basel as a teacher for almost a year. On his departure from Basel, the director of the Institute, Christian Blumhardt, expressed real regret at the loss of the pedagogical talent which Fjellstedt possessed. When he returned to Sweden, it was to organize and direct the Lund Institute. With that institution in its three locations at Lund, Stockholm and Uppsala, Fjellstedt was actively involved from 1846 to 1862.

In addition to these educational endeavors, Fjellstedt for a period of four years (1848-51) edited *Folkskolan*. His deep concern for the education of the Swedish people was expressed in the first issue of that journal. Two aims were articulated: first, to encourage the maintenance of folk schools which would teach children the difference between right and wrong, good morals, sound thinking and, above all, the Christian faith. "All children, regardless of individual physical or mental differences, were to have an opportunity to develop their unique talents." The aims for this journal were directed in a time when popular education was not yet a fact in Sweden's society.[187] In light of that truth, the second aim was to provide study helps to be used in the home. Lessons were given with questions on the Bible, essays on educational philosophy (e.g., Luther's views), lessons in music, methods of education, guides for teaching and learning astronomy, English, geography and history. Fjellstedt summed up this second aim:

> [It is] a paper for rural folks, children, school teachers and other friends and leaders in education. Its aim is to participate in the education of people, give instructions which are adaptable for the promotion of this important enterprise in the home as well as in the school and especially for the spread of the basic Christian principles for education in general.[188]

Fjellstedt's view of education was greatly shaped by the Bible and Luther. However, he was not restricted to those sources. Several articles showed his sympathetic inclination toward the educational philosophy of Johann Heinrich Pestalozzi (1746-1827), the Swiss educator.[189] Pestalozzi's ideas were considered revolutionary with their emphasis upon teaching as a process from the familiar to the new, stress on performance of the concrete arts, experience of emotional responses, and pacing of the educational process according to each child's development. His admiration for Pestalozzi's philosophy of education identified Fjellstedt as an educator with an open mind sympathetic to new ideas.

---

[186] Anshelm, *Peter Fjellstedt Och Hans Betydelses* . . . , p. 19.

[187] See above, p. 49.

[188] "Förord" (January 1848).

[189] August 1849, pp. 114ff. A series of articles on Pestalozzi appeared starting with the January issue of 1851 and through the July edition of the same year. Also, see above, p. 49.

From 1862 until his return to the School in 1877, he was occupied in parish work and preaching tours. Yet, even then, Fjellstedt continued to teach and give Bible studies. Allan Parkman, present rector of the Fjellstedt School, said that Fjellstedt's teaching attracted even larger crowds than his preaching and that he was more popular as a teacher than a preacher.[190]

His commitment to teaching leads one to suppose he could not easily disassociate himself from the central vocation of the Institution where he had spent so many years. One example of his continued interest was the use to which he put his journalism in behalf of the School. When the Institution faced financial crisis—which was often in the 1860's—Fjellstedt made pleas for the School. In the December issue (1866) of *Lunds Missions-Tidning*, he wrote that the congregations of the Lutheran Church in Sweden were badly in need of pastors. This placed them in a relationship of dependence upon the Fjellstedt School which at that time had thirty-two students. He wrote: "Do not forget this school. We pray that the love of Christ will enlighten and warm your hearts. Pray that with money and power this school may be established and supported. Success, obedience in prayer and blessings shall not fail and eventually to you shall come joy and gladness because your work in the Lord was not in vain."[191]

Another indication of his uninterrupted interest was the nature of Augustana's reliance upon Fjellstedt and the School. On July 27, 1869, Hasselquist wrote to his Swedish friend and asked his judgment about two students: "Joh. Sandén who is in the former Fjellstedt School in Uppsala and Wikstrand in Skara who has gone through 6 classes."[192] It is scarcely likely that Hasselquist would have written for such information had not Fjellstedt been actively associated with the Institution.

Finally, the invitation of the students at the School to the aged Fjellstedt in 1876 demonstrated that his connection with the School had been lively and well known. Certainly there must have been a near reverent respect for his name as the students wrote to him that they would receive him as eagerly as Jacob had received his son Joseph. They addressed him as the earthly father of the School. Such a letter bespeaks a close relationship between Fjellstedt and the School.

In the light of these facts—his deep concern and lifelong interest in education, his use of journalism in behalf of the School, his continuing reliance upon the School in his aid to Augustana, his concern for the continuation of the School as he urged his fellow Swedes to give generously for its support and his choice of the Institution as his last residence—it is difficult to argue that his absence from the School between 1862 and 1877 also meant withdrawal of his influence from it.

[190]Interview, December 2, 1979.

[191]21:186.

[192]Westin, p. 239. For several years after Fjellstedt's departure from the School, it was known as the Former Fjellstedt School. As late as mid 1875 correspondence collected by Westin employed that designation (p. 389). References thereafter again called the institution simply Fjellstedt School.

(2) *The character of the School*

The essential character of the School was articulated in the first of ten regulations:

> The Fjellstedt School has as its objective and hope the education of God-fearing and gifted youths to become faithful and diligent pastors for the Swedish Church. The educational program reaches out to those who have already reached some maturity and development and who desire a vigorous advance in studies. For such, the opportunity is given to enjoy strict Christian supervision and care and to acquire the knowledge and development such as a complete basic institution in the classical course is designed to impart.[193]

Apart from the purpose of the School to serve needy students who wanted to become pastors (which the document included in the fifth regulation), this statement expressed the nature of the Institution. There was an emphasis upon *discipline* ("Strict Christian supervision and care"), the *academic character* ("knowledge and development such as a complete basic instruction in the classical course is designed to impart") and *service* ("education of God-fearing and gifted youths to become faithful and diligent pastors").

Discipline.—This emphasis upon discipline began with the assumption that the students were God-fearing. Faithful attendance at religious functions was required. Students were expected to be diligent in their studies and to respect their teachers. Bad books, theaters and places of like nature were to be avoided. Exercise was not to be neglected and good care of health was to be observed. A day-book of how well each student handled his finances was to be kept and a report was to be made each week to the School treasurer. Lectures and presentations outside of the School could be attended only by permission of the authorities. Instruction of less capable students by the more advanced scholars under the direction of the School was encouraged. Even on vacation, when the students were away, its rules applied. During those absences, it was recommended that close assocation should be formed with a pastor.[194] Parents of boys as young as ten years of age were assured they need have no worries. Their sons would never be allowed to leave the School without adult companionship.[195]

An important aspect of this discipline related to studies. Would-be applicants were warned that they were expected to take seriously the opportunities for scholarship offered to them by the School. In *Bibelvännen* (May 1863), it was stated: "The directors perceive that it is not appropriate

---

[193]*Fjellstedtska Skolans Stadgar* [*The Regulations of the Fjellstedt School*] (Uppsala, Edv. Berlings Boktrycheri, n.d.), p. 1.

[194]"F. D. Fjellstedtska Skolan in Uppsala," *Lunds Missions-Tidning*, 21 (December 1866), pp. 182-83.

[195]"Missions-Skolan" ["The Mission School"] *Lunds Missions-Tidning*, 10 (July 1857), p. 110.

to allow entry into the school . . . to those who would tend to stay so long that they would not be able to gain the greater good from the school."[196]

Academic character.—The expectations which were assumed reflected the high standards Fjellstedt had set for the Institution. Of primary importance was the Christian character of the applicants. "Above all, they should have a well proven and decisive inner call to some Christian vocation whether it be the desire to become a missionary to the heathen or to go into the service of the Church in our fatherland."[197]

Fjellstedt's dominant concern for the spiritual character of the students, however, was by no means used to lower academic requirements. Under his influence, as well as that of his successors, high standards were set. Boys as young as ten years of age were allowed entry but only if they had sufficient ability. All applicants should have an elementary knowledge of Swedish grammar, history, geography and satisfactory skill in counting and writing in order to enter the School.

Successful matriculation was no guarantee that the student was assured of continuation at the Fjellstedt School. In June 1858, it was reported in *Lunds Missions-Tidning* that seven students had left the School basically because "of the inability to do adequate work."[198] In a later issue of that paper (August 1861), a similar report was given: "Some [students] have been separated from the School because they have lacked the needed gifts."[199]

The curriculum followed the classical tradition. There were four courses in Latin which included instruction in *Cicero, Caesar and the Gallican Wars* and *Aristides and Timon;* three courses in Greek including *Xenophon* and

---

[196]"Tillkännagifvande" ["Announcements"] 16:80.

[197]"Missions-Skolan," *Lunds Missions-Tidning,* 10 (July 1857), p. 110.

[198]"Missions-Skolan," 11 (June 1858), p. 84.

[199]The concern for excellence on Fjellstedt's part was continued in the work of the School. For example, in 1896, under the capable leadership of Johannes Kjerfstedt, it was reported that of the total number of students who were then studying theology at the University of Uppsala, one fifth of those had been students at the Fjellstedt School. (*Förhandlingar Vid Den Sjette Allmänna Svensk-Lutherska Prästkonferns I Stockholm Den 1-3 September, 1896* [*Deliberations of the Sixth General Pastors' Conference in Stockholm September 1-3, 1896*] (Stockholm: Tidningsaktiebolaget vårt Lands tryckeri, 1896), p. 202. The School was of sufficiently high calibre to serve as a model for other institutions. In 1923, the Church Society of the Evangelical Lutheran Faith was founded at Göteborg "to preserve and further the apostolic faith of our fathers according to the Lutheran Evangelical faith . . . and for the preservation and strengthening of our Swedish Church in that Spirit." The Göteborg Private Gymnasium for future pastors was founded in close relation to the Society, to be supported by free will contributions, and to serve as "a western counterpart to the Fjellstedt School in Uppsala." Fred Lindroth och Sven Norbrink, *Den svenska kyrkan: kyrkokunskap för kyrka, skola och hem* [*The Swedish Church: Churchly Knowledge For Church, School and Home*], femte, omarbetade upplagen [fifth revised edition] (Stockholm: Svenska Kyrkans Diakonistryrelses Bokförlag, 1960), p. 368.

grammar; three courses in German; one course in French; two, in Ancient History; four, in mathematics. Instruction in religion excluded the *Catechism* since all students had been confirmed. It was felt sufficient education in religion was available through the worship services which all students were required to attend. Students were expected to participate in the Bible studies which were conducted on Sundays both at the School and at the nearby *Trefaldighetskyrkan* (Trinity Church). Religious instruction was given in the upper classes in theology, New Testament, dogmatics and church history. Each student was allowed to study according to his own rate of progress.[200]

The Fjellstedt School appeared to have awakened in its students a lively curiosity and a strong desire for knowledge. Anders Olof Bersell (1853-1903) who came to America and had an impressive career as a teacher at Augustana College entered the Fjellstedt School in the autumn of 1872. He was a very capable student. Some years previous to his arrival at Uppsala, he had studied at the folk school in Mora where he demonstrated unique ability in language study. In 1868, he had entered the junior seminary in Mora where he completed its course in five weeks. That he studied for five years at the Fjellstedt School spoke well for the Institution in that such a good student at Bersell could occupy himself so long with the study opportunities it offered. He thought the teachers were very strict but he was drawn to them and admired them greatly.[201]

Bersell later studied at the University in Uppsala. There he belonged to the Christian Society, *Pro Facultate Dicendi*, which had its headquarters in a place called "Fjellstedtianum." This group was exclusively for those who had been students at the Fjellstedt School. Discussions were held on academic subjects. The inspiration gained from the Fjellstedt School was thus demonstrated to have been on a high and serious level. Later, at Augustana, Bersell taught Greek, which was his speciality, but his duties also included courses in Christianity, philosophy, German, Latin and Greek. The emphasis upon liberal arts at Augustana may well have been influenced by Bersell as a consequence of his five years as a student at the Fjellstedt School.

Service.—Beginning with Fjellstedt's departure as director of the School in 1862, the scope of its service was defined in a more limited manner. The new leadership announced that henceforth the School would no longer be a mission school. Hence, after Fjellstedt's departure, the School changed in character. It became a gymnasium. It was pre-university in its intention with the objective to prepare future pastors to enter the university. One likely reason for this change was the financial stringency which faced the Institution. The action was justified by saying that persons desiring to be educated for work in missions could go to other schools such as Basel or

[200]F. D. Fjellstedtska skolan i Uppsala," p. 181. "F. D." stands for "Fordom den"—the Former Fjellstedt School as it was known for several years after Fjellstedt's departure from the institution in 1861.

[201]*Korsbaneret*, 1905, pp. 155-74 *passim*.

Leipzig, but no other preparatory school existed in Sweden for those who wanted to be pastors.[202]

This view of service from the School to the Church was considerably limited from the intentions of Fjellstedt. He wanted it to remain true to its original purpose—to educate young men for the mission field as well as the ministry. In the year of the change of leadership, Fjellstedt warned that the School must not forget its ministry to educate persons for the service of the Swedish Missionary Society.[203]

The service which the School had contributed to the Church at large was impressive. In 1896, thirty-four years after Fjellstedt's departure as its first director, Professor C. Norrby represented the School at a pastor's conference in Stockholm. As a representative of the Uppsala Theological Faculty, he surveyed the achievements of the Fjellstedt School. Included in his report were the following statistics: of the 231 students of the Fjellstedt School who had passed the student examinations during its history, 119 had become pastors of the Church in Sweden; thirty had or were working among their countrymen in America;[204] three had become missionaries in Zululand; two worked as missionaries in East Africa, one in India and one in China. One was a university professor; two were heads of general education; four were adjunct teachers; two were professors in America [Olof Olsson and Anders Bersell] and one was head of a missionary school in Lapland.[205]

How many young men in addition to those who attended the Fjellstedt School were inspired to come to America by Peter Fjellstedt remains unknown. C. O. Hultgren, the capable and respected pastor of First Lutheran Church, Jamestown, New York for thirty-one years (1864-1895) attributed his early Christian awakening to the preaching he and his family heard from "Dr. Fjellstedt and other true, Christian minded pastors."[206] Another Augustana pastor who did not attend the Fjellstedt School was Nils J. Brink. He was recommended to Hasselquist by Fjellstedt in the autumn of 1870. Brink left Sweden and studied at Augustana College for two years after which he was ordained.

It was from the Fjellstedt School that Augustana most concretely benefitted from Fjellstedt's ministry. The confidence in him, so unqualifiedly shown throughout the years, extended also to the School. In a letter written to C. A. Torén from Paxton on March 18, 1871, Hasselquist rejected a student whom Torén had recommended. He did so on the basis of a sermon by the student which he had read. He justified his action in the

---

[202]*Ibid.*, p. 178.

[203]"Missions-Skolan," *Lunds Missions-Tidning* 15 (August 1862), 115.

[204]Present research indicates twenty-nine students from the School between 1858 and 1910 became pastors of the Augustana Lutheran Church. There may well have been some who came to America but returned to Sweden. Hence, the figure of thirty need not be a contradiction.

[205]*Förhandlingar . . . sjette allmänna svensk-lutherska prästkonferens*, pp. 200-202.

[206]*Korsbaneret*, 1902, p. 143.

following statement: "We need men, if possible, who are equipped with both knowledge and gifts but especially with hearts that are given to the Lord and so possess a lively desire to offer their strengths and days in his service; such shall have enough work and can be certain of finding blessing and bread." Hasselquist faulted the Mother Church for its lack of attention to the education of pastors and then added: "We are waiting for help from the Fjellstedt School. . . . [It] sends us a large number of Evangelicals."[207]

Hasselquist gave high tribute to his friend in Sweden when four and a half months after the death of Fjellstedt an article appeared in *Augustana och Missionären* (May 18, 1881) with comments over Hasselquist's signature. It incorporated a statement Fjellstedt had written in 1879 in regard to the Fjellstedt School. Fjellstedt had called the statement "a kind of Testament" which he wanted to lay upon the hearts of the friends of the School. The Testament was a plea for their continuing support. He justified the appeal on the ground that it was the Lord's work. He further substantiated his right to ask for their concern by noting that the regulations of the School were according to the Lutheran confessions.[208]

This invitation of Fjellstedt to friends of the School was very impressive to Hasselquist as he faced the struggles of Augustana College, so recently relocated in Rock Island. He wrote:

> Certainly our readers will be glad to note his "testament," for only through such a statement is one remembered. The undersigned feels no little desire to write a similar testament in relation to Augustana College and Theological Seminary which certainly needs faithful and continuing friends and which has an even greater significance than the Fjellstedt School inasmuch that it is the only tolerably good and complete educational establishment for our countrymen in America.[209]

Appreciation for Peter Fjellstedt and the Fjellstedt School was not an attitude limited only to Hasselquist and his generation contemporary with Fjellstedt's own life. Fifty-nine years later, Gustav Andreen, then president emeritus of Augustana College, following the death of two former Fjellstedt students who had been pastors in the Augustana Lutheran Church to which they had made rich contributions, wrote in tribute both to the Fjellstedt School and its founder:

> This Christian school was founded by P. Fjellstedt in 1856 with the special aim to instruct and prepare young men for theological studies in the university for the purpose to enter either in the office of the ministry or for mission work in heathen fields. In our early history as an Augustana Synod, Fjellstedt was a spiritual father who gave both good counsel and support to our churchly work in America. Hasselquist consulted with him about the procurement of men from Sweden, full of

---

[207]Westin, p. 296.

[208]The first paragraph of article two reads: "The School is established upon evangelical Lutheranism as defined by the Augsburg Confession and the "decision of the Upsala [*sic*) meeting [1593]" *Fjellstedtska Skolans Stadgar*, p. 1).

[209]"Dr. Fjellstedts Testamente," p. 308.

zeal for the Lord, who could become pastors in the many congregations which were continually being built during the period of large immigration. Fjellstedt also recommended among others several who attended the Fjellstedt School. There under God's leading they learned to appreciate both the need for inner spiritual life and the demanding requirements of congregational work. Some twenty could well be named who have come to us from the Fjellstedt School and worked with much blessing among our Swedish American church people. As a Synod we owe a great debt of gratitude to this school in Upsala [sic] for the blessed work which has gone forth both for the Swedish Church at large and for the spiritual power it sent to the Augustana Synod when it had a crying need and workers were few. The last of these Fjellstedters among us in our Synod have died during the year: namely, Dr. S. G. Öhman of the New York Conference and Dr. S. G. Youngert of the Augustana Seminary. Thanks be to God for Fjellstedt and the Fjellstedt School for the blessings which in the past have flowed to us![210]

[210]"Sven Gustaf Youngert," *Korsbaneret*, 1940, pp. 199-201. Dr. Andreen erred on one point. Youngert and Öhman were not the last of the "Fjellstedters." The last of the group was L. E. Sjölinder who died March 17, 1943.

Appendix

I. Biographies of "Fjellstedters"

I

Twenty-nine men who served the Augustana Lutheran Church had their early education in the Fjellstedt School (known as the Mission Institute until 1862). A brief biographical account of each of these men follows. The names will be given chronologically according to the year of ordination.

1. Olof Olsson

Olof Olsson was born to Anders and Britta Olsson March 31, 1841 at Björtorp (the name of their home), Karlskoga in Värmland, Sweden. He studied in the Mission Institute during the year 1858-59. The following year was spent at the Mission Institute in Leipzig. He studied theology at Uppsala University. On December 15, 1863, he was ordained and remained in Sweden until 1869. During those years he served the parishes of: Brunsko, Elgå, Persberg and Sunnemo. In 1869, he emigrated to Lindsborg, Kansas where he became the first pastor of the Bethany Lutheran Church. In 1876, he became professor of theology at Augustana Theological Seminary. In 1891, he was named president of Augustana College and Theological Seminary. For a brief time during this last period on leave for health reasons, Olsson served the Lutheran Church in Woodhull, Illinois.

Olsson wrote a number of books which included: *Vid Korset* [*At the Cross*]; *Helsningar från Fjerran* [*Greetings From Afar*]; *Det Kristna Hoppet* [*The Christian Hope*]; *Till Rom Och Hem Igen* [*To Rome and Home Again*]; and *Reformationen Och Socinianismen* [*The Reformation and Socinainism*]. He died at the age of fifty-nine on May 12, 1900.[1]

2. Gustaf Peters

Gustaf Peters was born January 4, 1832 at Åskeda in the province of Småland to Peter Emanuel Anderson and his wife, Eva (Jacobsdotter). In 1854 and 1855 he studied at a seminary for school teachers in Kalmar. In 1857 and 1858 he attended the Mission Institute in Stockholm. He also studied for one year at the catechetical school in Ahlborg.

Peters arrived in Chicago in 1859 and became assistant to Erland Carlsson. He was ordained June 10, 1860 at the organizational meeting of the Augustana Church. He served four congregations, two in Illinois (First, Moline and First, Rockford) and two in Nebraska (Swedish Lutheran, Omaha and Swedish Lutheran, York). He was a *"lasare* preacher." He had received no formal theological education; his preparation was confined to

---

[1]Johannes A. Nyvall, "Doktor O. Olsson," *Korsbaneret*, 1901, pp. 142-66 *passim.*

165

his years in the Fjellstedt and Ahlborg Schools and his apprenticeship with Erland Carlsson. He was respected by his colleagues and was elected to several offices including the office of secretary of the Synod. He died October 26, 1918, at the age of eighty-six.[2]

3. Anders Wilhelm Dahlsten

A. W. Dahlsten was born in Näshult, Småland November 7, 1836. It is not clear how many years Dahlsten attended the Mission Institute but certainly he was there in 1858-59. He may have been there longer because he wrote that he went through the Fjellstedt School.[3] Dahlsten left Sweden August 31, 1859, on the same boat which carried Gustaf Peters to America.

He began his education in the States under the professorship of Esbjörn at Illinois State University in Springfield and later continued his studies at the newly organized Augustana College and Theological Seminary in Chicago. He was ordained in 1861. He served seven congregations: two in Illinois (Rockford and Galesburg), four in Kansas (Fremont and Salemsborg, both of which he organized, and Assaria and New Andover) and one in Idaho Springs, Colorado. Dahlsten was motivated to move from Galesburg because so many of his members had moved to Kansas.

Dahlsten served as the first president of the Kansas Conference and in many positions of trust in the Church. His ministry was exercised not only in the Church but also in civic matters. While he was at Salemsborg, he organized seven public school districts. He retired in 1909. He died on March 4, 1918 at the age of eighty-one.[4]

4. Sven Gustaf Larson

Sven G. Larson was born January 20, 1833 in Kalmarlän, Småland. He studied at the Mission Institute until the fall of 1858 when he emigrated to the States. Like Dahlsten, Larson studied under Esbjörn both in Springfield and Chicago. He was ordained June 9, 1861. He served a total of ten congregations: two in Iowa (Burlington and Council Bluffs), four in Illinois (Knoxville, Altona, Sycamore and New Windsor), one in each of the following places: Omaha, Nebraska; Worcester, Massachusetts; Kansas City, Missouri; Pueblo, Colorado.

The simple record of the congregations where Larson was the pastor fails to tell the zeal of this dedicated man. Like his mentor, Peter Fjellstedt, he had a great enthusiasm for missionary endeavor. He went to Nebraska in 1868. There he organized the first Swedish Evangelical Lutheran Church in

[2]Autobiography in Norelius, *De Svenska Lutherska . . . historia i Amerika*, 1: 472-76 *passim*; L. G. Abrahamson, "Gustaf Peters," *Korsbaneret*, 1920, pp. 123-28 *passim*.

[3]"Anders Wilhelm Dahlsten," *Korsbaneret*, 1919, p. 142. There is confusion in that Dahlsten said the school was in Uppsala. Since, however, he left Sweden July 27, 1859, the interpretation of Dahlsten's statement must be that he was referring to its location at the time he wrote it. Fjellstedt's report showed that Dahlsten was a student at the School while it was in Stockholm.

[4]*Ibid.*, pp. 141-48 *passim*.

Omaha and built the first Swedish church building in that state. With Omaha as his base, he did missionary work in the area west of the city. That was an important center from which immigrants left for regions farther west. His work in Saunders County resulted in four strong congregations. He served the Church in a number of responsible offices.

He retired to a small farm three miles south of Mead, Nebraska, after thirty-nine years of service as a pastor in the Augustana Lutheran Church. On November 11, 1904, he died at the age of seventy-one.[5]

5. Jonas Petter Nilson Nyquist

J. P. N. Nyquist was born at Kristdala, Småland February 8, 1834, to a tenant farmer, Nils Petter Jönsson and his wife, Kristina (Jönsdotter). He began his studies in a parish school and then entered P. A. Ahlberg's School. In 1857, he studied at a seminary for teacher education at Kalmar. To prepare for the ministry, he entered the Fjellstedt School in the autumn of 1863.

In July, 1867, Nyquist received a call from the secretary of the Augustana Lutheran Church, Jonas Swensson, to become a pastor in America. In August, Nyquist sailed for America; he was ordained March 20, 1869. He combined the two aspects of pastor and educator. He served four parishes: three in Illinois (Baileytown, Chicago and Andover) and Edensburg, Nebraska. He also worked as a travelling preacher in Michigan for a brief period.

His educational ministry was exercised in two schools. He spent five years at Gustavus Adolphus College in St. Peter, Minnesota where he worked with some success against strong opposition to make the college co-educational.[6] He was one of the founders and the first president of the Board of Directors of Luther Academy, Wahoo, Nebraska. He was a member of that Board for the remainder of his life. He also served for one year as editor of the shortlived journal, *Missionären*.

His seventeen year ministry was brought to a close by his death in the autumn in 1886 at the age of fifty-two.[7]

6. Michael Sandell

Michael Sandell was born at Ström in the province of Jämtland November 7, 1844. From 1865 to 1868 he was a student at the Fjellstedt School. He emigrated to America in the latter year and from 1868 to 1871, he studied at Augustana College and Theological Seminary. He was ordained on June 11, 1871, at Chisago Lake, Minnesota.

His ministry consisted of four alternate periods in America and Sweden. From 1871 to 1874, he served four congregations at the same time: St. Peter, Sveadahl, Kansas Lake, and Mankato, Minnesota. Due to poor health, he

[5]"Pastor Sven Gustaf Larson," *Korsbaneret*, 1906, pp. 157-66 *passim*.

[6]Women were allowed finally to study at the School but they could not live on campus.

[7]"Pastor J. P. Nyquist," *Korsbaneret*, 1888, pp. 15-43 *passim*.

The Fjellstedt school in Uppsala, to the right, the older part, to the left, added in 1880.

returned to Sweden in 1874 and remained there until 1891. During this second period of his ministry, he established a preaching station in Hillsand, Jämtland. At the same time, he directed both a children's home (Fridsborg Children's Home) and a mission school for persons preparing for the ministry.

The second period of his ministry in America extended from 1892 to 1902. He returned to the congregation in St. Peter where he served for ten years before he returned to Sweden. While there, he served on the *Nya Hemlands-Sångboks-Kommittee* [New Homelands Song Book Committee].

In 1902, he returned to Sweden for the fourth and final period of his service. He again directed the work of the Fridsborg Home. He also assumed responsibility for the home for the aged as well as the direction for missionary work in Lapland. Of his ministry it was written: "Many who studied in Sandell's mission school later became pastors in the Augustana Synod and many who through his work were made acquainted with the nature of the Church in that land later became leading laymen in our [Augustana] congregations." Pastor Sandell died on February 21, 1919, at the age of seventy-four after a forty-eight year ministry.[8]

8"Michael Sandell," *Korsbaneret,* 1920, pp. 147-50 *passim.*

7. Anders Olof Bersell

Of all the "Fjellstedters" Anders Bersell was an exception in that he was never ordained. He chose instead to become a teacher, a work for which he was admirably talented.

He was born near Mora in the province of Dalarne. His father's name was Bärs Olof Olsson whose first name, Anglicized, became the beginning of the son's surname when the latter changed his name from Olsson to Bersell.

In preparation for his vocation as a teacher, he entered a seminary for elementary school teachers in 1868. He completed the course in five weeks. Bersell entered the Fjellstedt School in the autumn of 1872 where he studied until 1877. He entered Uppsala University in September of 1877. In December 1879, he passed his theological examinations at a high level of excellence. He accepted a call to become a teacher at the *Evangeliska Lutherska Fosterlandsstiftelsens Missionsskola* in Johannelund. While thus engaged in early 1880, he received two calls to come to America, one as a teacher of Greek and literature at Augustana College, the other, as a teacher at Gustavus Adolphus College. He chose to go to Augustana.

He began his teaching career in the autumn of 1880 and until his death in 1903, Augustana College was the locus of his ministry. He was an able linguist with a good knowledge of Greek, Latin, German and French. The congregation he served for two years as lay pastor in North Henderson, Illinois, wanted him to be ordained, a request which he refused. He edited *Augustana* for two years and assisted in the publication of two other church papers, *Ungdomsvännen* and *Hemvännen*. He was among those who organized the Augustana Book Concern. He translated many works for use in parish education (several from German to Swedish and one into English). Also among his publications was "Notes to Greek Grammar." The high regard Augustana College held for Bersell was shown in 1894 when the school conferred upon him the doctor of philosophy degree.

He died at the age of fifty on December 16, 1903. He had taught at Augustana for twenty-two years.[9]

8. Gustav Lundahl

Gustav Lundahl was born November 1, 1843, at Kil, Värmland. He attended both the Fjellstedt and Ahlborg Schools in preparation for the ministry. He emigrated to America in 1870 and completed his studies at Augustana College and Theological Seminary. Ordained June 29, 1873, he served only three parishes during his forty-four years of active ministry: LaPorte, Indiana (1873-87), Bethany in South Chicago, Illinois (1887-1907) and Hobart-Miller, Indiana (1907-17). At the conclusion of his ministry in Hobart-Miller, he moved to Chicago where for several years he assisted other pastors and preached in vacant congregations. He served as treasurer of the Illinois Conference and as a member of its executive council and of the board of directors of the children's home in Joliet, Illinois. He died January 6, 1934, at the age of ninety.[10]

[9]C. O. Granere, "Dr. Anders Olof Bersell," *Korsbaneret*, 1905, pp. 155-74 *passim*.

[10]"Gustav Lundahl," *Korsbaneret*, 1935, pp. 122-24 *passim*.

9. A. Palmström

A. Palmström was born in Häslöv, Skåne June 28, 1847. He studied at the Fjellstedt School and in 1875 emigrated to America. He was ordained in 1877. He served the congregation in Hastings, Minnesota. He also ministered to the congregation in Welch.[11]

Beginning with much promise, Palmström's career ended disappointingly. In the *Augustana Catalog* of 1884-85, it is written that he was deposed in 1882.[12] The subsequent life of Palmström is apparently unknown. Whatever the reason for the Church's action, there is a sense of pathos about Palmström who showed such promise and later went into obscurity.

10. John Torell

John Torell was born December 20, 1853, in Tengenäs, Västergötland. Following a period of study in the Vännersborg Public High School, he entered Fjellstedt School in the early 1870's. He was invited by Hasselquist to come to America and complete his studies at Augustana College and Theological Seminary. Two years after his entry into that institution, he was ordained in 1877.

Torell was pastor in four congregations: Saronville-Stockholm, Oakland and Swedeburg, Nebraska and Chesterton, Indiana. He was a home missionary for two years with his home base in Kearney, Nebraska. After a twenty-three year ministry at Swedeburg, he resigned to travel for the Augustana Church in behalf of missions in China. For five years, much as Fjellstedt had done in Sweden, Torell travelled over much of America to arouse interest and support for missionary work. He also worked for a time in the Augustana Colonization Association. The purpose of this group was to encourage and help Swedish Lutheran immigrants to establish their own homes under church influence in Minnesota, North and South Dakota, and Canada.

Another concern of Torell's was education. It was basically his initiative which brought about the establishment of Luther Academy at Wahoo, Nebraska. Torell was treasurer of the school for fifteen years.

The present archivist of the Lutheran Church in America wrote: "He was one of the most outstanding pastors in the pioneer period."[13] John Torell died on January 23, 1923, at the age of sixty-nine.[14]

[11]Emil Lund, *Minnesota-Konferensens Av Augustana-Synodens Och Der Församlingars Historia* [*History of the Minnesota Conference and Its Congregations of the Augustana Synod*] (Rock Island, Ill.: Augustana Book Concern, 1926), 1:467.

[12]I am indebted to Conrad Bergendoff for this data communicated to me in a letter dated May 3, 1980.

[13]Letter from Joel W. Lundeen, Lutheran Church in America Archivist, Lutheran School of Theology, Chicago, Illinois to Elmer Vedell, Chesterton, Indiana, May 13, 1970.

[14]C. A. Lönnquist, "John Torell," *Korsbaneret*, 1924, pp. 137-49 *passim*.

11. E. J. Nystrom

E. J. Nystrom was born May 8, 1860, in Borg, Östergötland. He attended
the Fjellstedt School, and at the age of nineteen, emigrated to America. He
completed his studies in America and was ordained June 16, 1889. He
served four parishes: Ottumwa, Iowa; St. Peter, Minnesota; Worchester,
Massachusetts; and the dual parish of Buffalo and Rush Lake, Minnesota
where he died while still in active service. He had completed thirty-seven
years of ministry to the Augustana Lutheran Church when he died on
August 31, 1926, at the age of sixty-six.[15]

12. Erik J. Werner

E. J. Werner was born March 27, 1852, in Tuna, Hälsingland. He began
his studies at a county seminary and spent four years at the Fjellstedt
School. In 1876, he emigrated to America and studied at Augustana College
and Theological Seminary from where he graduated in 1880. He was
ordained on June 20 of the same year. He served six parishes: five in
Minnesota (Chisago City, Tripolis-West Union-Rush City, Gibbon,
Monticello, and Cloquet) and Pierson, Florida. Following his ministry in his
first parish (Chisago City), he was called to be professor in Swedish
language and literature at Gustavus Adolphus College. He taught there
from 1886-1892.

Werner retired in 1916 in Minneapolis. He died on November 5, 1926, at
the age of seventy-four after a ministry of thirty-six years.[16]

13. Pehr Adolf Bergquist

P. A. Bergquist was born February 19, 1855, in Hellestad, Östergötland.
For three years, he was a student in the Fjellstedt School and later for a short
period in the secondary school in Norrköping. In the autumn of 1879, he
came to America, studied at Augustana College and Theological Seminary
and was ordained in July, 1881. During a ministry of thirty-one years, he
served four parishes, all in Pennsylvania: Antrim-Morris Run-McIntrye,
Kane-Wilcox, Wilkes-Barre and Sugar Notch, and Peale where he served
for twenty-four years. He died August 12, 1912, at the age of fifty-seven.[17]

14. Fredrik Nibelius

Fredrik Nibelius was born June 19, 1850 in Hedemore, Dalarne. He
entered the Fjellstedt School in 1871 and studied there until the spring of
1875. In July, 1880, he left for America to begin his studies at Augustana
College and Theological Seminary. He was ordained in 1882. During his
relatively short ministry of fifteen years, he served two Illinois parishes: one
in Englewood for seven years and the other in Ophiem for eight years.

Nibelius was co-editor for two years of *Nåd och Sanning* [*Grace and*

---

[15]A. G. Hammarberg, "E. J. Nystrom," *Korsbaneret*, 1927, pp. 291-94 *passim*.

[16]"Erik J. Werner," *Korsbaneret*, 1928, pp. 217-21 *passim*.

[17]"P. A. Bergquist," *Korsbaneret*, 1913, 193-202 *passim*.

Truth] and *Augustana*. He worked with the music committee for a publication entitled: *Zion's Sångbok för kyrkan och hemmet* [*Zion's Songbook for Church and Home*]. He wrote both articles of prose and poetry. He died on July 4, 1897, at the age of forty-seven.[18]

15. Daniel Renström

Daniel Renström was born June 9, 1855, in Ström, Jämtland. He entered the Fjellstedt School where he studied for four and one-half years (1878-82). His education for the ministry was continued in America at the Augustana College and Theological Seminary. He was ordained June 22, 1884.

His ministry was short. He served two congregations in Iowa: Creston and Swede Valley. He suffered for over a year with a pulmonary infection and died on August 14, 1888, at the age of thirty-three, just four years after his ordination.[19]

16. Victor Vixell

Victor Vixell was born September 3, 1853, in Torskoga, Dalsland. He entered the Fjellstedt School in the autumn of 1877 where he studied for five years. Upon completion of this work there, he emigrated to America and began his studies at Augustana College and Theological Seminary. With high commendation from the Fjellstedt School, he entered into his work at Rock Island in the autumn of 1882. Two years later, he was ordained on June 22 with seventeen others including another "Fjellstedter," Daniel Renström.

He served four parishes: three in Michigan (Manistee, Tustin-Dewings Siding, Menominee) and one in Illinois (Joliet). While at Tustin-Dewings Siding, he also preached in Traverse City and Mancelona. While in Joliet, he was the first president of the board of directors of the children's home which was begun in 1892; he later served as one of its directors.

After eighteen years in the ministry, he died on September 4, 1902.[20]

17. Lawrence Petrus Bergstrom

L. P. Bergstrom was born in Harbo, Västerås March 18, 1858, the son of factory owner Lars Bergstrom and Katarina (Norberg). He was accepted at the Fjellstedt School in 1878. There he achieved an excellent record as a scholar especially in Latin and botany.[21] When P. J. Sward, President of the Minnesota Conference, returned to America after a visit to Sweden in 1883, Bergstrom accompanied him. Following Bergstrom's graduation from Augustana College, he went to Austin, Texas to be a home missionary.

---

[18]"Fredrik Nibelius," *Korsbaneret*, 1898, pp. 85-94 *passim*.

[19]"Pastor Daniel Renström," *Korsbaneret*, 1889, pp. 213-19 *passim*.

[20]F. A. Johnson, "Pastor Victor Vixell," *Korsbaneret*, 1903, pp. 158-67 *passim*.

[21]The high educational quality of the Fjellstedt School is shown by the inclusion of scientific studies in its curriculum.

He returned to Rock Island to study for the ministry. He graduated from the Seminary and was ordained in 1887. He served eight parishes all in Minnesota (Winthrop and Swedhanda, Lancaster, two in St. Paul, Meneiska, Graston and Brunswick, and Minneapolis) except one: Winnipeg and Erickson, Manitoba, Canada.

Bergstrom's ministry went beyond the parish. Between the years 1889 and 1902, he directed campaigns through which a sum of $46,000 was raised to apply to debts on Gustavus Adolphus College and Bethesda Hospital in St. Paul. He was treasurer of the Minnesota Conference (1900-1902). Other offices he held were: president, St. Peter District (1896); president of board of directors, Gustavus Adolphus College (1902); member, board of directors, Augustana College, Bethesda Hospital and Home for the Aged, Chisago City; vice-president, Minnesota Conference (1904-1910); president, Canadian Conference (1914-1916).

Bergstrom gave notable service to the Canadian Conference as mission director. During his seven years there (1909-1916), he was instrumental in organizing thirty-two congregations, assisted in the erection of twelve church buildings, four parsonages, and helped gather funds for the payment of these projects.

He was honored in 1922 when Gustavus Adolphus College conferred upon him the degree of Doctor of Theology. In 1934, Sweden honored him with Knighthood in the Order of Vasa, Second Order, First Class.

Death occurred at the age of seventy-nine on April 28, 1937, after a rich ministry of forty-eight years.[22]

18. Nils Olof Grundén

N. O. Grundén, orphaned at an early age and cared for by a maternal aunt who became as a mother to him, was born March 20, 1857, at Attmar, Medelpad. For several years he studied at the Fjellstedt School. In the summer of 1882 together with several other students from the School, Grundén came to America. He enrolled in Augustana College in the autumn of that year. In 1885, he entered the Seminary for two years of study and was ordained June 26, 1887.

In a ministry of thirty years, he served six parishes, all but one in Minnesota: Lake City, Bernadotte, Moorhead, Oscars Lake, Fargo, North Dakota and Lafayette. During his stay in Fargo, a new church edifice and parsonage were built. On August 31, 1917, he died at the age of sixty.[23]

19. Five "Fjellstedters"

The rich contribution of the Fjellstedt School to the ministry of the Augustana Lutheran Church was dramatized in that five men who had been students at the School were ordained the same year into the Augustana ministry. They were: Sven Gustav Öhman, Johan Fr. Seedoff, Laurent Erik Sjölinder, Erick Wahlfrid Ståhlberg and E. S. Ternberg. They were

[22]Hugo Thorene, "Lawrence Petrus Bergstrom," *Korsbaneret*, 1938, pp. 178-85 *passim.*

[23]J. G. Hultkrans, "Nils Olof Granén," *Korsbaneret*, 1917, pp. 199-203 *passim.*

ordained June 24, 1888. The brief biographies of these men appear in the order of their age, from the oldest to the youngest.

i. Erik Wahlfrid Ståhlberg

E. W. Ståhlberg was born October 10, 1857, in Stjernsund, Dalarne. In 1878, he entered the Fjellstedt School where he studied for three years. In 1882, he emigrated to America and enrolled in the autumn of that year in Augustana College. In the fall of 1886, he entered Augustana Seminary from where he was graduated in 1888. On June 24 of that year, he was ordained on a call to Dahlsborg parish, Clay County, South Dakota.

From the time he was a student at the Fjellstedt School, he was plagued with poor health. In early 1890, he suffered an attack of influenza. On February 26, 1890, after less than two years as a pastor, he died at the age of thirty-two.[24]

ii. E. S. Ternberg

E. S. Ternberg was born November 23, 1858, in Junsele, Ångermanland. He attended the Fjellstedt School and completed his studies at Augustana College and Theological Seminary. He served eleven congregations in the course of a forty-two year ministry from which he retired in 1930: two in Nebraska (Malmö, Saronville), Houtzdale, Pennsylvania, East Greenwich, Rhode Island, two in Iowa (Freemount, New-Sweden-Lockridge), Montclair, New Jersey, three in Minnesota (Buffalo, Clear Lake-Gibbon, Moose Lake-Swede Park-Bloomskog-Oak Hill), and Port William-Port Arthur, Ontario, Canada. His services were also engaged in the following offices in the work of the Church at large: secretary of the New York Conference and member of four boards of directors (Uppsala College, Immigrants' Home in New York. Children's Home in Stanton, Iowa and the Deaconness Institute in Omaha, Nebraska.

Pastor Ternberg died three years after retirement at the age of seventy-five. His death occurred on December 24, 1933.[25]

iii. Laurent Erick Sjölinder

L. E. Sjölinder was born April 22, 1859 in Tuna, Medelpad, the son of farm owner Olof O. Sjölinder and his wife, Anna Maria (Brown). He entered the Fjellstedt School in 1881 when he was admitted to the third class. At the end of that year, his parents emigrated to America. Sjölinder accompanied them. Recommended to Augustana College by the Fjellstedt School, he entered the College in 1882 from where he graduated in June, 1886. He enrolled at the Seminary in the fall of the same year and was ordained at the end of a period of two years.

Sjölinder served eight parishes, most of which were multiple. They were located in Union-Lincoln Counties (South Dakota); Grand Forks, North Dakota-Polk County, Minnesota (he served this parish at two different

[24]"Pastor E. W. Ståhlberg," *Korsbaneret*, 1881, pp. 85-91 *passim*.

[25]"E. S. Ternberg," *Korsbaneret*, 1935, pp. 119-22 *passim*.

times); Tracy-Walnut Grove, Minnesota; Ivanhoe, Minnesota; Hager City-Bay City, Wisconsin; Minneapolis; and Morrison County, Minnesota.

In 1929, L. E. Sjölinder retired from the active ministry. He died March 17, 1943, at the age of eighty-three.[26]

iv. Johan Fr. Seedoff

J. F. Seedoff was born April 21, 1861, in Askeby, Östergötland. For five years from 1877 to 1882, he was a student at the Fjellstedt School. In the last year, he emigrated to America and completed his studies at Augustana College in 1886 and at the Seminary in 1888.

Following his ordination, he became pastor of Trinity Church in Topeka, Kansas. He later served parishes at Chisago City, Minnesota and First Lutheran Church in Rockford, Illinois where he served for thirty-one years.

His fine capabilities were recognized by the many offices of responsibility to which his peers elected or appointed him. Such positions of trust included: membership on boards of directors of Bethesda Hospital in St. Paul for five years, Augustana Hospital in Chicago for six years, four years for Charities of the Illinois Conference and many years for Augustana College and Theological Seminary. He served for awhile as vice-president of the Illinois Conference and also as co-editor of *Ungdomsvännen*. His church recognized his contributions by the bestowal upon him of the degree of Doctor of Theology from Upsala College, East Orange, New Jersey.

Pastor Seedoff retired in 1927 but continued working in the Rockford District until his death at the age of seventy-eight. He died July 27, 1939, after thirty-nine years in the active ministry and an additional twelve in semi-active work.[27]

v. Sven Gustav Öhman

S. G. Öhman was born in Neder-Luleå, Norrbotten on January 16, 1862. He studied at the Fjellstedt School. He completed his work at Augustana College and Theological Seminary and was ordained June 24, 1888. During his fifty years in the Gospel ministry, Öhman distinguished himself.

For awhile, he was superintendent of the Augustana Hospital in Chicago. For twenty-seven years, he was pastor in New Britain, Connecticut. During that period a beautiful cathedral-like church edifice was built and the congregation grew to be the largest in the Augustana Church. When the New England Conference separated form the New York Conference in 1912, Öhman became the first president of the new conference. He also served parishes in Rockford and Elgin, Illinois, New York and Jersey City.

In 1918, when fervent and serious debate occurred as to whether the Augustana Lutheran Church should become a part of the United Lutheran Church (a combination of the General Council, General Synod and United Synod of the South), Öhman was perhaps the most effective opponent

[26]"Pastor L. E. Sjölinder," *Korsbaneret*, 1944, pp. 97-100 *passim.*

[27]J. A. Benander, "John Fr. Seedoff," *Korsbaneret*, 1940, pp. 233-37 *passim.*

against such a merger.[28] His viewpoint won out, which was no little achievement when it is recalled that for nearly fifty years, since 1870, The Augustana Lutheran Church had been a member of the General Council.

His ministry was not confined to America. At the age of sixty, he fulfilled his desire to serve also in the Lutheran Church in Sweden. He became the chief pastor (*kyrkoherde*) in Storkåge, an independent division of the country parish of Shellefteå located not far from Öhman's birthplace. That congregation was ultimately organized into a new pastorate under the jurisdiction of the Diocese of Luleå. There he served for eleven years but by his own request, he remained on the rolls of the Augustana ministerium.[29]

Öhman's judgment of the Church in Sweden represents a one hundred eighty degree turn from the negative view taken in the early years by the leaders such as Esbjörn and Hasselquist. In 1931, Öhman wrote:

> The people here are very churchly and many of them are of an earnest Christian Spirit which makes my preaching and pastoral work very congenial and pleasant. Quite a few come to my room individually for special consultation in their spiritual troubles and anxiety. The Holy Spirit is certainly at work with these dear souls. I am very sorry that quite a number of the Augustana pastors know so little of the blessed work of the Church of Sweden.[30]

The accomplishments of S. G. Öhman were recognized by both his adopted and native countries. In 1907, he received an honorary doctorate from Muhlenberg College in Pennsylvania. He was one of few Americans to receive an honorary degree from Upsala University. Sweden also conferred upon him the distinctive honor of the Knight of the Order of Vasa.

Öhman returned to American after his eleven year ministry in Sweden and became pastor of the Augustana Church in Jersey City. He died there on April 17, 1939, at the age of seventy-seven.[31]

20. Johan Alfred Carlstrom

J. A. Carlstrom was born October 3, 1857, in Bråaryd, Småland. He was a student at the Fjellstedt School. He completed his education at Augustana Theological Seminary which he entered in 1886. After his ordination in

---

[28]The outstanding example of Swedish antipathy to merger, and the document which best summarized the synodical determination to maintain synodical independence on nationalistic grounds is S. G. Öhman, *Augustanasynodens Sälfständighetsförklaring* [*Clarification of the Independence of the Augustana Synod*], Worcester, Mass., 1918. Quoted in Arden, *Augustana Heritage*, p. 255, fn. 8.

[29]Letter to the Rev. Dr. G. A. Brandelle, President of the Evangelical Augustana Lutheran Church, Rock Island, Ill. from Öhman, Kåge, Västerbotten, Sweden, February 5, 1931 in Archives of the Lutheran Church in America, Lutheran School of Theology, Chicago, Illinois.

[30]*Ibid.*

[31]S. G. Hägglund, "Sven Gustaf Öhman," *Korsbaneret*, 1940, pp. 214-19 *passim*.

1889, he served for ten years in America and returned to Sweden in 1900. For two years, he was adjunct pastor in the Skäns congregation of the Härnösands parish. In 1902, he returned to America. He served one parish, Chandlers Valley, Pennsylvania, for twenty-four years. He also served congregations in St. Cloud, Minnesota; Princeton, Illinois; Ansonia, Connecticut; and Merrill, Wisconsin.

After a ministry of forty-two years, he died on May 16, 1932, at the age of seventy-four.[32]

21. Per Erik Åslev

P. E. Åslev was born to Franks Erik Petterson and Breta (Eriksdotter) at Östersund, Jämtland, Sweden, April 4, 1863. He attended the Fjellstedt School during the years 1885-1887. From 1887-1889, he studied at the Johannelund Mission Institute. He emigrated to America and completed his education at Augustana College and Theological Seminary. On a call to the dual parish of Arlington-Jersey City, New Jersey, he was ordained in 1892.[33] In addition to these congregations, he served parishes in Stanton, Iowa; Salt Lake City, Utah; Brattleboro, Vermont; Lowell, Massachusetts; and Lemont, Illinois.

Because he concluded his ministry in Sweden, the date of his death is not recorded in Augustana Church records.

22. Sven Gustaf Youngert

S. G. Youngert was born to Olof Persson and Anna B. (Olsson) at Sjunget, Småland on April 7, 1861.[34] After two years in a private school in Manhem, Västergötland, he entered the Fjellstedt School in 1882 where he studied until 1884. Well recommended by Johannes Kjerfstedt, director of the School, he was accepted into Augustana College in the autumn of 1886. He completed his theological education at Augustana Seminary and was ordained in 1892.

S. G. Youngert had a distinguished ministry of forty-three years. For twenty-seven years he was professor at Augustana Theological Seminary. He spent over sixteen years in the parish ministry which he carried on in congregations located in Kewanee, Illinois; Ottumwa, Iowa; Hartford, Connecticut; and Waltham, Massachusetts.

Both as pastor and teacher he was highly respected for his imagination and thoroughness. His energy and gifts were employed in many areas beyond his academic and pastoral work. He was editor of *Ungdomsvännen* (1899-1912) which Conrad Bergendoff has called "one of the finest examples of Christian and cultural publications which has come forth from any

---

[32]Carl Jacobson, "J. A. Carlstrom," *Korsbaneret*, 1933, pp. 249-51 *passim*.

[33]C. A. Swensson and L. G. Abrahamson, *Jubel-Album* [*Jubilee Album*] (Chicago: National Publishing Co., 1893), p. 334.

[34]*Ibid.* There is some confusion on the place of his birth. Gustav Andreen identified the place of Youngert's birth as "on [the Island of] Gottland" (Gustav Andreen, "Sven Gustaf Youngert," *Korsbaneret*, 1940, p. 198.

immigrant group in America."[35] He edited the *Augustana Theological Quarterly* from 1912 to 1917. He published the following works: *Handbok i undervisning* [*Handbook in Instruction*] in 1895; *Filosofiens historia* [*History of Philosophy*] in 1896; *Utkast till religionsfilosofi* [*An Outline of the Philosophy of Religion*] in 1921. He also wrote articles for *Hastings Encyclopedia of Religion and Ethics* (1912-22), assisted in the publication, *Svenskarna i Amerika* [*The Swedes in America*] (Stockholm, 1924-25), and several synodical and other works.

The Church also depended upon him for the execution of several important positons which included the offices of secretary of the Church Extension Society, vice-president and president of the New England Conference, and vice-president of Augustana College and Theological Seminary. At one time, he was president of the Board of Directors of the Lutheran Fire Insurance Association, Burlington, Iowa.

After World War I, the American Lutheran Council appointed Youngert as the chairman of a committee of five to be responsible for the disposal of funds to suffering fellow Lutherans in Europe. In 1919, the committee visited the beneficiaries of these monies which were used to restore churches, theological schools, hospitals and give encouragement to the war stricken people. In 1930, he visited the Holy Land and represented the Augustana Lutheran Church at Augsburg, Germany, for the four hundredth anniversary of the Augsburg Confession.

He was awarded an honorary Doctor of Philosophy degree from Bethany College in 1902. He also received the Doctor of Sacred Theology degree from Augustana College and Theological Seminary. In 1924, Sweden conferred on him the Knighthood of the Order of the North Star.

On February 26, 1939, Professor Youngert died at the age of seventy-seven.[36]

23. Magnus Theodore Andrén

M. T. Andrén was born August 15, 1863 in the village of Råneå, Norrbotten. He entered the Fjellstedt School in 1884. In the autumn of 1894, he emigrated to America and enrolled in Augustana Theological Seminary. On June 7, 1897, he was ordained on a call to Fridhems congregations in Funk, Nebraska. Other parishes he served during his thirty-nine year ministry were in Amery-Clayton, Wisconsin; Isanti-Long Lake, Minnesota; and St. Paul, Minnesota. Pastor Andrén also had literary ability. He had articles published in *Augustana* and *Korsbaneret*.

He retired from his pastoral work in May, 1936. Within a month thereafter, he died on June 12, 1936, at the age of seventy-two.[37]

24. Johan Carlson Westlund

J. C. Westlund was born on May 24, 1866, in Boda, Värmland. He

[35]Andreen, pp. 203-4.

[36]*Ibid.*, pp. 198-208 *passim.*

[37]Herman Söderberg, "Magnus Theodore Andrén," *Korsbaneret,* 1937, pp. 182-88 *passim.*

attended both Ahlborg and Fjellstedt Schools. He emigrated to America in 1891. He entered the newly opened Upsala College (begun in 1893) which at that time was located in the Swedish Lutheran Bethlehem Church in Brooklyn. He studied there from 1895 to 1902. He entered Augustana Theological Seminary and was ordained in 1904. During his twenty-seven year ministry, he served four parishes: Tabor, Brooklyn, New York; Sion, Brooklyn, New York; Tabor-Salem in Summit and East Orange, New Jersey; and finally, Salem as a separate congregation where he was pastor for twenty-one years.

He died at the age of sixty-five on July 26, 1931.[38]

25. Johannes Petrus Nordström

J. P. Nordström was born April 13, 1865, in Bungo, Gotland. He studied at the Fjellstedt School as well as in a preparatory school in Örebro. He emigrated to America and became a student at Gustavus Adolphus College. After his student days, he worked for some years as a lay preacher in the Minnesota Conference. He entered Augustana Theological Seminary and was ordained in 1910. He served four parishes, three of which were in Canada: Calgary, Alberta; Beatty-Kinistina, Saskatchewan; and a second pastorate in Alberta. His first five years were spent in the Marcus-Cherokee parish in Iowa.

He died April 3, 1933, at the age of sixty-seven.[39]

II. Some Concluding Observations

Geographically, the Swedish origin of these twenty-nine "Fjellstedters" was highly diverse. They came from fourteen different provinces of Sweden. The areas from which more than one came were: Småland, five; three from each of the following—Värmland, Jämtland, Dalarne, Östergötland; and two from Västergötland, Norrbotten and Medelpad. Other provinces represented were: Skåne, Hälsingland, Dalsland, Västmanland, Ångermanland, and Gotland.

Quantitatively, the contribution of the Fjellstedt School was immense. The twenty-nine students who became pastors in the Augustana Lutheran Church cumulatively served a total of 130 parishes for a minimum total of 869 years. In addition to this must be taken into account the years of service given in professor-and editorships and in numerous other functions and office of the Church.

The quantitative aspect is only a small part of the story. What was the qualitative contribution? To assess that statistically is impossible. Of John Carlson Westlund's ministry, C. W. Vetell wrote: "God alone perceives the significance of the work he did . . . "[40] So it must be said of all these men. What they did as faithful pastors, professors, editors, officers greatly enriched the lives of all who were touched by the ministry of the Augustana Lutheran Church.

[38]C. W. Vetell, "J. C. Westlund," *Korsbaneret*, 1932, pp. 259-63 *passim*.

[39]Anton A. Nelson, "Pastor Johannes Petrus Nordström," *Korsbaneret*, 1934, pp. 242-44 *passim*.

[40]"J. C. Westlund," p. 261.

BIBLIOGRAPHY
BOOKS

Ahnfelt-Laurin, Emilia. *Peter Fjellstedt, hans verksamhet i fosterlandet mellan åren 1843-1881.* Stockholm: A. V. Carlsons Förlag, 1881.

Ander, Oscar Fritiof. *T. N. Hasselquist: The Career and Influence of a Swedish-American Clergyman, Journalist and Educator.* Rock Island, Ill.: Augustana Historical Society/Augustana Book Concern, 1931.

Anshelm, Carl. *Peter Fjellstedt. Vol. 1: hans barndoms och ungdomstid samt utländska missionsverksamhet.* Stockholm: Svenska Kyrkans Diakonistyrelses Bokförlag, 1930.

——————. *Peter Fjellstedt. Vol. 2: hans verksamhet i hemlandet för den yttre missionen.* Stockholm: Svenska Kyrkans Diakonistyrelses Bokförlag, 1935.

——————. *Peter Fjellstedt. Vol. 3: hans verksamhet för kyrklig väckelse och inre mission 1850-1881.* Stockholm: Svenska Kyrkans Diakonistyrelses Bokförlag, 1957.

——————. *Peter Fjellstedt och hans betydelse för tillkomsten av Fjellstedska Skolan.* Uppsala: Almquist och Wiksells Boktryckeri-A.B., 1931.

Arden, G. Everett. *Augustana Heritage: A History of the Augustana Lutheran Church.* Rock Island, Ill.: Augustana Press, 1963.

——————. *Four Northern Lights: Men Who Shaped Scandinavian Churches.* Minneapolis: Augsburg Publishing House, 1964.

Bengel, Johann Albrecht. *Gnomen: det är handledning vid läsningen af nya testamentet.* Translated by J. Ternström. Jönköping, Sweden: J. H. Nordström and Sons Förlag, 1878.

Benson, Adolph B. and Hedin, Naboth. *Americans From Sweden.* The People of America Series, edited by Louis Adamic. Philadelphia: J. B. Lippincott Co., 1950.

Bergendoff, Conrad. *The Augustana Ministerium: A Study of the Careers of the Augustana Lutheran Synod/Church: 1850-1962.* Rock Island, Ill.: Augustana Historical Society, 1980.

——————. *The Making and Meaning of the Augsburg Confession.* Rock Island, Ill.: Augustana Book Concern, 1930.

Bergin, Alfred. *Lindsborg: en svensk-Amerikansk Kulturbild från Mellersta Kansas.* Rock Island, Ill.: Augustana Book Concerns Tryckeri och Bokbinderi, 1909.

Cornelius, C. A. *Handbok i Svenska kyrkans historia.* Uppsala: Edquist and Berglund, 1867.

Dowie, James Iverne. *Prairie Grass Dividing.* Rock Island, Ill: Augustana Historical Society, 1959.

Elmen, Paul. *Wheat Flour Messiah: Eric Janson of Bishop Hill.* Carbondale, Ill.: Southern Illinois University Press, 1976.

Fjellstedt, Peter. *Biblia det är all den heliga skrift, med förklaringar.* 3 vols. Stockholm: F. and G. Reijers förlag, 1890.

——————. *Bibliska betraktelser wid en konfirmations-underwisning.* Stockholm Tryckt på P. A. Huldbergs Förlag, 1863.

——————. *Bibliska framtidswinkar.* Uppsala: Esaias Edquists boktryckeri, 1881.

——————. *Guds swar på menniskan frågor: biblisk cateches med ett bihang af frågor och swar rörande den christna kyrkans största högtider.* Translated from German. 2d. ed. Stockholm: P. Palmquists förlag, 1855.

——————. *Några grunddrag af nya testamentets lära om det andeliga presterskapet och församlingens embeten.* Doctoral dissertation utgiven och till offentlig granskning framställes December 5, 1857. Uppsala: C. A. Leffler, Kong. Akad. Boktryckare, 1857.

__________. *Dr. P. Fjellstedts samlade skrifter i ordnadt urwal.* 3 vols. Stockholm: Tryckt hos Nya Tryckeri-Aktiebolaget, 1883-84.

Gustafsson, Berndt. *Svensk kyrkohistoria.* Handböcker i Teologi series. 5th ed. Stockholm: A B Tryckmans, 1973.

Hasselquist, T.N. *Försök Till en Grundlig och Dock Lättfattlig Förklaring af Paul's Bref Till Efeserna.* Rock Island, Ill.: Augustana Book Concern, 1887.

Helander, Dick, redactor. *Svenska kyrkans bekännelseskrifter.* Stockholm: Svenska Kyrkans Diakonistylrelses Bokförlag, 1944.

Holmquist, Hjalmar. *Handbok i svensk kyrkohistoria: från romantiken till första världskriget.* Part 3. 2d ed. Stockholm: Svenska Kyrkans Diakonistyrelses Bokförlag, 1952.

Hudson, Winthrop, *Religion in America.* 2d. ed. New York: Charles Scribner's Sons, 1973

Janson, Florence E. *The Background of Swedish Immigration 1840-1930.* Chicago: The University of Chicago Press, 1931.

Johansson, Emil. *Vinden drar från väster.* Jönköping: H. Halls Boktr., 1965.

Konglig placater resolutions och påbud: 1726. John Henry Werner, director öfwer all tryckeri i riket.

Lindahl, Goran. *Högkyrklight lågkyrkligt frikyrligt i svensk arkitektur 1800-1950.* Stockholm: Svenska kyrkans diakonistyrelses bokförlag, 1955.

Lindeberg, Gustaf. *Ett sekel i missionens tjänst.* Lund: C. W. K. Gleerups Förlag, 1945.

Lindquist, Emory. *Shepherd of an Immigrant People: The Story of Erland Carlsson.* Rock Island, Ill.: Augustana Historical Society, 1978.

__________. *Smoky Valley People: A History of Lindsborg, Kansas.* Lindsborg, Kansas: Bethany Press, 1953.

Lindroth, Fred and Norbrink, Sven. *Den svenska kyrkan: kyrkokunskap för kyrka, skola och hem.* Femte, omarbetade upplagen. Stockholm: Svenska Kyrkans Diakonistyrelses Bokförlag, 1960.

Lund, Emil. *Minnesota-Konferensens Av Augustana-Synoden Och Der Församlingars Historia.* Vol. 1. Rock Island, Ill.: Augustana Book Concern, 1926.

Lyttkens, Carl Henrik. *The Growth of Swedish-Anglican Intercommunion Between 1833 and 1922.* Translated by Neil Tomkinson. Bibliotheca Theologiae Practicae Series. Lund: C. W. K. Gleerups Förlag, 1970.

Norelius, Eric. *De Svenska Lutherska församlingarnas och Svenskarnas historia i Amerika.* 2 vols. Rock Island, Ill.: Augustana Book Concern, 1890-1916.

__________. *T. N. Hasselquist: Lefnadsteckning.* Rock Island.: Augustana Book Concern, 1900.

Olson, Ernst W. *Olof Olsson: The Man, His Work, and His Thought.* Rock Island Ill.: Augustana Book Concern, 1941.

__________. *The Swedish Element in Illinois: Survey of the Past Seven Decades.* Chicago: Swedish-American Biographical Association, 1917.

Olson, Oscar N. *The Augustana Lutheran Church in America: Pioneer Period 1846 to 1860.* Rock Island, Ill.: Augustana Book Concern, 1950.

__________. *Olof Christian Telemak Andrén: Ambassador of Good Will.* Rock Island, Ill.: Augustana Historical Society, 1954.

Olsson, Karl A. *By One Spirit.* Chicago: Covenant Press, 1962.

Olsson, Olof. *Helsningar från Fjerran: Minnen från en resa genom England och Tyskland.* Moline, Ill.: 1880.

Outler, Albert, ed. *John Wesley.* A Library of Protestant Thought Series. New York: Oxford University Press, 1964,

Rouse, Ruth and Neill, Stephen, eds. *A History of the Ecumencial Movement 1517-1948.* London: S. P. C. K., published in behalf of the Ecumenical Institute Château de Bossey, 1954.

Runblom, Harald and Norman, Hans, eds. *From Sweden to America: A History of the Migration.* Minneapolis: University of Minnesota Press, 1976.

Ruenby, Nils. *Den nya världen och den gamla: Amerikabild och emigrations-uppfattning i Sverige: 1820-1860.* Studia Historica Upsaliensia. Uppsala: Almquist and Wiksells Boktryckeri Aktiebolog, 1969.

Rönnegård, Sam. *Lars Paul Esbjörn och Augustana-Synodens uppkomst.* Stockholm Svenska Kyrkans Diakonistyrelses Bokförlag, 1949.

Scott, Franklin D. *Sweden: The Nation's History.* Minneapolis: University of Minnesota Press. 1977.

Seger, Olof. *En tidlös pedagog: rektor Johannes Kjerfstedt.* Uppsala: J. A. Lindblads Förlag, 1957.

Stephenson, George M. *The Religious Aspects of Swedish Immigration.* Minneapolis: University of Minnesota Press, 1932.

Sundkler, Bengt. *Svenska missionssällskapet: 1835-1876: missionstankens genombrott och tidigare historia i Sverige.* Stockholm: Svenska Kyrkans Diakonistyrelses Bokförlag, 1937.

Swanson, S. Hjalmar. *Foundation for Tomorrow.* Rock Island.: Augustana Book Concern, 1960.

__________. *Three Missionary Pioneers.* Rock Island, Ill.: Augustana Book Concern, 1945.

Sweet, William Warren. *The Story of Religion in America.* New York: Harper and Brothers Publishers, 1930.

Söderström, Hugo. *Confession and Cooperation: The Policy of the Augustana Synod in Confessional Matters and the Synod's Relations with Other Churches Up to the Beginning of the Twentieth Century.* Bibliotheca Historico-Ecclesiastica Lundensis IV. Lund: C. W. K. Gleerup Bokförlag, 1973.

Tappert, Theodore, G., ed. and translator. *The Book of Concord.* Philadelphia: Fortress Press, 1959.

Westin, Gunnar. *Emigranterna och kyrkan. Brev från och till Svenskar i Amerika 1849-1892.* Stockholm: Svenska Kyrkans Diakonistyrelses bokförlag, 1932.

Öhman, S. G. *Augustanasynodens sälfständighetsförklaring.* Worchester, Massachusetts, 1918.

FJELLSTEDT'S ARTICLES AND ESSAYS

Bibelvännen—Founded and edited by Fjellstedt 1848-1867.

"Friheten." 1 (May 1848), 69-79.

"Gustaf-Adolphs Stiftelsen." 18 (February 1865), 21-32.

"Gustaf-Adolphs Stiftelsen." 18 (March 1865), 36-38.

"Huru kan den bästa statsförfattningen åstadkommar?" 1 (October 1848), 151-55.

"Hura kan den bästa statsförfattningen åstadkommar?" 1 (November 1848), 160-71.

"Om den svenska kyrkan." 5 (July 1852), 100-110.

"Om församlingen och läro-embetet." 9 (June 1856), 82-93.

"Om församlingen och läro-embetet." 9 (August 1856) 126.

"Om Separatism." 12 (April 1858) 51-62.

"Samhallslifwets grundval." 2 (March 1849), 41-42.

"Skall jag taga wara på min bröder?" 12 (October 1859) 156-59.

"Socialism och kommunism." 3 (May 1850), 66-80.

"Tillkännagifvande." 16 (May 1863), 80.

"Utdrag ur ett bref angående Christendomens tillstånd i Nord-Amerikas förenta Stater." 5 (November 1852), 176-78.

"Wedergällningen." 20 (March 1867), 35-45.

Folkskolan—Founded and edited by Fjellstedt 1848-1851. Ceased publication 1851.

"Blick på Christenhetens närvarande politiska tillstånd." 1 (February 1848), 17-18.

"Förord." 1 (January 1848), 1-5.

"Något af Dr. J. A. Bengel's uppfastringsgrundsatser." 3 (December 1850), 178-80.

Lunds Missions-Tidning—Founded and edited by Fjellstedt 1846-1867.

"Den fria föreningswerksamheten." 18 (November 1865), 161-71.

"En resepredikant bland Svenskarne i Amerika." 13 (September 1859), 143-44.

"F. D. Fjellstedska skolan i Uppsala." 21 (December 1866), 182-86.

"Hwilka sammankomster äro förbjudna?" 4 (March 1851), 43-44.

"Indianerna i Nord-Amerikas förenta states." 22 (December 1867), 179-82.

"Indianer-missionen i Minnesota i Norra Amerika." 27 (January 1872), 6-10.

"Missions-Institute." 12 (February 1859), 29-30.

"Missions-Institute." 12 (July 1859), 98-101.

"Missions-Skolan." 10 (July 1857), 109-112.

"Missions-Skolan." 11 (June 1858), 83-86.

"Missions-Skolan." 14 (August 1861), 116-117.

"Missions-Skolan." 15 (August 1862), 114-115.

"Några ord om utwandring." 3 (April 1850), 59-64.

"Om kristens underdånighet under öfweheten och den borgerliga lagen." 9 (September 1856), 140-43.

"Rörande missionsinstitute." 4 (April-May 1851), 50-69.

"Slafhandeln." 2 (May 1847), 2-8.

"Slafhandeln." 2 (July 1847), 3-7.

"Upphäfwandet af 1726 års konventikelplakat." 12 (January 1859), 8-13.

"Utdrag af ett bref från America." 7 (April 1854), 50-52.

Samlade Skrifter. 3 vol. Collection of Fjellstedt's writings, 1883-84.

"Ännu några ord om nattvardens begående." 2:850-64.

"Den der träder i en annans embete." 2:583-590.

"Den helige Ande och hans werk." 3:111-128.

"Eder skäliga gudstjenst." 2:575-79.

"Finnes någon salighestswäg för de hedningar, som icke få höra evangelium?" 3:281-90.

"Guds olika sätt att uppenbara sig för menniskor." 1:32-39.

"Herren-Gud." 1:312-18.

"Jag tror på den helige Ande, en helig allmännelig kyrka, de heligas samfund."
2:501-26.

"Minnesord öfwer missionären C. J. Fast: uttalade i Lunds domkyrka den 3 Mars
1851, wid underrättelsen om hans död." 3:239-53.

"Olika slag af bekärmelse." 1:83-87.

"Om den helige Ande." 2:1-24.

"Om den helige Andes wägledande och tuktande nåd." 2:247-52.

"Om församling och läro-embets." 2:526-548.

"Om nödvändighetens af Diakonversksamheten åter." 2:595-604.

"Om staten och wåra pligter emot densamma." 1:192-200.

"Pröfwen andarne, om de äro af Gud." 2:579-83.

"Sjelfbiografi af P. Fjellstedt." 3:579-634.

"Socialism och kommunism." 1:203-24.

OTHER ARTICLES AND ESSAYS

"Bilder ur det Svenska Sion." *Ungdoms-Vännen* 7 (August 1902), 230-32.

Carlsson, Erland and Strömsberg, Carl. "Ett brev från de Svenska församlingarna i
Amerika till Gustaf-Adolphs stiftelsen i Göteborg." *Bibelvännen* 17 (February
1865), 23-26.

"Christlig Korresondens." *Hemlandet* 6-9 (March 1861), 41-44.

"Enhet i den Swenska Missionswerksambeten." *Hemlandet* 6-9 (December 1864),
175-76.

Esbjörn, Lars Paul. "Bref från en Swensk Prest i Nord-Amerika." *Bibelvännen* 6
(September 1852), 138-44.

__________. "Bref från en Svensk prest i Nord-America till en vän i Sverige."
Lunds Missions-Tidning 5 (February 1852), 26-30.

"Ett omdöm från Nord-Amerika om dem som invandra." *Bibelvännen* 3 (August
1850), 128.

"Fjellstedt's Johannes." *Augustana och missionären* 26 (February 1881), 153-55.

"Församlingswännen." *Rätta Hemlandet och Augustana* 16-18 (November 1872),
262-63.

Forsander, Nils. "Henric Schartau." *Lutersk Kvartalskrift* 3(1889), 1-20.

Från Sweriga: F. d. Fjellstedska Skolan." *Rätta Hemlandet och Augustana* 15 (May
1870), 115-116.

"George Scott's Journey to America in 1841." *Swedish-American Historical Bulletin*
5 (June 1932), 9-30.

Hasselquist, T. N. "Dr. Fjellstedts Testamente." *Augustana och missionären* 26
(May 1881), 308-312.

Herenius, A. M. L. "The Relation of the Augustana Synod to the Church of
Sweden." *The Augustana Quarterly* 9:296-300.

Josefson, Ruben R. "Hedningarna och Saligheten: en studie i Peter Fjellstedts teologi." *Ny Kyrkliga Tidskrift*, 1947, pp. 36-56.

"Kyrkliga underrättelser Från Swerige och Europa." *Rätta Hemlandet och Augustana* 16-18 (March 1872), 66-67.

"Peter Fjellstedt." *Augustana och missionären* 26 (February 23, 1881), 114-26.

"Peter Fjellstedt." *Ungdoms-Vännen* 3 (February 1, 1881), 40-44.

"Peter Fjellstedt." *Ungdoms-Vännen* 3 (February 15, 1881), 51-55.

"Peter Fjellstedt." *Ungdoms-Vännen* 3 (March 1, 1881), 66-68.

Reynolds, William R. "Brev från Doktor Reynolds." *Lunds Missions-Tidning* 2 (December 1849), 187-88.

Schweitzerbarth, G. "Prestbilding i Amerika för invandrade Swenskar." *Bibelvännen* 3 (September 1850), 144.

"Svenska missionswänners wal af missionsfält." *Hemlandet* 9-12 (April 1865), 56-60.

"Underrättelser från Nord-Amerika." *Bibelvännen* 11 (October 1858), 155-58.

"We behöfwa prester." *Bibelvännen* 15 (December 1862), 177-79.

Weidner, Revere. "John Albert Bengel." *Lutersk Kvartalskrift* 1 (1887), 24-35, 78-90.

Westin, Gunnar. "Emigration and Scandinavian Church Life." *Swedish Pioneer Historical Quarterly* 8 (April 1957), 35-48.

ALBUMS AND ANNUALS

Abrahamson, L. G. "Gustaf Peters." *Korsbaneret: Kristlig Kalendar för 1920*, pp. 123-28.

"Anders Wilhelm Dahlsten." *Korsbaneret*, 1919, pp. 141-48.

Andreen, Gustav. "Sven Gustaf Youngert." *Korsbaneret*, 1940, pp. 198-208.

Benander, J. A. "John Fr. Seedoff." *Korsbaneret*, 1940, pp. 233-37.

Cedarstam, P. A. "Lefnadsteckning af Fru Eva Helena Hasselquist." *Korsbaneret*, 1895, pp. 78-116.

Dahlberg, J. G. "Kommunikantafgiften och andra gåfvor." *Korsbaneret*, 1905, pp. 65-88.

"E. S. Ternberg." *Korsbaneret*, 1935, pp. 119-22.

"Erik J. Werner." *Korsbaneret*, 1928, pp. 217-21.

"Fredrik Nibelius." *Korsbaneret*, 1898, pp. 85-94.

Granere, C. O. "Dr. Anders Olof Bersell." *Korsbaneret*, 1905, pp. 155-74.

"Gustav Lundahl." *Korsbaneret*, 1935, pp. 122-24.

Hammarberg, A. G. "E. J. Nystrom." *Korsbaneret*, 1927, pp. 291-94.

Hultkrans, J. G. "Nils Olof Grundén." *Korsbaneret*, 1917, pp. 199-203.

Hägglund, S. G. "Sven Gustaf Öhman." *Korsbaneret*, 1940, pp. 214-19.

Jacobson, Carl. "J. A. Carlstrom." *Korsbaneret*, 1933, pp. 249-51.

Johnsson, F. A. "Pastor Victor Vixell." *Korsbaneret*, 1903, pp. 158-67.

Lund, Emil. "Peter Fjellstedt." *Korsbaneret*, 1932, pp. 20-28.

Lönnquist, C. A. "John Torell." *Korsbaneret*, 1924, pp. 137-49.

"Michael Sandell." *Korsbaneret*, 1920, pp. 147-50.

Nelson, Anton A. "Pastor Johannes Petrus Nordström." *Korsbaneret*, 1934, pp. 242-44.

Nyvall, Johannes A. "Doktor O. Olsson." *Korsbaneret*, 1901, pp. 142-66.

"P. A. Bergquist." *Korsbaneret*, 1913, pp. 193-202.

"Pastor Daniel Renström". *Korsbaneret*, 1889, pp. 213-19.

"Pastor E. W. Ståhlberg." *Korsbaneret*, 1881, pp. 85-91.

"Pastor J. P. Nyquist." *Korsbaneret*, 1888, pp. 15-43.

"Pastor L. E. Sjölinder." *Korsbaneret*, 1944, pp. 97-100.

"Pastor Sven Gustaf Larson." *Korsbaneret*, 1906, pp. 157-66.

Siljeström, O. J. "Barnens straff för fädernas skull." *Korsbaneret*, 1897, pp. 91-102.

Stiftelsens Styrelse. Evang. *Fosterlandsstiftelsen 50-åriga verksamhet 1856-1906.* Stockholm: Evang. Fosterlands-Stiftelsen Förlag-Expedition, 1906.

Swensson, C. A. and Abrahamson, L. G. *Jubel-Album, 1893.* Chicago: National Publishing Company, 1893.

Söderberg, Herman. "Magnus Theodore Andrén." *Korsbaneret*, 1937, 182-88.

Thorene, Hugo. "Lawrence Petrus Bergstrom." *Korsbaneret*, 1938, pp. 178-85.

Vetell, C. W. "J. C. Westlund." *Korsbaneret*, 1932, pp. 259-63.

MONOGRAPHS, UNPUBLISHED MATERIALS AND MISCELLANEOUS

Bergendoff, Conrad. "A Significant Enander Document." Typewritten. Rock Island, Ill,: Archives, Denkmann Memorial Library, Augustana College.

Carlson, Arthur B. "Pastoral Care in the Faith and Practice of Four Selected Swedish Churchmen." [Henrik Schartau, Carl Olof Rosenius, Erland Carlsson, Jonas Swensson]. Ph. D. dissertation, Boston University, 1962.

Enander, Johan. *Autobiography of Johan A. Enander: Student at Venersberg High School.* Translated by Conrad Bergendoff. Handwritten. Rock Island, Ill.: Archives, Denkmann Memorial Library, Augustana College, 1869.

Fjellstedtska Skolans Stadgar. Uppsala: Edv. Berlings Boktryckeri, n. d.

Förhandlingar vid den sjette allmänna svensk-lutherska prästkonferensens i Stockholm den 1-3 Sept. 1896. Stockholm: Tidningsaktiebolaget Vårt Lands Tryckeri, 1896.

Kinell, Andrew. *Memoirs.* Translated by Marie Kinell. Typewritten. Rock Island, Ill.: Archives, Denkmann Memorial Library, Augustana College, n. d.

Kjerfstedtska Deposition. Uppsala: Archives, Carolina Redivivi.

Lawson, Evald B. *Two Primary Sources For a Study of the Life of Jonas Swensson.* Rock Island, Ill.: Augustana Historical Association, 1957.

Svensk Uppslagsbok. 32 vols. Andra omarbetade och utridgade upplagan. Malmö: Förlagshuset Norden AB, 1947-1955.

Index

(The characters å, ä, and ö are placed according to the American order of the alphabet and not at the end as in the Swedish.)

Elgquist, Anders, Lund Society missionary, 70-71
Elohim, 41-42
Emigration. *See* Immigration
Enander, Johann A., editor of *Hemlandet,* 142
Enlightenment, 35, 47-48, 51-52
Ephesus, 9
Episcopacy, 62, 63, 64, 66, 72-73, 155
Episcopal Church in America, 16, 138, 151-153
Esbjörn, Lars Paul, Augustana Church, relation to, 97, 98, 99, 110-111,
    127, 135-136; Lutheran confessions, importance to, 107; pastor in Hille,
    Sweden, 12; relationship to Fjellstedt, 114-117, 118, 129; relationship to
    Hasselquist, 117-118; views on constitutional religious freedom, 102-106,
    108
Eschatology. *See* Apocalypticism
Eucharist, 75-76, 96
Evangelical Alliance, Fjellstedt's early appreciation for, 65, 66-67; later doc-
    trinal difficulties, 68, 69, 70, 73-74; relation to non-traditional groups,
    72-73
Evangeliska Fosterlandsstiftelsen, 68-69, 70, 73, 119-120, 137
Evolution, 89

Fjellstedt, Carlotta (daughter), 10
Fjellstedt, Joel Elisama (son), 11, 15, 84
Fjellstedt, Marie (daughter, Mrs. Philip Klett), 10, 17
Fjellstedt, Mrs. Peter. *See* Schweizerbart, Christina
Fjellstedt, Peter, as foreign missionary, 7, 8, 8-10, 19-20, 47, 94, 113-114; as
    linguist, 4, 6, 8; as promoter of missions, 7-8, 10-11, 14, 47; as preacher,
    5, 10-11, 14-15, 18-19, 23, 31-33, 114-115, 126, 131; availability of Bible,
    27; birth and parentage, 1, 26-27. *See* Larsson, Catherine and Larsson,
    Lars; confirmation and first communion, 3, 27; correspondence with
    Augustana leaders, 136-141; death, 18-19; financial aid to Augustana,
    143-145; journalism, 12, 141-142; relationship to Augustana leaders,
    114-142; theology, 40-42, 92-93. *See also* Apocalypticism; Atonement;
    Christology; Church and state; Church, doctrine of; Ecumenicity; Min-
    istry, doctrine of the; Priesthood of believers; soteriology; views on
    immigration, 97-99; Works. Books: *Biblia det är all den heliga skrift,
    med förklaringar.* 3 vols.; *Bibliska betraklteser wid en konfirmations-
    underwisning; Bibliska framtidswinkar; Evangelisk lutherska kyrkans
    symboliska böcker; Hvad lärer Bibeln om försoningen?; Några grund-
    dag af Nya Testamentets lära om det andeliga presterskapet och församl-
    ingens embeten.* Journals: *Bibelvännen; Folkskolan; Lunds Missions-
    Tidning; Samaritan.*
Fjellstedt, Richard (son), 9, 16-17, 107
Fjellstedt, Selma Natalie (daughter), 9, 84
Fjellstedt, Theodora Eugenia (daughter, Mrs. Axel Hermelin), 9, 17
Fjellstedt, Victor Nathaniel (son), 9, 15, 107
Fjellstedt School, 15-21, 34, 43, 155-157
Folk-church concept, 113

France, 81, 82, 87, 88
Franco-Prussian War, 17
Free Church of Scotland, 14, 19, 68, 101-102, 107-108, 132
Freedom, as belonging to the creature as creature, 81; concept of religious
    freedom, 81-82, 104-105, 106-107, 108; religious freedom in America,
    96-97, 98
Faxe, Wilhelm, 40
Finland, 96

Gamla och Nya Hemlandet, 130
Gavell, Jonas, Esbjörn's co-pastor in Hille, Sweden, 115
Genberg, Paul, 40
General Council, 138
General Synod, 138
Gnomen Novi Testament, 37, 90
Goldschmidt (Jenny Lind Goldschmidt). *See* Lind, Jenny
Grundén, Nils Olof, 173
Gustaf-Adolf Stiftelsen, 113-114, 144
Gustavus IV Adolphus, Swedish king, 95, 96

Haldeman, J. S., 97
Hallbeck, Hans Peter, Swedish missionary to South Africa, 5, 34
Halle pietism, 32, 33, 34, 37
Halle University, 14
Hallencreutz, Professor Carl, 146
Hälsingborg, 17
Hamburg, Theodor, Basel Mission Society missionary, 71-72
Hammar, H. B., Swedish pastor, 102
Hasselquist, Tuve Nilsson, belief in separation of church and state, 107;
    journalistic work, 101, 106, 118, 130; president, Augustana College and
    Theological Seminary, 132, 137; relationship to Episcopalians, 153-154;
    relationship to Fjellstedt, 113-114, 121-124, 137, 138-141, 143-144; repre-
    sentative of Augustana's theology, 148-150; view on slavery, 100-101;
    work in procuring pastors from Sweden, 99-100
Haugeanism, 40
Hedin, Naboth, 140
Hemlandet (successor to *Rätta Hemlandet, Det Rätta Hemlandet och
    Missionsbladet*), 100, 118, 120, 130
Hermansberg Mission, 119
Hermelin, Axel (son-in-law), 16-17
Herrestad, 11
Herrnhuters. *See* Moravians
Hindu Brahmans, 8
Hoffman, Wilhelm, successor to Blumhardt as head of Basel Institute, 66
Homestead Act of 1863, 95
Hoof, J. O., Swedish pastor, 31-32
Hultgren, C. O., 162

Wadström, Bernhard, 68
Wahlström, Matthias, 134
Waldenström, Paul Peter, 42-43, 74
Waldenströmian controversy, 18, 43-46, 137
Werner, Erik J., 156, 171
Wesley, John, 26-27
Westlund, Johan Carlson, 178-179
Whitehorse, Henry J., 152-153
Wiberg, Anders, 72
Wichern, J. H., 83
Wieselgren, Peter, leader of Swedish temperance movement, 116; one of
    founders of Lund Institute, 11; relationship to Augustana Lutherans, 67,
    107, 112, 121, 126, 140, 144; relationship to Fjellstedt, 10-11, 14, 15, 22
Wingård, Archbishop, 15, 99
World Council of Churches, 67
Würtemberg pietism, 33, 36, 37-38, 41, 48-49, 86, 90

Yahweh, 42
Youngert, Eugene, 43
Youngert, Sven Gustaf, 43, 164, 177-178

Zinzendorf, Nicholas, Ludwig Count von, 33

STUDIA MISSIONALIA UPSALIENSIA

I. *Peter Beyerhaus*, Die Selbständigkeit der jungen Kirchen als missionarisches Problem. 1956.

II. *Bengt Sundkler*, The Christian Ministry in Africa. 1960.

III. *Henry Weman*, African Music and the Church in Africa. 1960.

IV. *Tore Furberg*, Kyrka och mission i Sverige 1868-1901. 1962

V. *Eric J. Sharpe*, Not to destroy but to Fulfil: The Contribution of J. N. Farquhar to Protestant Missionary Thought before 1914. 1965.

VI. *Carl-Johan Hellberg*, Missions on a Colonial Frontier West of Lake Victoria. 1965.

VII. *Carl F. Hallencreutz*, Kraemer Towards Tambaram. A Study in Hendrik Kraemer's Missionary Approach. 1966.

VIII. *Johannes Aagaard*, Mission, Konfession, Kirche. Die Problematik ihrer Integration im 19. Jahrhundert in Deutschland. I, II. 1967.

IX. *Gustav Bernander*, Lutheran Wartime Assistance to Tanzanian Churches 1940-1945. 1968.

X. *Sigfrid Estborn*, Johannes Sandegren och hans insats i Indiens kristenhet. 1968.

XI. *Peter Beyerhaus* and *Carl F. Hallencreutz*, Ed., The Church Crossing Frontiers. Essays on the Nature of Mission. In Honour of Bengt Sundkler. 1969.

XII. *Sigvard von Sicard*, The Lutheran Church on the Coast of Tanzania 1887-1914 with special reference to the Evangelical Lutheran Church in Tanzania. Synod of Uzaramo-Uluguru. 1970.

XIII. *David Lagergren*, Mission and State in the Congo. A Study of the relations between Protestant missions and the Congo Independent State authorities with special reference to the Equator District, 1885-1903. 1970.

XIV. *Sigbert Axelson*, Culture Confrontation in the Lower Congo. From the Old Congo Kingdom to the Congo Independent State with special reference to the Swedish Missionaries in the 1880's and 1890's. 1970.

XV. *Per Østerbye*, The Church in Israel. A Report on the Work and Position of the Christian Churches in Israel with special reference to the Protestant Churches and Communities. 1970.

XVI. *Marja-Liisa Swantz*, Ritual and Symbol in transitional Zaramo society with special reference to women. 1970.

XVII. *Stiv Jakobsson*, Am I not a Man and a Brother? 1972.

XVIII. *Jonas Jonson*, Lutheran Missions in a Time of Revolution. The China experience. 1944-1951.1972.

XIX. *Tord Harlin*, Spirit and Truth. Religious Attitudes and Life Involvements of 2200 African Students. 1973.

XX. *Carl F. Hallencreutz*, *John Aagaard* and *Nils E. Bloch-Hoell*, Ed., Missions from the North, Nordic Missionary Council 50 Years. 1974.

XXI. *Josiah Kibira*, Church, Clan and the World. 1974.

XXII. *Axel Ivar Berglund*, Zulu Thought-Patterns and Symbolism. 1975.

XXIII. *Ingemar Bergmark,* Kyrka och sjöfolk. En studie i Svenska kyrkans sjömansvård 1911-1933. 1974.

XXIV. *Håkan Eilert,* Boundlessness Studies in Karl Ludvig Reichelt's Missionary Thinking with Special Regard to the Buddhist-Christian Encounter. 1974.

XXV. *Sven Arne Flodell,* Tierra Nueva. Svensk grupputvandring till Latinamerika. Integration och församlingbildning. 1974.

XXVI. *Håkan Zetterquist,* Stad och stift. Stiftsbildning och församlingsdelningar i Stockholm 1940-1956, Ett bidrag till stadens missiologi. 1974.

XXVII. *Olav Saeveraas,* On Church-Mission Relations in Ethiopia 1944-1969 with special reference to the Evangelical Church Mekane Yesus and the Lutheran Missions. 1974.

XXVIII. *Ingvar Kalm,* Missionen i Linköpings stift, Biträdesmissionssällskapets verksamhet 1841-1875. 1977.

XXIX. *Bengt Sundkler,* Zulu Zion and some Swazi Zionists. 1976.

XXX. *Herman Schlyter,* Der China-Missionar Karl Gützlaff und seine Heimatbasis. 1977.

XXXI. *Carl F. Hallencreutz,* Dialogue and Community. Ecumenical Issues in Interreligious Relationships. 1977.

XXXII. *Gustaf Arén,* Evangelical Pioneers in Ethiopia. Origins of the Evangelical Church Mekane Yesu. 1978.

XXXIII. *T. E. Yates,* Venn and Victorian Bishops abroad. The missionary policies of Henry Venn and their repercussions upon the Anglican Episcopate of the colonial period 1841-1872. 1978.

XXXIV. *Carl-Johan Hellberg,* A Voice of the Voiceless. The involvement of the Lutheran World Federation in Southern Africa 1947-1977. 1979.

XXXV. *John Hultwall,* Mission och revolution in Central Asien. Svenska Missionsförbundets insats i Östturkestan. 1981.

XXXVI. *Emmet E. Eklund,* Peter Fjellstedt: Missionary Mentor to Three Continents. 1983.

SWEDISH INSTITUTE OF MISSIONARY RESEARCH
UPPSALA, SWEDEN

SPCK, LONDON, GREAT BRITAIN